CLINICAL
BEHAVIOR
THERAPY

CLINICAL BEHAVIOR THERAPY

MARVIN R. GOLDFRIED
GERALD C. DAVISON
State University of New York
at Stony Brook

HOLT, RINEHART AND WINSTON
New York   Chicago   San Francisco   Atlanta
Dallas   Montreal   Toronto   London   Sydney

The authors wish to thank the following authors and publishers for permission to quote from copyrighted material:

Excerpt from Sarbin and Allen, "Role Theory" from *The Handbook of Social Psychology*, Second Edition, Volume I, edited by Lindzey and Aronson, 1968, Addison-Wesley, Reading, Mass.

Excerpt from A. Ellis, *Reason and Emotion in Psychotherapy*. Copyright © 1962 Institute for Rational Living. Published by arrangement with Lyle Stuart.

Excerpt from Goldfried, M. R., and Pomeranz, D. Role of assessment in behavior modification, *Psychological Reports*, 1968, 23, 75–87.

Excerpt from *Principles of Behavior Modification* by Albert Bandura. Copyright © 1969 by Holt, Rinehart and Winston, Inc. Reprinted by permission of Holt, Rinehart and Winston.

Library of Congress Cataloging in Publication Data

Goldfried, Marvin R.
Clinical behavior therapy.

Includes index.
1. Behavior therapy.   I.   Davison, Gerald C., joint author.
II.   Title.   [DNLM: 1.   Behavior   therapy.   WM420   G617c]
RC489.B4S23   616.8'91   75-25665

ISBN 0-03-008151-3

1234567890 038 09876

To
Anita and Carol

Photograph by A. O. Ross

Marvin R. Goldfried (left) received his B.A. from Brooklyn College in 1957, and his Ph.D. from State University of New York at Buffalo in 1961. After holding teaching positions at Buffalo and the University of Rochester, he moved to the State University of New York at Stony Brook, where he currently is Professor of Psychology and Psychiatry. He has also been a Visiting Professor at Bar-Ilan University in Israel. He is a Diplomate in clinical psychology from the American Board of Professional Psychology, a Fellow in the American Psychological Association, and a member of the Association for Advancement of Behavior Therapy. He has served as an ad hoc consultant to several professional journals, and has published in the areas of self-control and behavioral assessment. His previous co-authored books include *Rorschach Handbook of Clinical and Research Applications* and *Behavior Change through Self-Control*. He is also currently involved in the practice of clinical behavior therapy.

Gerald C. Davison (right) received his B.A. from Harvard in 1961, studied the following year in Germany on a Fulbright scholarship, and obtained his Ph.D. from Stanford in 1965. After a postdoctoral clinical fellowship at the Veterans Administration Hospital in Palo Alto, California, he joined the faculty at the State University of New York at Stony Brook, where he is Professor of Psychology and Psychiatry. He has published widely in the general area of behavior therapy and personality, particularly on theoretical and philosophical issues, and is co-author of *Abnormal Psychology: An Experimental Clinical Approach*. He is a Fellow of the American Psychological Association and has served on the Executive Committee of the Division of Clinical Psychology. He is also a Past-President of the Association for Advancement of Behavior Therapy. He has been on the editorial board of several professional journals, including the *Journal of Abnormal Psychology*, the *Journal of Consulting and Clinical Psychology*, and *Behavior Therapy*. In addition to his teaching and research, he is a practicing clinical psychologist.

A NOTE TO
THE READER

A colleague of ours once alluded to a "therapeutic underground" among clinical workers of various orientations. He struck a resonant chord, for we are continually impressed by the distance between written descriptions of behavior therapy and what occurs in practice. In *Clinical Behavior Therapy*, we have tried, within the constraints of the printed word, to describe in detail the complexities inherent in effective and humane intervention into the lives of others.

As behavior therapists, we are ever-mindful of the importance of tying our clinical procedures to our data base. Whenever possible, we present material that is consistent with available research. But as any knowledgeable student of behavior therapy can appreciate, more is required of the behavioral clinician than familiarity with well-established principles and procedures. Much of what you will find in this book will necessarily be based on clinical experience, our own and that of our students and colleagues. While some readers may be uncomfortable with an appeal to clinical experience, for the time being this seems to us the most straightforward way of talking about clinical behavior therapy and, most important, communicating our thinking to others. A special virtue of the behavior therapy approach is that we are answerable to data, and are prepared to alter or give up entirely any suggestion contained in this book that is found wanting in the light of controlled research.

Our overall goal is to present behavior therapy as we know it in our roles as teachers, researchers, practitioners, and clinical supervisors. We have tried to describe the way behavior therapists analyze clinical problems and move from general principles to clinical applications. We discuss those behavior therapy techniques with which we are intimately familiar, paying special attention to the complexity of employing various procedures in a clinical context. We have intentionally omitted aversion and implosion therapy, which have not been a part of our clinical practice, and the graded sexual approach procedures of Wolpe, Lazarus, and Masters and Johnson, which are already well described in the literature. Though written primarily from the vantage point of individual therapy, the considerations and techniques described are relevant across a range of applied areas—including the classroom, the college counseling center, the mental health clinic, the psychiatric ward, and the domain of the community worker. We hope that the book will serve a heuristic purpose in helping the reader generate clinical innovations within a broad behavioral framework.

Our intended audience is varied. This is by no means a book only for behavior therapists. We discuss behavior therapy in a broad context, allowing clinicians from other theoretical orientations to integrate behavioral procedures into their own practice. Among the professional groups for whom we have written this book are clinical psychologists, psychiatrists, social workers, counselors, and teachers, as well as peer counselors and paraprofessionals, who are taking more and more responsibility for helping others. Undergraduates can find much of value and interest in our sampling of clinical experience, enriching their understanding of the fascinating and difficult links among theory, research, and application.

We have been influenced by many people. To acknowledge by name all those who have contributed to the substance of this book would be to list most of our colleagues, students, and former teachers. We must satisfy ourselves with mentioning just a few particularly influential people to whom we owe a special debt. Albert Bandura impressed upon us the importance of theory and research in behavior therapy; Arnold A. Lazarus provided a model of clinical work that highlights the intellectual and emotional challenges of translating abstract principles into viable, realistic clinical procedures; and Perry London sensitized us to the ethical and societal issues in therapeutic intervention.

There is a special group of people who have influenced us profoundly as our thinking and practice have evolved over the years. By allowing us to share their experiences, difficulties, and joys, our clients have given us what theory and research alone could not provide, namely the constant challenge of coping both practically and conceptually with human problems. By not always changing the way theory and research suggest they should, our clients have at times forced us to revise and even to abandon accustomed ways of approaching clinical problems. We are most grateful for having been able to learn from them.

Several valued colleagues and friends offered incisive criticisms of earlier drafts of this book, and we have incorporated many of their suggestions. We thank Paul L. Wachtel, G. Terence Wilson, David M. Pomeranz, and Alan O. Ross. We wish to thank Deborah Doty, for her infinite patience and understanding, Johnna Barto, for her expert copy editing, and especially Sharon Worksman, for typing the many revisions of the manuscript. Our work was greatly facilitated by National Institute of Mental Health grant #24327.

In the final stages of the manuscript, we were made painfully aware of the sexism that was inherent in what we had written. It was easier to realize that not all teachers are "she" nor all parents, women, than to deal with the fundamentally sexist nature of the English language. We have tried to be sensitive to the societal role biases that work against women, but not being true revolutionaries, we decided to retain conventional references to "he" rather than to innovate with neuter pronouns or to follow more cumbersome practices such as "he/she."

Finally, we express our loving thanks to Anita Powers Goldfried and Carol Davison, who labored long hours clarifying what was often obscure in the manuscript, and who successfully changed some of our sexist attitudes. It is to them that we dedicate the book.

Stony Brook, New York　　　　　　　　　　　　　　　M. R. G.
October 1975　　　　　　　　　　　　　　　　　　　　G. C. D.

CONTENTS

PART II
CURRENT BEHAVIOR THERAPY TECHNIQUES

PART III
DECISIONS FOR CLINICAL APPLICATIONS

CLINICAL BEHAVIOR THERAPY

PART

BASIC
CONSIDERATIONS

Chapter 1

The Essence of Behavior Therapy

It may not come as a surprise to the reader that unanimity is not to be found in the definition of behavior therapy. To be sure, the earliest vocal proponents tied the new field to "modern learning theory" (Eysenck, 1960), or to classical and/or operant conditioning (Ullmann & Krasner, 1965; Lazarus, Davison, & Polefka, 1965; Skinner, 1953; Wolpe, Salter, & Reyna, 1964). Since that time, however, investigators from both the experimental and clinical camps have begun to question the limited scope of these definitions.

One frequently hears professionals discussing behavior therapy as if it were a "school" of therapy, defined primarily in terms of a particular set of concepts or techniques. We have found it undesirable, indeed impossible, to restrict ourselves to this narrow conception of behavior therapy (Davison & Goldfried, 1973). Instead, we believe that behavior therapy is more appropriately construed as reflecting a general orientation to clinical work that aligns itself philosophically with an experimental approach to the study of human behavior. The assumption basic to this particular orientation is that the problematic behaviors seen within the clinical setting can best be understood in light of those principles derived from a wide variety of psychological experimentation, and that these principles have implications for behavior change within the clinical setting.

There are several important consequences of this basic point of view. Behavior therapists, like their experimental colleagues, are operational in their use of concepts. High level abstractions such as anxiety or depression are always operationalized in specific terms, such as a particular score on a behavioral assessment device, or a concrete description of behavior. Also very much within the spirit of experimental psychology, the behavior therapist is interested in the search for and manipulation of the strongest controlling variables (Bandura, 1969; Mischel, 1968). That is, the behavior therapist assumes that behavior is lawful and that it is the function of specifiable antecedent, organismic, and consequent conditions. In this regard, every clinical interaction constitutes a kind of experiment.

● A HISTORICAL VIEW OF BEHAVIOR THERAPY

In its historical development, behavior therapy can be viewed as a confluence of several relatively distinct trends. The first, represented by the work of Joseph Wolpe and Arnold Lazarus in South Africa in the 1950s and by experimental and clinical work at the Maudsley Hospital in London by M. B. Shapiro and H. J. Eysenck, tended to emphasize Hullian learning theory, as well as Pavlovian conditioning. The emphasis here was largely on neurotic anxiety. Both sets of workers were attempting to extrapolate from experimental research in the acquisition of anxiety and its elimination in laboratory animals to the amelioration of unrealistic fears and their consequences in humans. For example, Wolpe's thesis (1948) for his medical degree at the University of the Witwatersrand in Johannesburg entailed the induction of persistent fears in laboratory cats and their successful elimination by combining graduated exposure to the conditioned stimuli with feeding. The idea was that (as Mary Cover Jones [1924] had demonstrated years before in her successful treatment of little Peter) one could successfully eliminate fear by inducing a nonfearful state, in this instance by eating, while exposing the fearful subject to increasing doses of what had previously been associated with an unconditioned stimulus. In his clinical work, Wolpe began to experiment with analogues to the animal situation. In a massive and fruitful extrapolation to his work with human patients, he substituted the response of deep muscle relaxation and, instead of limiting himself to real-life exposures, used the human capacity to imagine situations and thereby was able to present fearsome items to the person in the consulting room. The technique of systematic desensitization, discussed extensively in Chapter 6, is a good example of the attempt by behavior therapists to apply in the clinical situation what appear to be established principles of learning from the experimental laboratory.

Related to this largely British tradition in behavior therapy is the work of Andrew Salter in this country. In 1949 Salter published a polemical yet cogent book called *Conditioned Reflex Therapy*, in which he proposed that human neurotic problems result from an excess of cortical inhibition. His theoretical framework was Pavlovian. While many would disagree with the relationship between his theory and his therapeutic practices, he nonetheless occupies a central role in the development of behavior therapy, particularly in his emphasis on assertion training, discussed later in this book in Chapter 7.

A second trend in the development of behavior therapy seems to be largely an American one, with an emphasis on the consequences following behavior. This operant orientation seems to have begun with an unpublished report by O. R. Lindsley and B. F. Skinner, working with mental patients in a state hospital in Massachusetts (Lindsley & Skinner, 1954). Subsequently, numerous reports were published demonstrating the utility of regarding much human behavior, particularly that of patients diagnosed as psychotic, as instrumental in nature and therefore amenable to various Skinnerian reinforcement procedures. Stated simply, hospital wards were regarded and treated as huge Skinner boxes, in which the environmental events surrounding the emission of behavior by patients were controlled so as to extinguish or shape desired responses. As is characteristic of the operant orientation in experimental psychology, there was a high degree of experimental control and an emphasis on reducing observer bias in these various clinical studies. This work is discussed in greater depth in Chapter 10.

A third trend in the development of behavior therapy can be seen in the early work of Julian Rotter (1954) and the later work of Perry London (1964) and of Goldstein, Heller, and Sechrest (1966), as well as in the important contributions of Albert Bandura (1969). Perhaps as a reaction to the earlier insight therapies, the first developments in behavior therapy tended to downgrade the importance of human cognitive capacities. Both the classical conditioning behaviorists and the operant conditioning behavior modifiers eschewed any appeal to the thinking processes of the individuals concerned. Interestingly enough, the tendency in much of the earlier psychodynamic thinking was to regard cognitive processes as basically distorting in nature, entailing such defenses as denial and rationalization. They were, moreover, thought to be generally under involuntary control only. In contrast, more recent developments in behavior therapy emphasize the adaptive, voluntary nature of cognitive processes (D'Zurilla & Goldfried, 1971; Goldfried, Decenteceo, & Weinberg, 1974; Mahoney, 1974; Meichenbaum, 1974). The result of these efforts has been, in essence, to make the consideration of cognitive processes a legitimate domain for behavior therapists. At the same time, as will become evident throughout this book, it brings behavior therapy somewhat closer to more recent developments in ego psychology (Wachtel, in press). Cognitive approaches in behavior therapy are examined in Chapters 8 and 9.

Regardless of the concepts employed or procedures proposed, it will be seen that the common denominator in all behavior therapy theorizing and research is the insistence on rigorous standards of proof and a commitment to an experimental analysis of therapeutic processes.

● SOME MISUNDERSTANDINGS ABOUT BEHAVIOR THERAPY

To elaborate further on our conceptualization of behavior therapy, we can turn to a discussion of several misunderstandings about the field.

Behavior Therapy, Not Behavior Modification

As a result of some ill-conceived programs in mental hospital and prison settings, the year 1974 saw lobotomy, electric convulsive therapy, and even such techniques as psychodrama and transactional analysis all lumped together under the rubric of "behavior modification." A confusion arises inasmuch as all therapy techniques aim at the modification of behavior. Thus, the desired end product is the same. However, to regard the goals and processes involved as the same is to make a serious definitional error. It is for this reason alone that we prefer in this book to use the term behavior therapy rather than behavior modification (although the latter term has been widely used to encompass the entire field).

The Mechanistic Nature of Behavior Therapy

As will be shown in many of the succeeding chapters, behavior therapists tend to use a rather mechanistic language system, conceptualizing behavior in terms such as "stimulus," "response," and "reinforcement." These metaphors convey the impression that behavior therapists are cold-hearted and detached from other human beings, that indeed to practice behavior therapy is to discourage honest and intimate relationships with one's clients. This need not be the case, for words like "stimulus" and "response" are nothing more than scientific metalanguage that we judge useful in understanding behavior. Because of the "scientific" stance taken by behavior therapists in conceptualizing human functioning and the behavior change process, it is often assumed that they place no emphasis on the therapist-client relationship. One can find little comfort in the experimental literature for this radical viewpoint. The simple fact is that all clinical procedures take place within an interpersonal context, and this interpersonal context itself is amenable to a scientific analysis (Wilson, & Evans, in press). As we try to point out and illustrate throughout the book, a tough-minded approach to conceptualizing human problems in no way precludes a warm, genuine, or empathic interaction with clients.

Related to the above view is the belief that behavior therapists regard people as nothing more than animals. Laboratory experiments do indeed isolate phenomena and study them under conditions that are more controlled than what is possible in everyday life. However, when we use a pigeon rather than a human being in an experiment and then extrapolate our findings to the real-life situation, we are engaging in analog work. We are not saying that a human being is nothing but a pigeon; rather we are suggesting that something might be learned from analog experiments—done under better controlled conditions than is possible with humans—that will possibly be useful in helping people. Ample clinical research demonstrates the usefulness of many principles and procedures that are derived from experiments with infrahuman organisms.

The Superficiality of Behavior Therapy

Another view of behavior therapy stems perhaps from the word "behavior." We have often wished that the term had never been used at all, for it fosters the impression (which, to be fair, *is* held by many respected workers in the field, e.g., Bijou & Baer, 1961; Ullmann & Krasner, 1969) that we restrict our attention entirely to external events. As will become amply clear in this book, we are not radically behavioristic for we do not eschew the use of inferred concepts. Provided that we anchor internal mediators to observable stimuli or responses, behaviorists do not have to ignore the private life of the human being. Indeed, we have argued and will argue in this book that it is essential to make such inferences. Related to this point is our use of cognitive variables in understanding and modifying behavior. Of course, all of this is quite consistent with contemporary experimental psychology.

It is often alleged that behavior therapists are interested only in symptomatic treatment and do not attempt to deal with "underlying causes." This is perhaps the most widespread misconception of behavior therapy. A determinant of behavior that is assumed to lie in the unconscious need not be viewed as more "underlying" or "basic" than a controlling variable that is in the environment. This issue, crucial in any therapy endeavor, is discussed in greater depth in Chapter 2.

The Ahistorical Nature of Behavior Therapy

Because behavior therapists frequently emphasize the role of current determinants of behavior, they are often mistakenly interpreted as belittling the significance of the client's past. While it is true that few of the behavior therapist's discussions with clients center around early childhood experiences, it would be a mistake to assume that the behavior therapist considers the past to be unimportant. Quite the contrary. A working assumption under which behavior therapists function is that past learning experiences were *indeed* very significant in determining the way in which a person is currently behaving. The reason that little emphasis is placed on past events is the belief that they seldom are still functional, in the sense of maintaining current problematic behaviors. While acknowledging the importance of past learning experiences, the behavior therapist places most of the emphasis on providing the client with *new* learning experiences. This view is most elegantly summarized by Skinner (1953), who observed: "By accounting for a given example of disadvantageous behavior in terms of a personal history and by altering or supplementing that history as a form of therapy, we are considering the very variables to which the traditional theorist must ultimately turn for an explanation of his supposed inner causes" (p. 379).

Manipulation and Self-Control

Behavior therapists are frequently criticized for their open attempts to "manipulate" and "control." The assumption is made that the client's integrity and potential for self-direction is being undermined. There are several reasons why this is not the case. To begin with, the very fact that a client has sought professional assistance is an open admission that he has been unable to adequately control certain aspects of his own life. Although we readily acknowledge the therapist's deliberate attempts to do what he can to influence the client, the ultimate goals for change are typically decided on by the client himself. There are clearly ethical and value-laden issues associated with the behavior change process, particularly with children and institutionalized patients, but these are basically no different from those associated with any therapeutic intervention (see Chapter 13). Moreover, behavior therapists place considerable emphasis on the development of therapeutic procedures by which the client might be provided with greater *self*-direction (Goldfried & Merbaum, 1973; Thoresen & Mahoney, 1974). Unlike other therapeutic approaches that may have as their goal a natural unfolding of the client's potential, behavior therapy views self-direction and self-control as involving certain skills that may effectively be taught to the client by deliberate and systematic therapeutic interventions.

The Simplicity of Behavior Therapy

Finally, it is sometimes asserted that behavior therapy entails a straightforward application of psychological principles. Would that this were so! In all instances, a behavior therapist might be guided by a general principle, but he has to rely on his inventiveness as demanded by the clinical situation in order to translate that principle into clinical practice. That this creativity is characteristic also of experimental psychology is illustrated by the following quote from a respected chapter in the *Handbook of Social Psychology*:

> In any experiment, the investigator chooses a procedure which he intuitively feels is an empirical realization of his conceptual variable. All experimental procedures are "contrived" in the sense that they are invented. Indeed, it can be said that the art of experimentation rests primarily on the skill of the investigator to judge the procedure which is the most accurate realization of his conceptual variable and has the greatest impact and the most credibility for the subject (Aronson & Carlsmith, 1968, p. 25).

One need only substitute "client" for "subject," "therapist" for "investigator," and "clinical" for "experimental" to capture the essence of behavior therapy. Thus, like their experimental colleagues, behavior therapists are faced with the same kinds of decision-making challenges. Or, as we have stated elsewhere,

> ... the theoretical notions to which a clinician subscribes seem to bear importantly on the specific decisions he makes in a particular case. The clinician in fact approaches his work with a given set, a framework for ordering the complex data that are his domain. But frameworks are insufficient. The clinician, like any other applied scientist, must fill out the theoretical skeleton. Individual cases present problems that always call for knowledge beyond basic psychological principles (Lazarus & Davison, 1971, p. 203).

● A BEHAVIORAL VIEW OF PERSONALITY

In many respects, the behavioral view of personality bears great similarity to H. S. Sullivan's (1953) orientation. According to Sullivan, the concept of personality is best defined according to the individual's interpersonal relations. Once having presented this general view, however, Sullivan went on to postulate a number of hypothetical constructs with which he believed one could adequately understand human functioning. From within a behavior therapy framework, however, the concept of personality represents a high level abstraction, which is *nothing more* than the sum total of the individual's behavior. In other words, "personality may be construed as an intervening variable that is defined according to the likelihood of an individual manifesting certain behavioral tendencies in the variety of situations that comprise his day-to-day living" (Goldfried & Kent, 1972, p. 412).

Mischel (1968) has argued most convincingly for the need to explain human behavior in terms of what the individual does in various life situations, as opposed to what traits he possesses more globally. Wendell Johnson, in his little-read *People in Quandaries* (1946), emphasized the importance of using operational terms in assessing and changing behavior:

> To say that Henry is mean implies that he has some sort of inherent trait, but it tells us nothing about what Henry has done. Consequently, it fails to suggest any specific means of improving Henry. If, on the other hand, it is said that Henry snatched Billy's cap and threw it in the bonfire, the situation is rendered somewhat more clear and actually more hopeful. You might never eliminate "mean-

ness," but there are fairly definite steps to be taken in order to remove Henry's incentives or opportunities for throwing caps in bonfires. . . .

What the psychiatrist has to do . . . is to get the person to tell him not what he *is* or what he *has*, but what he *does*, and the conditions under which he does it. When he stops talking about what *type* of person he *is*, what his outstanding *traits are*, and what type of disorder he *has*—when he stops making these subject-predicate statements, and begins to use actional terms to describe his behavior and its circumstances—both he and the psychiatrist begin to see what specifically may be done in order to change both the behavior and the circumstances (p. 220).

The behavior therapist's view of personality has been construed by Wallace (1966; 1967) as referring basically to the individual's abilities or skills in dealing with various life events. Wallace uses the term "response capability" to refer to the person's behavioral potential, which may be seen as being determined by early social learning experiences. In many respects, the concept parallels what is typically referred to as an acquired skill, such as the ability to ride a bicycle, to drive a car, or to demonstrate any other learned proficiency. Whether or not the individual then actually engages in certain activities depends not only on the availability of the behavior within the person's repertoire, but also on the extent to which certain situational determinants elicit and/or reinforce this particular response.

In 1935, Kurt Lewin discussed the importance of construing human behavior as the joint function of the individual and his particular environmental circumstances. Most traditional personality theorists, however, have tended to be more centralistic in their orientation, believing that human behavior might best be understood in terms of the individual's characteristics, such as inner dynamics, needs, expectations, and other similar motivational variables. At the other extreme there have been the radical behaviorists, whose peripheralistic approach maintains that the study of human behavior may be carried out by focusing entirely on environmentalistic variables. We would ascribe to a more interactionalistic viewpoint, for such an orientation seems best to fit the available data (Bowers, 1973; Ekehammar, 1974; Mischel, 1973).

In acknowledging that behavior is the result of the individual's characteristics and current life situation, are we saying that all behavior is specific to the particular situation at hand? Although there appears to be some controversy over this issue, our clinical experience as well as experimental data (Mischel, 1973) tell us that behavioral consistencies *do* exist. In fact, the very nature of most presenting problems within a clinical setting reflects an undesirable cross-situational behavioral consistency, whereby the client's typical behavior pattern tends to be maladaptive across a variety of situational contexts (Wachtel, 1973). The key question is not whether any behavioral consistency exists, but the range of situations and the types of behaviors in which one may find such consistency. Although work is currently being done on this topic (Bem & Allen, 1974), there is little available to provide us with a comprehensive behaviorally oriented theory of personality.

● COGNITION AND BEHAVIOR CHANGE

As mentioned above, it is our firm conviction that to ignore the role of cognitive factors in the conceptualization and modification of human behavior would seriously interfere with the behavior therapist's ability to deal with many of the problems he is confronted with clinically. Although there was a time when behavior therapists assiduously avoided any reference to mediational concepts, more recent presentations of behavior therapy have clearly emphasized the importance of cognitive factors (Bandura, 1969; Davison, 1969; Goldfried & Merbaum, 1973; Kanfer & Phillips, 1970; Lazarus, 1971; London, 1964; Meichenbaum, 1974; Mischel, 1968; Peterson, 1968; Peterson & London, 1964).

In many ways, the early behavior therapists' wariness in introducing cognitive conceptualizations into their understanding of the behavior change process may be viewed as a reaction against the various insight-oriented therapies. The fact that contemporary behavior therapy focuses on cognitive variables, however, does not mean that its approach is identical to the classical psychodynamic viewpoint. As mentioned earlier, within the dynamic frame of reference, cognitively related concepts such as denial, rationalization, or intellectualization were believed to be involuntary and defensive. In contrast, behaviorally oriented cognitive concepts refer to symbolic operations that are more voluntary in nature, and that function primarily to *clarify* the true state of affairs and to contribute to more "healthy" functioning.

Although there are obvious differences between psychodynamic and behavioral conceptions of symbolic processes, we hasten to add that the distinction is not clear-cut. The ego psychoanalytic orientation of such theorists as Hartmann (1958) and Rapaport (1958) has emphasized the conflict-free, deliberate, and conscious use of cognitive processes in order to assist the individual to adapt more effectively to the demands of his world. Consistent with this view, the therapeutic approaches of ego analysts emphasize working with the here and now, and enlarging the individual's areas of conscious control.

In reviewing the history of experimental psychology, it becomes apparent that learning theorists have long recognized that a totally peripheralistic view of human behavior is insufficient. In 1913, Edward L. Thorndike spoke about the importance of "attitude" or "set" in an individual's subsequent learning experiences. According to Hilgard and Bower (1975), Thorndike's view of learning stressed that:

> Responses are determined in part by enduring adjustments characteristic of individuals raised in a given environment or culture. The attitude or set determines not only what the person will do, but what will satisfy or annoy him. . . . Roughly, the notion is that an individual has his own internal standard regarding how well he should perform a given task, and he judges and reinforces (or punishes) his own performance accordingly as it is above or below his standard in quality (p. 35).

In Dollard and Miller's (1950) classic work *Personality and Psychotherapy*, which they dedicated to "Freud and Pavlov and their students," an attempt was made to use the concept of "cue-producing responses" to explain human symbolic processes. Dollard and Miller maintained that the response to a given situation is frequently determined not by the nature of the situation itself, but rather by the individual's interpretation of that event. Thus, if an individual labels a situation as being potentially dangerous, he will then take whatever steps he can to escape or avoid the potential negative consequences associated with that situation. One important implication of such a conceptualization is that the individual may *mislabel* events and then react to this distorted label. In many respects, his reaction to the label is completely appropriate (i.e., it is natural to want to avoid danger); it is the label itself that is inappropriate (i.e., the situation may actually be harmless). Dollard and Miller also made use of the cue-producing response as a means of explaining the time-binding function of symbolic processes, as in the case where we can work many long hours in the absence of any external consequences, providing ourselves instead with periodic self-reinforcement.

Within the field of contemporary experimental psychology—an area that behavior therapists presumably look toward for principles that will bear on their clinical work—it is not at all unusual to find researchers and theorists conceptualizing learning in mediational and cognitive terms. By carefully anchoring their concepts operationally, they often appear considerably more willing to deal with such issues than are some more radical behavior therapists. In fact, Estes (1971), a prominent contemporary learning theorist, has concluded:

> For the lower animals, for very young children, and to some extent for human beings of all ages who are mentally retarded or subject to severe neurological or behavior disorders, behavior from moment to moment is largely describable and predictable in terms of responses to particular stimuli and the rewarding or punishing outcomes of previous stimulus-response sequences. In more mature human beings, much instrumental behavior and, more especially, a great part of verbal behavior is organized into higher-order routines and is, in many instances, better understood in terms of the operation of rules, principles, strategies, and the like than in terms of successions of responses to particular stimuli. Thus, in many situations, an individual's behavior from moment to moment may be governed by a relatively broad strategy which, once adopted, dictates response sequences, rather than by anticipated consequences of specific actions. In these situations it is the selection of strategies rather than the selection of particular reactions to stimuli which is modified by past experience with rewarding or punishing consequences. (p. 23)

As will be seen in subsequent chapters, we find it essential to consider certain cognitive conceptualizations of behavior and of the behavior change process. This ranges from the initial exploration of the client's expectation of what therapy will be like to actual intervention procedures such as rational restructuring and problem solving.

● THE SCOPE OF BEHAVIOR THERAPY

As stated above, most early writers in behavior therapy avoided the use of cognitive conceptualizations. They also took special pains to dissociate their approach from what held sway in the previous clinical work of others. This understandable attempt to stake out a contrast in domain is, we believe, best replaced at the present time by a serious examination of rapprochements with other therapeutic orientations. This is not to say that, as an approach, behavior therapy has nothing unique to contribute in its own right. Rather, it is to say that in the attempt to expand knowledge and to improve the quality of our clinical services, it is time for behavior therapists to stop regarding themselves as an outgroup and instead to enter into serious and hopefully mutually fruitful dialogues with their nonbehavioral colleagues. Just as we firmly believe that there is much that behavior therapy can say to clinicians of other orientations, we reject the assumption that the slate should be wiped clean and that therapeutic innovations should be—and even can be—completely novel. Thus, for example, Sullivan's suggestions on interviewing procedures, client-centered techniques for establishing rapport, and Gestalt therapy procedures for encouraging open expression can all have important applications in clinical behavior therapy.

Although it is not our goal to review the points of overlap between behavior therapy and psychodynamically oriented approaches—such a review has already been most impressively accomplished by Wachtel (in press)—there are some remarkable similarities that are worth noting. For example, Freud's ultimate goals for therapy were essentially behavioral in nature, focusing on helping the patient to love and to work. Similarly, on occasion he described the role of the therapist as an educator, and emphasized that the patient should be educable. He was also among the first to recognize that problems in adulthood may be explained on the basis of early childhood experiences. Where Freud's approach dramatically differs from the behavioral is with regard to the nature of the learning process, and the way in which the patient can be retaught new ways of functioning.

In a careful reading of the psychoanalytic literature, there are numerous instances that reflect a striking similarity to what currently exists in clinical behavior therapy. A prime example is in the classic book of Alexander and French (1946), where they spoke of the "corrective emotional experience." By this they refer to the fact that the patient need not always require insight into the historical origins of his problem in order to effect behavior change. They suggested that the individual might be encouraged to engage in new experiences in the current life situation, which in some way or other might pay off, thereby freeing him to behave differently in the future. They even observed that "Freud himself came to the conclusion that in the treatment of some cases, phobias for example, a time arrives when the analyst must encourage the patient to engage in those activities he avoided in the past" (Alexander & French, 1946, p. 39). In other words, the job of the therapist at times might be to instigate the client to try out new behaviors.

One is tempted to draw a distinction between behavior therapy and other clinical approaches on the basis of techniques. To define behavior therapy in terms of certain techniques, however, is illusory. With continued clinical ingenuity in more effectively implementing various principles of psychology, and also with the formulation of more principles themselves, it is obvious that the pool of techniques available to the behavior therapist in the future will probably be very different from those currently at hand.

While the definition of behavior therapy as deriving its techniques from the well-established body of knowledge in psychology sounds reasonable, it often does not occur that way in clinical practice. We have found instances where "insights" occurred to us in the midst of clinical sessions, prompting us to react in specific ways that paid off handsomely in the therapeutic progress of our clients. These may have entailed personal revelations that we provided to our clients, vaguely articulated hunches that we followed up, or therapeutic moves that we blindly stumbled upon, but which yielded therapeutic benefits well beyond our hard-headed comprehension. In accordance with most common definitions of behavior therapy, this might be viewed as heresy. Perhaps in some way it is. Nonetheless, our contact with reality is relatively veridical, and what we have observed under such instances is not terribly unique. If, in fact, some of these phenomena are reliable, even if they are not easily derived from basic principles of psychology, should we ignore them because we call ourselves behavior therapists?

The assertion that behavior therapy involves the implementation of principles of psychology assumes that all of the principles have been established, and that anything different we see in the clinical situation is accidental and without meaning. To assume this, however, places us in direct contradiction with the clinical working assumption that the phenomena we see in this setting are a reflection of lawful behavior that can readily be explained in light of what we know of people in general. Clearly, it is possible to see things clinically that have not yet been established scientifically.

There is yet another very good reason that behavior therapists should not be overly enamored with their current pool of techniques. As has been aptly observed by Maslow (1966): "If the only tool you have is a hammer, [you tend] to treat everything as if it were a nail" (pp. 15–16). We at times find ourselves most concerned over the possibility that we may be overlooking some important concerns of our clients simply because we have no techniques to deal with such problems. An excellent case in point is the so-called existential crisis that one frequently reads about in the nonbehavioral literature. All too often, behavior therapists dismiss such complaints on the grounds that available behavior therapy concepts and techniques cannot readily deal with such issues. However, it is just such problems that provide the greatest challenge to behavior therapy. When confronted with such complaints, we indirectly blame the client, indicating that his problem is "not appropriate" to our procedures. Similarly, when progress in therapy for any given client does not proceed smoothly, we frequently accuse the client of either not being motivated enough or perhaps "not being ready for" behavior therapy. We would like to suggest, however, that *the client is never wrong.* If one truly accepts the assumption that behavior is lawful—whether it be deviant or nondeviant—then *any* difficulties occurring during the course of therapy should more appropriately be traced to the therapist's inadequate or incomplete evaluation of the case. We are not implying that this always means the behavior therapist has been incompetent in the way in which he has conceptualized or handled the case. It may very well be that our knowledge of certain problems, or the unavailability of certain concepts, principles, or techniques at this point in the development of the field simply does not provide us with the ability to meet certain types of challenges. We firmly believe, however, that behavior therapy, when viewed as an experimental clinical approach to human difficulties, provides us with the most workable framework within which to expand the effectiveness of the behavior change process.

● PURPOSE OF THIS BOOK

Behavior therapy is entering a new phase. We believe current and future developments will not only reflect a more sophisticated cognizance of clinical activity, but will at the same time make the field more palatable to those hitherto put off by some of the narrow conceptualizations and polemics that marked the beginnings of behavior therapy.

Our attempt in this book is to convey as best one can with the printed word the subtleties and decision-making processes that, in our view, are crucial for the successful implementation of the behavioral approach. We shall try to explain as clearly as possible the cognitive activities of the behavioral clinician confronted by a variety of clinical exigencies. In essence, what we shall try to do is to emphasize those aspects of behavior therapy that are discussed far more often in private supervisory sessions than in textbooks or scientific articles. We believe that the considerations enumerated in the following chapters must be confronted if one is to operate effectively and responsibly as a clinical behavior therapist.

Chapter  2

Conceptual Issues in Behavioral Assessment

The topic of behavioral assessment has only recently begun to receive serious attention in the literature. Most clinicians of all theoretical orientations regard therapeutic activities as much more prestigious than assessment and testing. Thus, some of the early neglect of assessment by behavior therapists may well have stemmed from the fact that it was not personally very "reinforcing." And yet, without an appropriate assessment, it is unlikely that any of the currently available behavior therapy techniques, no matter how powerful, can be effective. In this chapter, we discuss a number of conceptual issues in behavioral assessment, including the differences between behavioral and traditional approaches to assessment. We also deal with those variables upon which the clinician must focus in carrying out a behavioral analysis of the presenting problem, as well as the considerations associated with the selection and implementation of the most appropriate intervention procedures.

● ROLE OF ASSESSMENT IN BEHAVIOR THERAPY

The early neglect of assessment by behavior therapists may also have been due in part to the traditional conceptualization of personality associated with most assessment procedures. Personality theorists have, for the most part, employed *dispositional* concepts, such as "instincts," "needs," "drives," and "traits," in an attempt to understand human behavior. This general approach of looking solely "within" the individual for motivational determinants has been referred to by Murray (1938) as representing the *centralistic* orientation to the study of human functioning. Perhaps it is behavior therapy's partial or total rejection of the centralistic orientation itself that has led to the tendency to neglect the area of assessment. Some of the more radical behavior therapists have completely rejected the role of inner determinants, and have focused solely on environmental variables in their quest for increased prediction and control. While we would agree that this focus is appropriate in some cases, the complete neglect of intraindividual variables places a serious limitation on the types of problems one can deal with clinically.[1]

As noted above, assessment procedures have traditionally been directed at measuring a relatively stable set of dispositional variables that would explain and predict behavior. These dispositional concepts were viewed as being useful not only in describing personality functioning, but also in attempting to modify personality structure, thereby producing behavior change. In other words, the questions that the centralistically oriented clinician has typically asked himself are, "What is there about the client's personality structure which is causing him to have certain problems?" and "What aspects of his personality should be altered in order to minimize these problems?"

Although this close connection between assessment and therapy would seem to be a logical one, relatively few therapists rely on traditional assessment procedures (Meehl, 1960), perhaps because they have doubts about the validity of the instruments themselves. More likely, however, is the fact that within many schools of therapy, the same procedure is used across a wide variety of problems

---

[1] It is of interest to note that this neglect of internal processes is not intrinsic to a Skinnerian approach (Skinner, 1953). And yet, we would argue, operant behavior therapists have, in practice, eschewed such inferred variables.

(London, 1964). As will become apparent in this chapter and succeeding ones, effective clinical behavior therapy requires a thorough
and detailed assessment prior to the selection and implementation
of the most appropriate intervention procedure.

● COMPARISON OF BEHAVIORAL
AND TRADITIONAL ASSESSMENT

As indicated above, traditional approaches to personality assessment generally have focused on understanding the individual's underlying *personality characteristics or traits*. This approach is
reflected in most currently available personality tests, including the
Rorschach, Thematic Apperception Test, Draw-A-Person, and Min-
nesota Multiphasic Personality Inventory In contrast, the behavioral
approach to personality assessment involves more of a direct sampling of the individual's *response to various life situations* The
techniques typically associated with behavioral assessment include
the observation of individuals in various life situations, a simulation
of real-life situations through role playing, physiological measurement, and self-reports of how the client behaves in specific situations (Goldfried & Sprafkin, 1974).

Although the methods of traditional versus behavioral assessment are different, the primary distinction rests with certain
underlying assumptions and not with the methods per se. Traditional and behavioral assessors may at times use the same procedure—such as the interview, but the *way* in which it is used is
likely to differ (Goldfried, 1976; Goldfried & Kent, 1972; Peterson, 1968; Mischel, 1968). As noted by Goldfried and Kent (1972),
the two approaches to assessment may best be differentiated in
terms of those assumptions underlying (a) the conception of what
is meant by "personality," (b) the selection of test items, and (c)
the interpretation of test responses.

Conception of Personality

Most traditional personality tests are based on a common conception of human functioning, and have been directed toward
obtaining information about the individual's "personality structure."
Depending on the specific theoretical orientation, these inferred
characteristics may consist of "motives," "needs," "drives," "defenses," "traits," or other similar constructs. Central to this view
is the notion of psychic determinism, whereby a person's actions
are assumed to be motivated by certain underlying dynamics. Ac-

cording to this concept of personality, then, the most appropriate way to predict human behavior should be based on a thorough assessment of those inferred characteristics of which the overt actions are believed to be a function.

In contrast to this classical psychodynamic orientation, which focuses on the characteristics an individual "has," the behavioral view places greater emphasis on what a person "does" in various life situations (Mischel, 1968). That is, the basic unit of assessment involves the individual's response (overt or covert) to specific aspects of his environment. As noted earlier in this chapter and also in Chapter 1, human behavior is viewed as being determined not only by the person's interpersonal abilities resulting from previous social learning history, but also by current environmental antecedents and/or consequences of behavior.

It should be mentioned that more recent trends in psychodynamic circles have begun to place greater emphasis on concurrent environmental influences and the extent to which the individual is capable of responding to such events. A discussion of the current status of psychodynamic thinking can be found in Wachtel (in press).

Selection of Test Items

A significant consequence of the more classical psychodynamic view that consistencies in behavior exist independently of situational variables has been the fact that relatively little emphasis seems to have been placed on the importance of the stimulus items employed. In the case of behavioral assessment, which construes personality more in terms of the individual's specific response to situations, a crucial requirement is that the appropriate stimulus situations be adequately represented. For example, in surveying fear behavior, it is necessary to obtain measures of fear in certain situations that sample the population of potentially anxiety-producing situations. In behavioral assessment, then, the issue of content validity becomes particularly relevant; procedures for conducting situational analyses may be found in Goldfried and D'Zurilla (1969).

Interpretation of Test Responses

In considering the assumptions underlying the interpretation of traditional and behavioral tests, one can refer to the "sign" and "sample" distinction originally made by Goodenough (1949). The sign approach assumes that the response may best be construed as

an indirect manifestation of some underlying personality characteristic. The sample approach, on the other hand, assumes that the
test behavior constitutes the subset of some larger pool of responses.
Whereas traditional personality tests have typically taken the sign
approach to interpretation, behavioral procedures approach test interpretation with a sample orientation. The assumption that behavioral test responses are sampling certain behavioral tendencies
is closely linked to the assumption that the test items themselves
consist of a representative sample of certain types of situations. In
the assessment of assertiveness toward authority figures, for example, a sampling interpretation of an individual's test responses
would assume that the test items themselves represent an adequate
sample of interpersonal situations involving authority figures.

● VARIABLES IN NEED OF ASSESSMENT

It is useful to make a conceptual distinction between (a) those
variables associated with a behavioral analysis of the maladaptive
behavior and (b) those which have implications for the selection
and implementation of the most relevant therapeutic procedures.
In essence, the first set of variables sheds light on *what* has to be
manipulated in order to bring about behavior change, while the
second set provides information about *how* best to bring about this
change.

Variables Associated with Maladaptive Behavior

Viewing the client's maladaptive behavior as a dependent variable, the therapist's task becomes one of deciding which of many
potential independent variables he can best "manipulate" to bring
about behavior change. There has been some confusion in the
literature as to whether or not behavior therapists actually are
manipulating "underlying causes" when attempting to modify problem behaviors. If by "underlying causes" one necessarily means
early social learning experiences, then the answer is no. This does
not imply, however, that the treatment always focuses on the presenting problem. Take, for example, the client whose marriage is
faltering due to the frequent arguments he has with his wife. In
carrying out a behavioral analysis, it may be revealed that the
arguments typically occur when he has been drinking. When does
he drink? Whenever he's had a hard day at work. What contributes
to the pressure at work? The excessively high standards he imposes

on his own performance. Here the therapist would probably focus more on the husband's unrealistic standards for self-evaluation, and not on the fighting behavior itself. In other words, the behavioral analysis may "uncover" other relevant variables—not early social learning experiences, but additional concurrent variables within the chain of potential determinants of behavior.

In deciding on which variables should be manipulated, the behavior therapist can select from one or more of the following: (a) the antecedent stimulus variables, which may elicit or set the stage for the maladaptive behavior; (b) organismic variables, whether of a psychological or physiological nature; (c) the overt maladaptive behavior itself; and (d) the consequent changes in the environmental situation, including the reactions of others to the maladaptive behavior. While the distinction among these four types of variables may at times be arbitrary, it is useful to discuss each separately.

Stimulus Antecedents

Although once highly centralistic, clinicians and personality theorists have begun to recognize the significant role of the environment as an important determinant of behavior. In considering the role of antecedent stimulus events, one may draw a distinction between those that elicit emotional or autonomic responses and those that function as discriminative cues for the occurrence of maladaptive instrumental responses.

In dealing with such maladaptive emotional responses as anxiety or depression, the behavior therapist operates under the assumption that there exists some external situation which is eliciting the behavior. We must admit, however, that at times it may be no easy task to specify exactly which events in the client's life are determining his emotional response. There are individuals who report being anxious all of the time or being in very chronic and pervasive states of depression. In such a case, the client's emotional reaction apparently becomes so salient that he is unable to pinpoint its functional antecedents. Other clients may be able to indicate general classes of situations to which they are reacting (e.g., heights, enclosed spaces, social evaluative situations). Although this clearly simplifies the task of assessment, the need nonetheless exists for greater specification of those situations which have been eliciting the emotional upset.

In the assessment of discriminative stimuli that set the stage for maladaptive instrumental behaviors that will be reinforced, the therapist must obtain detailed information on the precise nature of the situation, such as time, place, and frequency. Mischel (1968) has argued convincingly that an individual's response, whether it be deviant or nondeviant, is greatly influenced by the specific nature of the situation in which the behavior occurs. We have all had the experience of being surprised when a friend or colleague acts "out of character" in certain situations. Clinically, it is not uncommon to observe a child who presents a behavior problem at home, but creates no difficulties in the school setting. As in the specification of stimuli that elicit maladaptive emotional responses, relevant discriminative stimuli must be described in detail (e.g., what is it about the school setting which differs from the home environment?).

The way an individual interprets an event is often important in determining the stimulus antecedents of his behavior. The issue of defining the effective stimulus has prompted those involved in research on perception to focus on the significant role played by physiological and cognitive states of the individual. We refer to these factors as organismic variables.

Organismic Variables

While the increasing recognition of environmental variables as determinants of behavior is a welcome trend, the exclusion of all inferential concepts and the refusal to consider mediating factors can seriously limit the therapist's ability to understand and modify behavior. The completely environmentalistic, noninferential orientation to the study of human functioning, which Murray (1938) has called the *peripheralistic* approach, can limit one's understanding of human behavior as much as an entirely centralistic orientation can. Although an individual's attitudes, beliefs, and expectations may often be modified by changes in overt behavior, there are times when such organismic variables should themselves be the target for direct modification.

One type of mediator consists of the client's expectations or set about certain situations. As suggested by Dollard and Miller (1950) and by Ellis (1962), the way in which a person labels or categorizes events can greatly color his emotional reaction in such situations. In addition to interpreting situations in ways that can create problems, a person may also create difficulties by the way he labels his own behavior. To the extent that an individual construes his maladaptive behavior as indicative of his "going crazy," being out of control, or manifesting a serious physical illness, his problem will be compounded. Another important mediating variable consists of

the standards one sets for self-reinforcement. Although a client 2
may be functioning at an appropriate level of proficiency according
to societal standards, his primary problem may result from the fact
that he construes his behavior as being substandard; in such instances, it would appear that the standard is unrealistic and in need
of modification.

In the assessment of organismic variables, one should attend
also to any physiological factors which may contribute to the mal- 3
adaptive behavior. Included here would be direct and side effects of
any psychoactive drugs, the client's general energy level, states of
fatigue, and other similar physiological and constitutional factors
which might influence his behavior. It is not uncommon, for example, for depression to coincide with some women's menstrual
periods. It is clear that, with presenting problems such as headaches,
forgetfulness, sexual inadequacy, and other potentially biologically
mediated problems, a thorough physical examination should be
done.

Response Variables

The primary focus here should be consistent with the general
guidelines suggested by Mischel (1968): "In behavioral analysis
the emphasis is on what a person *does* in situations rather than on
inferences about what attributes he *has* more globally" (p.10). In
other words, the assessment of response variables should focus on
situation-specific samples of the maladaptive behavior, including
information on duration, frequency, pervasiveness, and intensity.

Although the distinction is at times difficult to make, it is important to differentiate responses which are primarily *respondents*
from those which are *operants*. Respondents, where consequences
play a relatively minimal role in maintaining the response, typically
include such emotional reactions as anxiety, depression, anger, and
sexual arousal. Operant or instrumental behavior, on the other hand,
includes those responses for which the consequent reinforcement
plays a significant role. Examples of maladaptive instrumental
behaviors are typically seen in children, particularly where the
primary difficulty consists of "behavior problems." The extensive
work done with token economies in schools and institutional settings
has similarly focused on instrumental behaviors. Still further examples of operant behavior seen in clinical settings are social skill
deficits, such as lack of assertiveness and inappropriate heterosexual behaviors.

There are times when one cannot distinguish between operants and respondents. For example, the child who consistently delays going to bed at night because he is "afraid to be by himself" may pose assessment problems. The same is true of a multitude of other problems of a primarily avoidant nature, which may be maintained both by an emotional reaction to antecedent stimuli and by consequent changes in the environment following the avoidance response.

Consequent Variables

To a great extent, many of our day-to-day responses, both adaptive and maladaptive, are maintained by their consequences. In determining whether something "pays off," the timing of the consequences can play a significant role. For example, the so-called neurotic paradox (Mowrer, 1950) refers to behaviors having immediate positive consequences, but long-term negative ones, as in the case of the alcohol or drug addict. A frequently existing positive reinforcement may consist of the reactions of significant others. Such reinforcements can include approval and praise, but in some cases may simply be attention, as when a parent or teacher becomes angry over a child's refusal to obey a given command. In addition to the delay and content of reinforcement, one should note also the frequency of reinforcement, as in the case of the depressed person who has few reinforcing events in his life situation.

Variables Associated with Selection and Implementation of Techniques

In addition to using assessment procedures to determine which variables—whether antecedent, organismic, response, or consequent—need to be modified, the clinician must also assess for the most appropriate therapeutic technique. Unlike most other clinicians, behavior therapists choose from a wide range of possible procedures. In part, the selection of therapeutic technique will be determined by the target in need of modification. For example, if a detailed behavioral analysis done with a test-anxious client reveals that his difficulties are due to the fact that he does not study, one would obviously not utilize a technique such as desensitization. Or, for a client whose anxiety in social situations is due to an actual behavioral deficit, some sort of skill-training procedure would be more appropriate than desensitization.

At present, we have relatively little empirical data on specific variables associated with the effective implementation of the various behavior therapy procedures. Some findings are just beginning to become available, such as Kanter's (1975) report that rational restructuring may be more appropriate than desensitization in cases of social anxiety. However, most of our clinical decisions are based on the intrinsic nature of the procedure itself (e.g., you cannot use systematic desensitization with a client who is unable to conjure up an aversive image) as well as on clinical experience in the use of the various procedures.

There are certain client characteristics that are relevant for the selection and implementation of therapeutic procedures. The client's ability to report specific concrete examples is frequently crucial in the implementation of a number of therapeutic techniques. What we have observed clinically is that those clients who have the greatest initial difficulty in reporting actual behavioral samples tend to be brighter and more "psychologically sophisticated." Clients who have this difficulty must be trained to be more specific (e.g., via repeated instructions, selective reinforcement, homework assignments) before anything can be done therapeutically.

A number of techniques used by behavior therapists include ongoing homework assignments, in which the client must keep a record of various behavioral events between sessions, or practice certain skills *in vivo*. If the client tends to be disorganized or to procrastinate, which may or may not be part of the primary target behaviors towards which the therapy is being directed, he will probably be less likely to carry through on the between-session assignments. In such instances, the therapist must decide to rely less on homework, or must attempt to persuade the client to follow through on these tasks.

The therapist should also be attuned to the client's standards for self-reinforcement. Clients with perfectionistic standards may expect too much too fast, and consequently may become discouraged with the gradual nature of behavior change. We take great care to discuss this potential difficulty with such clients prior to the actual implementation of whatever technique is to be used. We also dispel potential dissatisfaction by focusing continually on the client's appropriate evaluation of behavior change as it begins to occur.

In addition to client variables, certain environmental variables may be important in the selection and implementation of therapeutic procedures. (We are referring to considerations such as the availability of appropriate role models in a client's life, or the extent to which certain reinforcers are likely to be available for certain behaviors.) In the treatment of sexual problems, for example, the availability of a partner can have obvious implications for the specific therapeutic procedures utilized. Other examples occur with various phobias, where the feasibility of *in vivo* desensitization depends upon the availability of fear-related situations or objects.

At present, one typically uses clinical intuition and experience as an aid in determining what seems to be the most appropriate behavior therapy technique for a particular client. Clinical practice involves selecting a few seemingly relevant techniques, and then trying each in turn until one proves to be effective. A better strategy would seem to involve the use of a thorough "criterion analysis" of each behavior therapy procedure, with the goal being the determination of those variables necessary for the selection of the most effective treatment for any given client. In the most comprehensive sense, the relevant research question to be answered is: "*What* treatment, by *whom*, is most effective for *this* individual with *that* specific problem, and under *which* set of circumstances?" (Paul, 1967, p. 111).

● CLASSIFICATION OF BEHAVIOR DISORDERS

The Kraepelinian system of classifying deviant behavior has been criticized on a number of counts, not the least of which is its scant relevance for a behavioral approach to the understanding and modification of behavior (Kanfer & Saslow, 1969). Although there is not, at present, any alternate comprehensive classification system available, Staats (1963) has offered some suggestions that have been elaborated upon by Bandura (1968) and Goldfried and Sprafkin (1974). In outlining various categories of deviant behaviors, this interim approximation attempts to take into account stimulus as well as client variables. Further, it categorizes deviant behaviors according to the variables that are probably maintaining them.

I. Difficulties in Stimulus Control of Behavior

Within this general category, the distinction is drawn between the failure of environmental stimuli to control maladaptive *instrumental* behavior and the tendency of some stimuli to elicit maladaptive *emotional* reactions.

A. Defective Stimulus Control

In instances of defective stimulus control, the individual presumably possesses an adequate behavioral repertoire, but is unable to respond to socially appropriate discriminative stimuli. An extreme example of defective stimulus control would be an individual who tells jokes at a funeral. Although the jokes may be objectively funny (i.e., the behavioral repertoire is adequate), they are clearly out of place in that particular situation. An example with more clinical relevance is a child who is so eager to show the teacher he knows the correct answer, that he continually speaks out of turn in class. Assuming the child is capable of maintaining silence at times, he must learn to respond to those situational cues that indicate when it is appropriate for him to speak up. There are numerous clinical examples that show how parents inadvertently train their children to respond to incorrect discriminative stimuli. For example, a parent may complain that his child will not obey him when he speaks quietly, but only when he shouts. The child has probably learned that neither aversive nor positive consequences follow ordinary requests, but that failure to heed an angry parent's request can result in a variety of aversive consequences. The child is clearly capable of obeying, but does not do so when the parents want him to.

B. Inappropriate Stimulus Control

In this category one would include intense aversive emotional reactions elicited by objectively innocuous cues. These emotional reactions have presumably been conditioned to these specific stimuli, either by direct or by vicarious social learning experiences. Anxiety, gastrointestinal disturbances, insomnia, and other direct or indirect manifestations of intense emotional reactions would be included in this category. Such problems are frequently complicated by attempts to avoid these emotional states (as in the case of phobias), and also by the symbolic presentation of aversive stimuli, that is, ruminating about fears.

II. Deficient Behavioral Repertoires

This category includes behavior problems in which an individual lacks skills needed to cope effectively with situational demands. For example, the person may never have learned what to say or do in social, academic, or vocational situations. Although the problem may be construed as a skill deficit, the clinical picture is often complicated by such an individual's failure to achieve adequate social reinforcement. He may even experience punishing consequences, such as loss of status, ridicule, and rejection. As a result, clients manifesting behavioral deficits frequently report negative subjective attitudes, including anxiety, depression, lack of self-confidence, and sometimes generalized anger toward others.

III. Aversive Behavioral Repertoires

The defining characteristic of this category is a maladaptive behavior pattern that is aversive to other individuals surrounding the client. Included here, then, would be persons who manifest anti-social behavior, who are overly aggressive, or who in some other ways are inconsiderate of others. Some writers have characterized these individuals as manifesting a "behavioral excess." In contrast to behavioral deficiencies, individuals with aversive behavioral repertoires know what to say and do in various situations, but they ultimately make life difficult for themselves by being obnoxious or otherwise bothersome to others.

IV. Difficulties with Incentive Systems (Reinforcers)

Included here are deviant behaviors that are functionally tied to reinforcing consequences, either because the incentive system of the individual is deficient or inappropriate, or because the environmental contingencies are creating problems.

A. Defective Incentive System in Individual

In these instances, social stimuli that are reinforcing for most people are not capable of controlling the individual's behavior. Thus, attention, approval, and praise may not be positively reinforcing, nor criticism or disapproval negatively reinforcing. Two clinical examples are autistic children, whose behavior cannot be readily controlled by conventional social reinforcers (Rimland, 1964), and delinquents for whom social reinforcers in the larger society have little relevance, as their behavior conforms to the standards of a subculture.

B. Inappropriate Incentive System in Individual

This category includes those persons for whom the incentive system itself is maladaptive, that is, those things reinforcing to the individual are harmful and/or culturally disapproved. Excessive involvement with alcohol, drugs, and sexual practices such as pedophilia are some clinical examples.

C. Absence of Incentives in Environment

Problems in this category include situations in which reinforcement is lacking in an individual's particular environment. The most clearly delineated example is a state of prolonged depression resulting from the loss of a spouse. More subtle examples are apathy and boredom.

D. Conflicting Incentives in Environment

Much maladaptive behavior stems from conflicting environmental consequences. The clearest clinical examples are children whose maladaptive behavior appears to pay off, where there is a contradiction between what has been labeled by the environment as maladaptive and what, in fact, the environment is inadvertently reinforcing. Sometimes certain individuals in the environment are positively reinforcing a deviant behavior, as with the class clown who attracts the attention of his peers, despite the fact that his teacher disapproves of his actions. More subtly, a parent or teacher may reinforce a child for lack of persistence by helping him as soon as he experiences some difficulty in handling a situation. Problems associated with conflicting incentives in the environment are not limited to children. As pointed out by Goffman (1961), Rosenhan (1973), and others, institutional settings, including psychiatric hospitals, may inadvertently foster behavior which is then labeled as deviant. On the more interpersonal level, an individual may verbally encourage his spouse to behave in one way but may act otherwise to discourage or even outrightly punish such attempts.

V. Aversive Self-Reinforcing Systems

Assuming that cognitive processes are capable of maintaining various forms of behavior, it is important to recognize that an individual is capable of reinforcing himself for adequate behavior. If an individual's standards for "adequacy" are unrealistically high, he is likely to find himself in few situations where his performance merits self-reinforcement, regardless of how adequate he may be according to external criteria. The consistent lack of self-reinforcement may lead to chronic states of depression and subjective feelings of inadequacy.

Although the system outlined above can be useful in carrying out a behavioral analysis of deviant behavior, it should be viewed as only a first attempt to categorize maladaptive behavior within a social learning context. Obviously, the categories are not mutually exclusive. Any one person may manifest a number of behavior problems, which can be classified according to several of the headings. Further, certain behavior problems may be so complex as to warrant a multiple classification. Still, the system can serve its purpose by isolating those environmental or client variables which can be manipulated for maximum therapeutic benefit.

● FURTHER CONSIDERATIONS IN THE SELECTION OF TARGET BEHAVIORS

A reading of the behavior therapy literature often conveys the impression that behavior therapists typically deal with simple phobias or otherwise clearly delineated problems. This is far from being the case. Except in rare instances, clients seen in behavior therapy usually manifest a multitude of different problems. Assuming a finite amount that a therapist can accomplish during consultation sessions and can require of a client between sessions, he must decide on treatment priorities.

In the difficult decision of where to begin, the most obvious consideration would be whether there might be a functional relationship among the presenting problems. With a client who complains of both unassertive behavior and feelings of depression, for example, it is possible that the depressed feelings might be a consequence of his lack of assertiveness. During the initial stages of therapy, such interpretations are obviously speculative, and must await confirmation by therapeutic intervention.

Another consideration in determining treatment priorities is the potential consequence of delaying the modification of any particular problem. If, for example, a client were phobic and also severely depressed, it would probably be more appropriate to place a higher priority on the depression, for two reasons. First it is frequently possible to avoid being in contact with phobic objects; secondly, severe depression may lead to serious consequences, such as hospitalization and/or suicide.

There are times, however, when the therapist might want to begin with a problem behavior that is not terribly important within the larger scheme of things, but which can readily be modified. He may thereby encourage a client who is particularly skeptical about the likelihood of changing. The goal would be to modify the client's expectation and increase his motivation to carry through with the behavior therapy procedures yet to come. Before using such a tactic, the therapist must predict that the "cost" (i.e., time and effort expended) will be worth the "payoff" (i.e., change in client attitude).

Any discussion of the ordering of treatment priorities that fails to mention the client's own preferences is obviously incomplete. It is remarkable how many therapists fail to take the client's own desires into consideration. A behavior therapist might mistakenly assume that his goals coincide with the client's, with the result that therapist and client may find themselves working at cross-purposes. Of course, there may be times when the client's problems themselves prevent him from adequately evaluating his plight, as in the case of the socially inappropriate individual who feels his interpersonal relationships would improve if only he could lose some weight. One of us was asked by a parent to assist in toilet training her four-year-old son, only to find that the child was autistic. Clearly, the therapist must use his professional judgment in deciding to overrule the treatment goals as stated by the client. Having done so, however, he should make every effort to arrive at a mutually agreeable set of goals. We shall return to this important issue in Chapter 3.

● CASE DESCRIPTION

The following case description, which has been taken from Goldfried and Pomeranz (1968), can serve to illustrate a number of the points made above.

> Consider the hypothetical case of a fifty-year-old man who comes to therapy because he has difficulty in leaving his house. The situation has reached the point where merely contemplating getting out of bed results in such anxiety that most of his time is spent in a prone position. As a result, he must be constantly looked after by his wife. Further questioning reveals that his most salient fear is having a heart attack, which he states is the reason for remaining at home and in bed. Upon carrying the assessment further—this time evaluating the nature of his current life situation—it is found that this man has recently been promoted in his job to a position where he now has the responsibility for supervising a large staff. Prior to this promotion, he led a fairly normal life, and his fears of having a heart attack were nonexistent.

Further assessment reveals that the client has always tended to become anxious in unfamiliar situations and is the type of person who would prefer to have other people look after and care for him. Additionally, questioning his wife reveals that she does not find the current situation entirely noxious; rather she feels important and needed now that she has to care for her husband, and she lavishes much attention and affection on him in his incapacitated state.

Prior to the delineation of the appropriate target for modification, the clinician must conceptualize the data more systematically. As we have noted above, a formulation of the case should focus on: (a) the relevant environmental antecedents, (b) the significant, mediational responses and cues, (c) the observable maladaptive behavior itself, and (d) the consequent environmental changes.

Using this paradigm, a formulation of this case might be as follows: the change in this individual's work situation elicited a number of mediational (labeling) responses (e.g., this is a situation requiring direction and supervision of others, judgments must be made about other people's performance, inadequate work of others reflects negatively on a supervisor, etc.). Because of this particular individual's previous learning experiences, these responses, associated with a change in job status, elicit anxiety. Among the many manifestations of this anxiety reaction is increase in heart rate. Because of the client's mislabeling of this state of increased arousal (i.e., he associates the increased activity of the heart in a man of his age and position with the possibility of having a heart attack), he becomes concerned with thoughts that this might be happening to him. These thoughts serve as mediating responses which tend to elicit additional anxiety, thus adding to his distressed condition. Remaining at home and confined to bed, which belong to a class of behaviors relatively high in his behavioral repertoire, serve as successful avoidance responses which keep him out of a situation which initially elicited the anxiety; it is also appropriate behavior for a person who might be having a heart attack. His behavior elicits attention and care from his wife, providing additional reinforcement for the maladaptive behavior.

Following the translation of the data into conceptual terms, the clinician is then faced with the task of selecting the most relevant target for change. The most salient target in this case—the *observable maladaptive behavior* of staying at home and remaining in bed—does not appear to be the most appropriate for direct modification. We have conceptualized this behavior as an avoidance response, where the stimuli eliciting the anxiety continue to be present. The direct alteration of this overt behavior without any change in the mediating anxiety could very well result in the manifestation of other avoidance responses lower in the client's repertoire. In considering possible modifications in the *current life situation*, we also encounter difficulties. Although a change in the situation that was *antecedent* to the appearance of this maladaptive behavior—his promotion at work—might successfully eliminate the problem, it would also result in a financial and status loss for this individual; the modification of other targets that might eliminate the problem and yet avoid these other negative consequences would be preferable. Modification of the *consequent* aspect of the client's current life situation—the attention he is receiving from his wife—would only be focusing on the additional reinforcers and not on the stimuli that are concurrently eliciting the avoidance response.

Having considered the observable maladaptive behavior and the current life situation as possible areas for modification, we turn to the *mediational responses*. The client's distorted labeling of the psychological cues that were a concomitant of the anxiety reaction seems to be of only secondary importance. Antecedent to this inappropriate labeling are the anxiety responses elicited by those situations requiring him to supervise and make decisions about others. It is his fear of functioning in this type of situation that seems to have resulted in a chain of internal and external maladaptive responses. It appears that the most crucial area toward which any therapeutic endeavors should be directed would be the client's anxiety regarding the supervision of others.

Following the selection of the most important target for modification, some decision must be made in the choice of an appropriate treatment procedure. It is here that behavioral assessment is most inadequate. While the assessment of the target makes the task of selecting the appropriate therapeutic procedure less difficult, the situation is certainly not clear-cut. Indeed, what we often find is that the assessment enables us to *eliminate* certain therapeutic techniques more than to indicate which would be most appropriate. In the case of our hypothetical client, the determination of whether or not to employ systematic desensitization, assertion training, rational restructuring, or perhaps problem-solving training in the reduction of his anxiety regarding decision making cannot easily be made on the basis of any currently existing assessment information. Although it may well be that one particular approach to anxiety reduction would be most effective with this client in his particular life situation, we currently have little empirical data about which variables would be relevant in making this choice. At best, we can only speculate about the variables . . . pertinent to the successful application of the above-mentioned techniques, and then to use each of the several possible procedures until one turns out to be effective in modifying the maladaptive behavior in question (pp. 83–85).

● SUMMARY

This chapter has discussed several conceptual issues associated with behavioral assessment. In addition to approaching the behavior change process from a different vantage point, clinical behavior therapists have also adopted a different orientation in their assessment procedures. The behavior therapist has at his disposal a wide variety of therapeutic techniques, necessitating a detailed assessment to determine which particular intervention procedure is likely to be appropriate to each particular client. To select the client's problems and to select the proper therapy procedure, the clinical assessment focuses on several types of variables: antecedent stimulus variables, organismic variables, the overt maladaptive behavior itself, and consequent changes in the environmental situation. The chapter outlined a classification system for categorizing a client's difficulties according to those variables likely to be maintaining the problem behaviors. The chapter also discussed several clinical considerations important in the selection and priority-ordering of target behaviors. The next chapter describes a variety of procedures for gathering the kind of assessment data discussed above.

Chapter  3

Methods of Behavioral Assessment

Having outlined some of the conceptual issues associated with behavioral assessment, we can now turn to the translation of these principles into actual clinical assessment procedures. In the clinical practice of behavior therapy, assessment is usually carried out by interview, behavioral observations conducted in real life, the observation of behavior in simulated situations, paper-and-pencil questionnaires, or some combination thereof.

● INTERVIEW

In light of the behavior therapist's emphasis on the importance of assessing problem behaviors directly, it may come as a surprise that the interview is the most frequently used assessment procedure. This is due largely to the practical difficulties inherent in the direct observation of behavior, such as the lack of a controlled environment, the unavailability of trained observers, the relative infrequency of certain behavior patterns, and the complex and sometimes intimate nature of the problem behavior itself (e.g., sexual inadequacy). In the interview, the attention of the behavior therapist is typically focused on those variables discussed earlier, namely antecedent, organismic, response, and consequent variables.

The use of interview procedures rather than more direct observational techniques clearly involves a trade-off. Along with the economy and flexibility of the interview comes a degree of uncertainty as to how accurately the client's verbal report will reflect what is happening in real life. Although Mischel (1968) has offered evidence to suggest that verbal report is a good predictor of real-life behavior, there are limitations in the use of the interview as an assessment device. In attempting to obtain a detailed account of the client's reactions to specific situations, it is not unusual to find that he has difficulty providing the data required for an adequate behavioral assessment. He may have forgotten what happened, may omit certain details that he thinks are irrelevant, or may simply be ashamed to reveal certain things to another person. Further, if the relevant behavior consists of overlearned responses, the client may simply be unaware of what he is doing.

Like any other user of interview procedures, the behavior therapist must be sensitive to leads provided by the client, must be willing to follow up on his own hunches, and must frequently make use of traditionally oriented interview techniques, such as reflection of feeling, clarification, use of transitions, summary statements, and open-ended questions. Sullivan's classic work, *The Psychiatric Interview* (1954), contains a number of valuable suggestions on how to conduct an interview, many of which are compatible with a behavioral orientation. Sullivan stresses the importance of the therapist assuming the role of expert, generally controlling the interview, being attentive to nonverbal cues, and eliciting information regarding the client's expectations for treatment. Storrow (1967) and Peterson (1968) also describe several techniques useful to the behavior therapist in obtaining information.

Intake Interview Guideline

Apart from the question of how to elicit specific information from the client, there are some general guidelines for conducting an intake interview. Depending on the complexity of the particular case, whether adult or child, one or more interviews may be necessary to obtain intake information. Although the guideline provided below is presented within the context of the initial contact with the client, various portions may have to be repeated during the course of treatment, in order to determine whether change has occurred, and if not, why not.

Initial Greeting

In making the initial contact with the client, the therapist should remember that the purpose of the interview is actually twofold: to get information and to give information. Just as the therapist wants to learn more about the client, the client is himself sizing up the therapist. Thus, the behavior therapist's activities during the intake interview should be directed toward obtaining relevant assessment information and simultaneously establishing the rapport needed to implement a therapeutic program.

It would be beyond the scope of this outline to detail how the behavior therapist should handle himself in this initial contact; some of these issues will be discussed in Chapter 4. Suffice it to say that he should do all he can to make the client feel comfortable (e.g., by smiling, referring to the client by name, indicating where he might sit), and also provide enough structure to make clear to the client the assessment goals of this initial contact.

Description of Presenting Problem and Maintaining Variables

Although there are a number of similarities between behaviorally and traditionally oriented interviews, behavior therapists tend to focus more on concrete details relevant to the client's problem and on current maintaining variables. The reasons for this focus should be obvious when we consider what is involved in conducting a behavioral analysis. What may not be so apparent, however, are the potential negative side effects associated with getting details from clients. One potential problem is that pressing for specifics may interfere with the establishment of rapport. By continually having to use concrete examples to illustrate what he means, the client may get the feeling that he is not understood, either because of his own inability to communicate or the therapist's insensitivity. This pitfall can be avoided, however, if the therapist clarifies the reasons for his particular line of questioning, and also conducts himself in such a way that he communicates to the client that he understands what the client means. The therapist should point out to the client that details will provide the thorough comprehension of his plight necessary for successful therapy.

A second drawback to focusing on details is that it may blind the therapist to other significant problems not yet discussed. One way to avoid this difficulty is to give the client an opportunity to describe the nature of his problems in general terms before proceeding with a detailed analysis of a specific problem. One should remember, however, that even with a general description of presenting problems, a certain amount of operationalization may be required. That is, rather than accepting the client's label for his problem behavior at face value (e.g., "I am dependent"), the therapist should seek some examples of what is meant. He may then reconceptualize the presenting problem, if necessary. Once a general evaluation of the various problems has been made, detailed information about duration, frequency, pervasiveness, strength, as well as data on relevant maintaining variables, can be specified. Such information may be obtained directly during the interview, or additional assessment procedures as outlined below, including direct observation, the use of additional informants, and self-observation, may be required.

The following transcript illustrates some of the problems of getting specific information during the interview:

Client: I just feel nervous a lot of the time.

Therapist: What is the feeling like?

Client: I don't know. It's hard to describe . . . I just feel nervous.

Therapist: [*I think I'm going to have some difficulty in getting her to elaborate on her problems. Maybe I'll hold off on trying to push for specifics for a little bit, and instead try to get her to feel more comfortable about describing and elaborating on her feelings, and just talking in general.*] So you know what the feeling is like, but it's kind of difficult to describe it in words.

Client: Yes, it is. You know, it's just a feeling of uneasiness and apprehension. Like when you know something bad may happen, or at least you're afraid that it might.

Therapist: So emotionally, and perhaps physically, there's a fear that something might happen, although you may not be certain exactly what.

Client: Yes.

Therapist: When you're feeling that way, what do you experience physically?

Client: Well, my heart starts pounding and I feel myself tense up all over. It's not always that bad; sometimes it's only mild.

Therapist: [*I can make a smooth transition at this point and try to find out the situations in which the intensity of her anxiety varies. Whether or not I'll ever use this information for hierarchy construction remains to be seen.*] In other words, depending upon the circumstances, you may feel more or less anxious.

Client: Yes.

Therapist: Tell me something about the situations that make you *most* anxious.

Client: Well, it's usually when I deal with other people.

Therapist: I would find it particularly helpful to hear about some typical situations that may upset you.

Client: It's hard to come up with something specific.

Therapist: [*I'm having doubts as to how hard to press her for details. If she has too much difficulty in coming up with specifics, the whole process of questioning might just make our relationship too aversive. Perhaps I can give her a homework assignment to self-observe during the course of the week. Let me try to get one or two examples, perhaps confining them to the past week, suggesting certain kinds of situations to her. I can then use this as a lead to question the extent to which the situations were typical of a broader class of events. I sense by the expression on her face that she may be somewhat uneasy about her inability to give me the information I want. I should probably attend to that before moving on.*] I can understand how it may be hard to come up with specific examples right on the spot. That's not at all uncommon. Let me see if I can help to make it a little easier for you. Let's take the past week or so. Think of what went on either at work, at home, or when you were out socially that might have upset you.

Client: O.K. Something just occurred to me. We went out to a party last weekend, and as we were driving to the place where the party was being held, I felt myself starting to panic.

Therapist: Can you tell me more about that situation?

Client: Well, the party was at my husband's boss' house, and I always feel uncomfortable about events like that.

Therapist: In what way?

Client: Well, I find it difficult for me to be natural in that kind of situation.

Therapist: [*In my personal and clinical experience, there are a number of components that might be relevant in creating anxiety. There is the obligatory nature of the occasion, the perceived evaluations in such situations, to say nothing of the broader class of social interactions to which she may be responding with apprehension. Let's see if I can find out from her what this situation was a sample of.*] Do you typically become nervous when you go to social gatherings?

Client: Well, a lot depends on the situation.

Therapist: In what way?

Client: It depends on how comfortable I feel with the people.

Therapist: [*We seem to have come full circle. I think I have to be less open-ended in my line of questioning.*] O.K., so there are certain situations and certain types of people that make you feel more comfortable, and others that make you more apprehensive.

Client: Yes.

Therapist: I think it would be helpful if we focused a little more on the kinds of people and the kinds of situations which upset you to varying degrees.

Client: A lot has to do with how loud or how aggressive the people are. I think I get very intimidated when people seem so self-confident.

Therapist: [*Among the possibilities that I should check out a little later in the session is whether or not a social deficit may be operating here, as well as any associated problems in general unassertiveness. For now, though, I should stick with getting general classes of situations that upset her.*] What other kinds of individuals do you find you react negatively to?

Relevant Historical Information

There is some misunderstanding in the behavior therapy literature regarding the relevance of historical information. For the most part, a behavior therapist tends to deemphasize his client's past, undoubtedly because the therapist does little to provide insight into the early determinants of the problem behaviors. Instead, the focus is on current situations. In his eagerness to convey a behavioral orientation, the behavior therapist may inadvertently communicate to the client that he believes the past has had little influence on the client's current problems. Unfortunately, this may detract from the therapist's credibility, for the client may be quite convinced of the importance of his past experiences.

What role, if any, does past history information have in behavioral assessment? This is not an easy question to answer. With clearly delineated problems, such as phobias, knowledge of the historical antecedents will probably provide little help on how to proceed therapeutically. In other instances, however, past information may help the therapist understand the client's current difficulties in such a way as to have implications for treatment. This would be particularly true in more complex cases, where the exact nature of the current problems and of their maintaining variables is not clear-cut. On the assumption that early social learning is responsible for later functioning, the behavior therapist may frequently learn more about the client's current problem areas and their maintaining variables by virtue of his knowledge of past learning experiences.

Positive Characteristics

In addition to information about the client's problems, a thorough assessment by interview should also include some data on the client's strengths. For example, what are the client's behavioral assets, and what does he enjoy doing? Such knowledge may later be used therapeutically by either the therapist or the client himself, for it provides an understanding of potential reinforcers in the client's life.

Past Attempts to Cope with Problems

Information about the client's past successes and failures in dealing with his problems can have a direct bearing on the particular therapeutic technique the therapist decides to use, as well as the way he introduces it to the client. For example, if a client reports that he has been successful in coping with his anxiety by taking hot showers, the therapist might later want to construe relaxation training as fulfilling a similar function. On the other hand, if a client reports having unsuccessfully tried to relax on his own, it would be important for the therapist to convey that the particular relaxation procedure to be used in therapy is different—and presumably more effective.

In line with the client's previous attempts to cope, past therapy experiences, if any, should also be reviewed. If past experiences have been favorable, then the therapist can attempt to point out the *similarities* to the procedures he will be using. If the client has been dissatisfied with his therapy in the past, no matter what its orientation, the *differences* between past and current methods should be emphasized. Certainly, if a previous well-executed course of therapy was not helpful, the therapist would do well *not* to follow the same tack.

Expectations Regarding Therapy

In addition to obtaining indirect information, such as the client's past experiences in attempting to cope, it is important to assess more directly the client's expectations, both with regard to the likelihood of changing, and with respect to the particular treatment approach to be used in bringing about such change. Research shows that a client's favorable expectations regarding treatment are positively correlated with actual change (Goldstein, 1962). Failure to adequately assess the client's expectations can result in client and therapist working at cross-purposes, which will doom to failure even the most powerful of therapeutic techniques. A more detailed discussion of client expectations appears in Chapter 4.

Establishing Goals

A good way to establish therapeutic goals is by means of what Sullivan (1954) has called the "summary statement." Once the therapist feels that he has obtained sufficient data on the potential target behaviors, he can provide the client with a summary of those behaviors as he, the therapist, views them at that time. The client can then have an opportunity to comment on the accuracy of the therapist's view, after which priorities for treatment may be ordered. As will be discussed in Chapter 4, some sort of therapeutic contract, in which expected behaviors for both client and therapist are outlined, should be established.

● BEHAVIORAL OBSERVATION

To the extent that it is practically feasible, direct observation of behavior frequently proves the most clinically useful of all the assessment procedures. These observations may be made by trained individuals, by significant others in the client's life, by the therapist, or by the client himself.

Trained Observers

The use of persons who have been trained in behavioral observation procedures constitutes the most desirable, although not
necessarily the most practical, approach to assessment. Although
it is theoretically possible to follow someone and observe his behavior on a 24-hour basis, trained observers have typically been employed only in more controlled settings, such as hospitals, schools,
and home environments.

In using direct behavioral observation, it is necessary to develop
some sort of classification system, so that attention can be drawn
to specific aspects of the environment, as well as to the individual's
response to it. A number of different observational guidelines are
available for use in hospitals (Ayllon & Azrin, 1968; Honigfeld,
Gillis, & Klett, 1966), schools (O'Leary & Becker, 1967; Werry &
Quay, 1969), and homes (Lewinsohn & Shaffer, 1971; Patterson,
1971). Some of the methodological problems associated with the
use of such procedures, as well as suggested means of coping with
them, have been reviewed by Goldfried and Sprafkin (1974).

Significant Others

In the absence of a controlled environment and/or available
trained personnel, the therapist may enlist the cooperation of significant others in the client's life. This is in marked contrast to some
of the more traditional approaches to therapy, in which there is reluctance to involve others in the therapeutic process. Although their
observational skills seldom match those of trained observers, the
client's parent, spouse, friend, or roommate can frequently provide
valuable information about the client's reactions to various situations. Such an approach is particularly useful in a child case, where
parents and teachers have frequent opportunities to observe the
child's behavior. In such instances, a minimal guideline for observation of certain classes of adaptive and deviant behavior patterns may be provided, such as a simple A-B-C format, in which
the informant is asked to record antecedents, behavior, and
consequences.

Therapist Observations

As mentioned by such writers as Sullivan (1954), Fromm-Reichmann (1950), Reich (1949), and various Gestalt and experientially
oriented therapists (Corsini, 1973), the client's interactions with

the therapist in the consultation room may frequently provide a sample of his problem behaviors. In working with severely disturbed hospitalized patients, for example, Farina, Arenberg, and Guskin (1957) have provided a checklist for assessing an individual's social behavior as manifested within the interview setting itself. One cannot always be certain, however, whether the client's behavior is actually a sample of how he reacts to the particular therapist, or is indicative of a more generalized problem. In any event, observation of in-therapy behavior can provide useful leads for further assessment.

Observations in Simulated Situations

Another way that the therapist may observe a client's behavior is in role-playing situations (McFall & Lillesand, 1971; McFall & Marston, 1970; Rotter & Wickens, 1948; Stanton & Litwak, 1955). In certain circumstances, the role playing may be carried out in imagination, for example, in attempting to obtain a measure of subjective anxiety to situations which are not readily simulated in the consultation room (e.g., sexual behavior).

It has been demonstrated by Wahler, Winkel, Peterson, and Morrison (1965) that problems in parent-child interactions can be seen easily by using one-way observational facilities. In order to obtain a sample of relevant problem behaviors, the situation is structured in such a way that the behaviors have a high probability of occurring during the observation period. With a child client who has difficulty independently carrying out homework assignments, for example, the child may be given some academic problem to work on while the parent is engaged in some other activity (e.g., reading a newspaper or completing a questionnaire). Then the frequency of the child's requests for aid and the parent's reactions to such requests may be noted. Following such observations, the therapist may emerge with a hypothesis about the circumstances under which the child is unable to work independently, as well as the likelihood that the parent may be reinforcing the child's unnecessary requests for aid. At this point the therapist may have the unique opportunity to employ a highly sophisticated assessment procedure through the manipulation of variables believed to be maintaining the problem behavior. By providing the parent with signals, either by lights or wireless earphones, telling him when to attend to the child and when to ignore him, the therapist may test his hypothesis that certain reactions on the part of the parent have been maintaining the child's problem behavior. One may ask whether such a procedure constitutes therapy, rather than assessment. Although the two are inextricably entwined in such instances, it would probably be called therapy if it produced beneficial change, and assessment if it did not.

● SELF-REPORT

An assessment strategy that is used almost routinely consists of having the client observe his own behavior or emotional reactions in particular target situations. Such an approach may take the form of having the client use a golf counter to tally the frequency of certain behaviors, or keep a written record of his anxiety level in different situations. Sometimes it is useful to ask the client to notice when he becomes tense and then to use those feelings of tenseness as a reminder to stop and examine what is taking place. One of the "problems" with the use of self-observation as an assessment device is that the individual frequently changes (typically for the better) as a function of observing his own behavior. This seems to occur in those instances where the problem behaviors involve instrumental responding (e.g., study behavior). Although it is not entirely clear why change comes about as a function of this self-monitoring, a more objective, even detached, perspective on one's own behavior may disrupt what was previously an overlearned and automatic chain, and may also make more apparent the negative consequences which ensue.

Another form of self-report involves having the client complete various questionnaires. Personal data forms for both college students and adult outpatients, such as those appearing in Storrow (1967) and Lazarus (1971), can be used. A number of behaviorally oriented questionnaires have appeared in the literature in recent years: for example, the Fear Survey Schedule (Geer, 1965); the Reinforcement Survey Schedule (Cautela & Kastenbaum, 1967); the assertiveness questionnaire (McFall & Lillesand, 1971); the Irrational Beliefs Test (Jones, 1968); and the Test Anxiety Behavior Scale (Suinn, 1969). These questionnaires, however, have been used primarily for research purposes and may lack the specificity or comprehensiveness required in an adequate clinical assessment procedure.

● AN INTAKE REPORT OUTLINE

Although the lines between behavioral assessment and behavior therapy are frequently blurred, there is usually a period at the very beginning of treatment when the therapist gathers information and attempts to organize it so that he can tentatively decide which targets to focus on and which therapeutic procedures to employ. Depending on the complexity of the case and the nature of the setting, this period may encompass one or two interviews, supplemented by other assessment procedures. At all times, however, the therapist's conceptualization must remain open to change.

In the process of compiling and organizing assessment information for a written report, one is faced with the decision of what to include and what to discard. Much of what we learn about clients, although intrinsically interesting, is nonfunctional in planning treatment programs. Unfortunately, such information frequently finds its way into written assessment reports. The problem of this plethora of data has been dramatically stated by Storrow (1967), who observed:

> Case reports . . . [often] contain massive collections of useful as well as useless information, with the useful usually so well buried that it, too, becomes useless. I have long suffered from an acute boredom syndrome from reading too many such reports. They read like poorly written biographies, full of information that has no bearing on the problem at hand. I usually find I can't even *remember* all the data, much less utilize it to make predictions and treatment plans (p. 41).

In an attempt to avoid such chaos in reporting assessment information, Pomeranz and Goldfried (1970) have suggested an intake report format that not only guides the clinical assessor in obtaining relevant data, but also organizes the case material to allow the therapist to select the target behaviors and therapeutic procedures most appropriate for each particular client. The report is usually structured as follows.

I. Behavior during Interview and Physical Description

Included here are the therapist's observations of what may be a sample of the client's behavior in the therapeutic relationship, and perhaps even outside of the therapy interaction as well. Any aspect of the client's physical appearance that might categorize him as being typical or different from his reference group is noted as well, since it might provide leads for the impact he may have on others.

II. Presenting Problem(s)

A. Nature of Problem(s)

Although this category covers the presenting complaint as described by the client himself, it may include more than the client's own construction of the problem. If the intake interviewer believes that the presenting problem may best be construed in other terms, the interviewer's reconstruction of the client's original conception of his difficulty should also be included in this section. For example, a client may present a problem of being nervous in certain social settings, but further questioning may reveal that the problem is primarily one of unassertiveness.

B. Historical Setting Events

This material is useful primarily with those clients for whom an evaluation of the current situation proves to be somewhat difficult (e.g., the client states his problems in vague and abstract terms). Thus, the report should include any early developmental data that may provide a context for current problems and give clues to the dimensions of the problems, such as the exact nature of the deviant behavior (e.g., deficiency versus inhibition) and the situations where it is more likely to occur.

C. Current Situational Determinants   *not emphasized by psychoanalytic*

The antecedent situational variables—whether they serve to elicit respondents or act as discriminative stimuli for operants—should be described in this category.

D. Relevant Organismic Variables

In addition to physiological states of the client and any potential effects of medication currently being taken, the clinician should note the client's covert labeling activity—either as a primary determinant of the problem (e.g., "I must be perfect in this situation") or as a secondary attribution of the difficulty (e.g., "My rapid heartbeat must mean that I am having a heart attack").

E. Dimensions of Problem

Any information relevant to the duration, pervasiveness, frequency, and magnitude of the problem should be included in this category.

F. Consequences of Problem

In addition to information about what may be reinforcing the client's problem behaviors, positive and negative consequences for the person's current or future functioning should be included here as well (e.g., job status, interpersonal functioning).

III. Other Problems

This category includes those problems not raised by the client himself, but instead observed by the therapist. Such problems need not be related to the presenting problems, may not have been discussed with the client himself, and may not actually be targets for modification.

IV. Personal Assets

In addition to providing information relevant to prognosis, such personal assets as physical characteristics, aptitudes, abilities, and interests can provide leads to possible social reinforcements for use in altering the client's maladaptive behavior. Also included in this category can be any aspect of the client's environment which has the potential for eliciting and/or reinforcing adaptive behaviors (e.g., a cooperative spouse).

V. Target(s) for Modification

This category is used to specify the exact variables that need to be modified, whether situational antecedents, organismic variables, aspects of the problem behavior itself, and/or maintaining reinforcers. A tentative ordering of priorities should be indicated here as well.

VI. Recommended Treatment(s)

Included here would be any one or combination of several procedures deemed to be most appropriate for modifying the targets outlined above.

VII. Motivation for Treatment

Some general classification—such as high, medium, or low—should be indicated, together with the data on which the inference has been made (e.g., verbal commitment to change, past attempts at behavior change).

VIII. Prognosis

On the basis of considerations such as duration of problem, likelihood of manipulating the relevant variables (environmental as well as client), appropriate therapeutic procedures, and other factors, a general prognosis (very poor, poor, fair, good, or very good) can be made.

IX. Priority for Treatment

This is a particularly useful category in a clinic setting, especially where therapeutic time may be at a premium. A "low," "medium," or "high" priority can be given on the basis of a consideration of the consequences of *not* seeing this particular client in treatment.

X. Expectancies

The client's expectations regarding the likelihood of his changing as well as his general view toward therapy should be included here.

XI. Other Comments

This is a catchall category where information not easily included elsewhere can be included. For example, one can use this section to note any additional information that should be obtained, or as a place to alert the therapist to difficulties he might encounter in dealing with the client.

In providing the above intake report format, we do not wish to imply that all categories of information will be relevant to each clinical case. In some instances, certain information may be unavailable or irrelevant. The outline should function as a guideline, not as a straightjacket. The following sample intake report shows how the outline has been used within a college clinic.

```
                        SAMPLE INTAKE REPORT

Name: BRIAN, James (fictitious name)        Age: 22   Sex: Male

Class: Senior                    Date of interview: March 25, 1974
                                 Therapist:  John Doe

  I.  Behavior during interview and physical description:

      James is a clean-shaven, long-haired young man who appeared for the
      intake interview in well-coordinated college garb: jeans, wide belt,
      open shirt, and sandals.  He came across as shy and soft-spoken,
      with occasional minor speech blocks.  Although uneasy during most of
      the session, he nonetheless spoke freely and candidly.

 II.  Presenting problem:

      A. Nature of Problem: Anxiety in public speaking situations, and
      other situations in which he is being evaluated by others.

      B. Historical setting events:  James was born in France, and arrived
      in this country seven years ago, at which time he experienced both a
      social and language problem.  His social contacts had been minimal
      until the time he entered college, at which time a socially aggressive
      friend of his helped him to break out of his shell.  James describes
      his father as being an overly critical and perfectionistic person
      who would, on occasion, rip us his homework if it fell short of the
      mark.  The client's mother is pictured as a controlling, overly
      affectionate person who was always showing concern about his welfare.
      His younger brother, who has always  been a good student, was con-
      tinually thrown up to James by his parents as being far better than he.

      C. Current situational determinants: Interaction with his parents,
      examinations, family gatherings, participation in classes, initial
      social contacts.

      D. Relevant organismic variables: The client appears to be approaching
      a number of situations with certain irrational expectations, primarily
      unrealistic strivings for perfection and an overwhelming desire to
      receive approval from others.  He is not taking any medication at this
      time except as indicated under X below.

      E. Dimensions of problem: The client's social and evaluative anxiety
      are long-standing and  occur in a wide variety of day-to-day situations.

      F. Consequences of problem: His chronic level of anxiety resulted in an
      ulcer operation at the age of 15.  In addition, he has developed a skin
      rash on his hands and arms, apparently from excessive perspiration.  He
      reports that his nervousness at one time caused him to stutter, but this
      appears to be less a problem in more recent years.  His anxiety in exam-
      ination situations has typically interfered with his ability to perform
      well.
```

● SUMMARY

This chapter has focused on some of the assessment procedures used in behavioral clinical practice. The use of the interview in clinical behavior therapy is both similar to and different from its use by clinicians with other therapeutic orientations. Like all clinicians, the behaviorally oriented interviewer should be sensitive to leads provided by the client, must be willing to pursue his own clinical hunches, and will often employ interviewing techniques used by clinicians of other persuasions, such as reflection of feeling, clarification, summary statements, appropriate use of transitions, and open-ended questions. Particular attention should also be paid

III. Other problems:

A. Assertiveness: Although obviously a shy and timid individual, James said that lack of assertiveness is no longer a problem with him. At one time in the past, his friends would take advantage of him, but he claims that this is no longer the case. This should be followed up further, as it is unclear what he means by assertiveness.

B. Forgetfulness: The client reports that he frequently misses appointments, misplaces items, locks himself out of his room, and generally is absent-minded.

IV. Personal assets:

The client is fairly bright and comes across as a warm, friendly, and sensitive individual.

V. Targets for modification:

Unrealistic self-statements in social-evaluative situations; possibly behavioral deficits associated with unassertiveness; and forgetfulness.

VI. Recommended treatment:

It appears that relaxation training would be a good way to begin, especially in light of the client's high level of anxiety. Following this, the treatment should move along the lines of rational restructuring, and possibly behavior rehearsal. It is unclear as yet what would be the best strategy for dealing with forgetfulness.

VII. Motivation for treatment:

High.

VIII. Prognosis:

Very good.

IX. Priority for treatment:

High.

X. Expectancies:

On occasion, especially when going out on a date with a female, James would take half a sleeping pill to calm himself down. He wants to get away from this, and feels what he needs is to learn to cope with his anxieties by himself. It would appear that he will be very receptive to whatever treatment plan we finally decide on, especially if the emphasis is on self-control of anxiety.

XI. Other comments:

Considering the brief time available between now and the end of the semester, between-session homework assignments should be emphasized as playing a particularly important role in the behavior change process.

to the client's behavior in the therapeutic interaction per se, bearing in mind, however, that the behavior sample observed may be specific to the particular interaction. Unlike his counterpart of a traditional persuasion, the behavior therapist interviewer focuses strongly on specifics, and systematically attempts to obtain information about situational antecedents, organismic variables, the dimensions of the behavior problem itself, and consequences of the problem behaviors. Other methods of behavioral assessment include observations in real-life situations and in simulated situations, and paper-and-pencil questionnaires. The chapter also included an intake report outline that can help the clinical assessor obtain relevant information, as well as organize the case material to allow the therapist to select the target behaviors and therapeutic procedures most appropriate for each particular client.

Chapter

The Therapeutic Relationship

Any behavior therapist who maintains that principles of learning and social influence are all one needs to know in order to bring about behavior change is out of contact with clinical reality. We have seen therapists capable of conceptualizing problems along behavioral lines and adept at the implementation of the various behavior therapy techniques, but they have few opportunities to demonstrate their effectiveness; they often have difficulty keeping their clients in therapy, let alone getting them to follow through on behavioral assignments.

While it is true that behavior therapy stresses the importance of the client-therapist relationship less than do other therapeutic approaches, instead attending more to specific therapeutic procedures, this in no way implies that behavior therapists need be cold and mechanical in their clinical dealings. One may be both tender-hearted and tough-minded at the same time when it comes to clinical behavior therapy. In fact, it is entirely likely that there are times when the nature of the therapeutic relationship between behavior therapist and client is indistinguishable from that which may be observed within other orientations. The behavior therapist may be saying and doing things for very different reasons than the non-behavior therapist, but his actions may come across to the client as quite similar. What we are maintaining, in essence, is that while one views human behavior according to principles of conditioning, reinforcement, social influence, and the like, these concepts involve the therapist's scientific metalanguage and are not descriptive or prescriptive of the way he should interact with his client. The truly skillful behavior therapist is one who can both conceptualize problems behaviorally and make the necessary translations so that he interacts in a warm and empathic manner with his client.

Clinical and research evidence suggests that a therapeutic relationship, even in the context of a behavior therapy orientation, can contribute significantly to the behavior change process (Frank, 1961; Goldstein, 1971; Goldstein, Heller, & Sechrest, 1966; Morris & Suckerman, 1974; Wilson & Evans, in press). There are findings to indicate that the therapeutic relationship can interact with even as effective a technique as systematic desensitization. For example, Morris and Suckerman (1974) found that desensitization was more effective in reducing fear of snakes when carried out by a "warm" therapist (e.g., demonstrating concern, speaking in a soft voice, having good eye contact) than by a "cold" therapist (e.g., unconcerned, aloof and impersonal, and otherwise mechanical).

Perhaps one of the reasons that behavior therapists have tended to deemphasize the importance of the therapeutic relationship is the fact that their therapeutic techniques have been shown to be effective in their own right. For example, Lang, Melamed, and Hart (1970) have demonstrated that the Device for Automated Desensitization—consisting of tape-recorded therapeutic desensitization instructions, and affectionately referred to as DAD—can reduce fear in the absence of any therapeutic relationship. Despite the effectiveness of DAD, it would be misleading to conclude that the therapeutic relationship itself is unimportant. One may ponder how such an automated procedure might work in an actual clinical case, where the target problem is less clear-cut, and where the client may be somewhat reluctant to change—let alone use this procedure.

The specific ways in which relationship factors interact with behavior therapy procedures have yet to be determined empirically. Extrapolating from basic research and drawing on our own clinical experience, the remainder of this chapter will focus on those aspects of the therapeutic relationship that seem important in the behavior change process.

● THE RELATIONSHIP AS A SAMPLE OF BEHAVIOR

Within the psychoanalytically oriented therapies, the relationship between patient and therapist represents the primary vehicle through which change is assumed to take place. By allowing transference feelings to develop, the therapist is able, within the consultation session, to bring to the fore indirect representations of underlying conflicts. The major focus of the therapy, then, is on the distorted nature of the patient's attitudes and reactions toward the therapist.

In describing the significance of the therapeutic relationship, Sullivan (1954) has presented a view somewhat more consistent with a social learning orientation. In contrast to the classic psychoanalytic notion of transference—which is believed to exist primarily within the context of a therapeutic relationship—Sullivan describes a client's behavior in terms of "parataxic distortions." According to Sullivan, the individual learns various attitudes and behavior patterns on the basis of his early interactions with his parents, which in turn serve as prototypes for his reactions when he is placed in similar situations later in life. Thus, the client's reactions toward the therapist represent a sample of his current behavior, which may also be manifesting itself in other interpersonal situations in his life.

The primary distinction between the Sullivanian and behavioral views of client behavior in the therapeutic relationship concerns what the therapist should do when such behaviors occur. According to Fromm-Reichmann (1950), who has amplified on the Sullivanian approach to therapy, parataxic distortions should be used as a means for allowing the patient to gain insight into the origins of his problems. Within the context of a behavioral orientation, on the other hand, the therapist would provide direct feedback, primarily to help the client realize how his maladaptive behavior manifests itself. The unassertive or socially inappropriate behavior we see during the consultation session, for example, may well provide us with a useful—albeit potentially biased—sample of how the client reacts outside the session.

In construing the therapeutic relationship as providing a sample of the client's interaction, it is important for the therapist to focus on his own reactions during the therapeutic sessions. The therapist should continually observe his own behavior and emotional reactions, and question what the client may have done to bring about such reactions. Provided the therapist is in relatively good contact with reality, such a seemingly paranoid stance can offer important clues about how other individuals in the client's natural environment may be reacting toward him. For example, in working with a family, one of us became particularly angry and put off by the mother's way of dominating the session. These feelings of anger were used as a cue to raise the question: "What is she doing to make me feel this way, and is there any likelihood that other significant individuals in her life may be having similar reactions?" This assessment strategy helped to change the focus of the therapeutic intervention, enabling us to deal with the relevant variables that were maintaining the son's behavior problem.[1]

Although the therapist can generally make good therapeutic use of the client's problem behaviors as they occur within the therapy session, there are certain behavior patterns that can directly interfere with the progress of therapy. For example, the excessively critical client can sabotage the efforts of even the most skilled therapist. The individual with high standards for self-reinforcement may terminate prematurely because of his disappointment with the gradual pace of behavior change. And the socially anxious or inappropriate client can make the communication process within the session painful for both therapist and client. Under such circumstances, the primary target for modification should consist of those very behaviors manifested within the session that are likely to undermine the course of treatment. Even if there is no generalization to the "real world," a change within the therapeutic relationship would at least allow the therapist and client to work together more effectively.

In contrast to problem behaviors that interfere with the course of therapy, there are client behaviors that serve to facilitate therapy. We are referring here to the client who, because of his own problems, may be more susceptible to the therapist's influence. For example, the so-called dependent individual may welcome any suggestions or guidance offered by the therapist. The client whose problems consist primarily of social-evaluative anxiety can be very

---

[1] This suggested use of the therapist's own reactions in therapy raises the important and controversial—at least for behavior therapy—issue of whether a personal course of therapy is desirable or necessary for the behavior therapist in training.

conscientious in carrying out homework assignments, for fear of being disapproved of by the therapist. Under such circumstances— when the client's problem may be "working for" the therapy—the therapist might decide to continue to "use" the situation as long as it is therapeutically productive. Although there will come a time toward the end of therapy when one should have the client change his behavior vis-à-vis the therapist, it may be wise to wait until it is no longer productive for the therapist to serve as an instigator and reinforcer. The ultimate goal is to help the client achieve total independence from his therapist.

● THE THERAPIST AS A SIGNIFICANT OTHER

On the basis of his socially defined role alone, the therapist has the potential for exerting an important influence on a client's behavior. This has been documented in the classic work by Frank (1961), who has written about the placebo factors involved when someone goes to a professional with the expectation that he will somehow be changed. The placebo effect can help the change process up to a certain point. Beyond that point, the effectiveness of the therapeutic procedures and the characteristics of the therapist play an important role.

With regard to the specific nature of the therapeutic relationship, Frank (1961) has suggested the following:

> . . . the good psychotherapist has qualities such as self-confidence, energy, and controlled emotional warmth. These enable him to offer his patients a pattern of active, personal participation, which arouses their expectation of help and facilitates attitude changes (p. 141).

We would agree with Frank's observation. In follow-up interviews with clients who had completed a course of behavior therapy, Ryan and Gizynski (1971) found that, in addition to the confidence they had in the therapeutic procedures, clients felt that the persuasiveness of the therapist, the therapist's ability to create positive expectations, and their liking of the therapist all contributed significantly to their behavior change. While such findings are of considerable interest, it should be emphasized that these post hoc data do not unequivocably demonstrate that these factors actually accounted for the behavior change.

Regardless of how powerful a therapeutic procedure may be, active cooperation on the part of the client is nonetheless necessary

(Davison, 1973). The potential reinforcing value of the therapist becomes particularly important when between-session homework is required of clients, as is the case with so many of our behavior therapy procedures. Relaxation exercises, self-observation, and attempts simply to try out new behavior patterns *in vivo* all depend greatly on the therapist's influence. There are no set rules that guide the therapist in exerting a personal influence on his client. The social influence process may take the form of continually inquiring about and otherwise showing interest in the client's between-session attempts at certain activities, or it may even involve having the client periodically phone the therapist following certain attempts at behavior change.

With a female client who was having difficulty utilizing rational restructuring to cope with her anxiety, the therapist instructed her to "take me home with you," that is, to imagine that he was following her around and reminding her how to go about coping with her anxiety. The client reported that this suggestion worked, describing one incident when its effect was most dramatic. She had been out shopping during a busy holiday season, and was starting to become overwhelmed by the surrounding noise and crowds. Although she had been making some attempts to cope with her anxiety, it seemed to be getting the best of her. While attempting to relax and rationally reevaluate her reason for becoming upset, she noticed a man pushing a baby carriage containing a noisy and unruly child. While thinking to herself, "If he can handle that situation, then I should be able to cope as well," she suddenly noticed that the person behind the carriage was the therapist! The impact on the client was dramatic. Her anxiety rapidly dissipated, and she was able to continue shopping for the remainder of the day in a relatively anxiety-free state.

Inadvertently or deliberately, the therapist frequently serves as a model for the client. Thus, the therapist should be aware continually of his impact on the client, making every effort to model behavior, attitudes, and emotions likely to enhance therapeutic progress. For example, it is not uncommon for clients to describe problems that are part of the therapist's own personal experience. By disclosing the way he himself changed his thinking or behavior with positive consequences, the therapist can often use his own life experiences to help facilitate the client's behavior change.

The personal influence of the therapist is particularly important for facilitating behavior change. For example, certain problem behavior patterns may exist primarily because of the client's tendency to become involved in relationships likely to be fraught with conflict, or because of other similarly generalized deviant life styles. In such instances, the therapist's personal influence in having the client try out a different behavior pattern becomes especially important. The therapist's genuine concern for the client's welfare and his ability to point out potential negative consequences associated with the maladaptive behaviors and to suggest alternate courses of action could be employed to instigate behavior change.

● RESISTANCE TO BEHAVIOR CHANGE

An understanding of therapy would be incomplete without consideration of the client's receptivity to behavior change. A person's set to resist the influence of others—even so-called significant others—can effectively undermine attempts at behavior influence.

A client's resistance to the behavior change process can take many forms, from open oppositional statements to persistent forgetfulness in carrying out homework assignments. Although one may be tempted to conclude that the client is "not ready for behavior therapy," we maintain that one of the roles of the behavior therapist is to make him ready. The need to work on resistance within the therapeutic relationship has long been recognized as a significant component of psychodynamically oriented therapies. Within very recent years, behavior therapists themselves have also begun to attend to this problem, recognizing the need to overcome the client's attempts at countercontrol (Davison, 1973) and to facilitate commitment to change (Marston & Feldman, 1972). Some behavior therapists have tried to overcome resistance by means of contingency contracts, such as making a subsequent therapy session contingent on the client's fulfilling an agreed-upon homework assignment.

The power struggle that seems intrinsic to a dyadic relationship in which one person is trying to persuade the other to do something has been analyzed by both Erickson (1959) and Haley (1963). Although their discussions were within the context of hypnosis (see Chapter 5), many of their suggestions are directly applicable to the therapeutic interaction itself. For example, Erickson and Haley advise the hypnotist, especially with a resistant subject, to *utilize* whatever behavior the subject exhibits at any given time in order to gain increasing control. The hypnotist may suggest, for example, that minute muscle twitches, not yet visible, may soon become visible. Inevitably, *some* kind of movement occurs; the hypnotist must be careful to comment on it. He reminds the subject that this was precisely what was supposed to happen and then suggests that perhaps additional movements will take place. The important empirical principle is that the hypnotist phrase suggestions in a way that enables or constrains the subject to construe *anything* that happens as being due to the hypnotist's suggestion. Thus, the hypnotist should suggest things like "Perhaps you will soon note a tendency for your hand to rise," and not "your hand will rise." If the hand does not rise, the hypnotist may then imply that it was not supposed to anyway. The principle underlying this utilization technique is that it reinforces the client's perception of the hypnotist's credibility and power.

The utilization technique may be employed at various points in therapy. At the beginning of relaxation instructions, for example, the therapist can suggest that the client may find a tendency for his mind to wander during the instructions. The therapist can then wait 5 to 10 seconds so that the client will indeed think of something else. Similarly, in suggesting that the client apply his relaxation skills *in vivo*, the therapist can forewarn him that he sometimes may not be successful in relaxing away his anxiety and that the primary purpose of these initial attempts at coping is to have him start to do something different when he becomes upset. Thus, whether the attempts at relaxation are successful or not, the client can nonetheless interpret his efforts as meeting the demands of the therapeutic instructions. Utilization may also be fruitfully employed when the client is asked to self-observe some behavior pattern, such as the number of social contacts he makes in a week. Although this self-observation may be presented to the client as an assessment procedure, what one frequently finds is that the procedure is reactive, that is, some behavior change occurs. The therapist may use such change to therapeutic advantage by attributing it to the client's motivation and ability to change.

In many respects, the utilization technique provides one with a therapeutic "foot-in-the-door." Freedman and Fraser (1966) demonstrated dramatically how compliance with an initial small request can increase the likelihood of compliance with a more demanding request at a later time. They found, for example, that asking homemakers first to reply to some questions about soap products significantly increased their later willingness to allow a group of investigators to come into their kitchens and carry out an intensive classification of all their household products. In another study, Freedman and Fraser found that requesting car owners to place "Drive Carefully" stickers on their car windows greatly increased the probability that they would later agree to place large "Drive Carefully" signs on their front lawns. With the foot-in-the-door, 76 percent of the people agreed to display the sign; without it, only 17 percent complied. These findings illustrate how compliance can be brought about with minimal, though gradually increasing, pressure.

A study bearing greater similarity to an actual therapeutic relationship was carried out by Davis (1971), who investigated the way an underlying power struggle may be related to verbal conditioning. Subjects were found to emit more verbal behavior on a target topic when the experimenter first disagreed and then agreed with what the subject was saying. The verbal conditioning effect was greater under this condition than it was when the experimenter either agreed or disagreed all of the time. These findings are discussed by Davis in terms of the subject's preferring a relationship where he did not see himself being controlled by the experimenter. This low profile of influence was apparently more readily achieved when the subject perceived himself as having power over the experimenter, rather than vice versa.

A description of the therapeutic relationship in terms of the influence the therapist has over the client does not imply that the therapist should come on strong in his attempts to change behavior. Evidence indicates that an empathic reflection of feeling can serve as an effective means of reinforcing a client's verbal behavior (Merbaum & Southwell, 1965). In fact, in a detailed analysis of one of Carl Rogers' own therapeutic interactions, Truax (1966) determined that many of the reflective statements used during the course of therapy were contingent on certain client statements, and that such statements increased as an apparent function of the reflective feedback offered by Rogers.

The tendency of people to actively resist being influenced by others has been studied at great length by Brehm (1966) and has evolved into a theory of "psychological reactance." Stated simply, the theory maintains that a state of reactance is aroused whenever a person feels that his freedom has been threatened. When an individual perceives himself as having some choice, and when he perceives that this choice is restricted, threatened, or eliminated by some external authority, he will not only experience a subjective state of discomfort but will also strive to restore this lost freedom.

Does this mean that psychological reactance will occur in every therapeutic interaction? Probably not. On any given topic, including the issue of how best to go about changing one's behavior, there are undoubtedly individual differences in a person's perceived freedom of choice. Crucial to the theory of psychological reactance is whether or not the individual *perceives himself* as capable of exercising free choice in the situation. Within the context of behavior change, the two extreme attitudes on a continuum would be "I want someone to take over and tell me what to do" and "I have to be the one to determine what is best for me." The behavior therapist's attempts at overt control within the therapeutic relationship should vary as a function of where any given client falls on this continuum.

● PREPARING THE CLIENT FOR BEHAVIOR CHANGE

In their writings, behavior therapists have frequently emphasized the importance of structuring therapy for the client. This structuring includes a description of the social learning orientation to maladjusted behavior, presentation of the general rationale underlying the treatment procedure, and specification of the therapy steps themselves. It is our contention that the manner, style, and pacing of these preparatory steps have important implications for increasing the client's motivation and enlisting his cooperation.

In laying the groundwork for behavior therapy, the therapist must be sensitive to the client's expectations of what therapy holds in store for him. Many a client has terminated prematurely because he did not feel he was getting what he thought he would, and many a behavior therapist has become annoyed on learning that the client's main goal all along was to reach some "understanding" of his problem. Despite the fact that the therapist may have a clear idea about what target behavior should be pursued and what procedures would most readily effect change, any specific attempts at therapeutic intervention should take place only after the therapist's and client's expectations are aligned. Needed specifically are a distinct agreement on goals, a clear understanding of the client's expectations regarding the nature of the therapeutic procedures to be used, the likelihood of change, and a tentative commitment to follow through with what will be expected during the course of therapy.

Determination of Goals

As a part of the initial behavioral assessment described in Chapters 2 and 3, treatment goals are specified and ordered according to their priority. In a large number of cases, client and therapist will fully agree on which problem behaviors are in need of change. In other instances, however, some disagreement may exist. Take, for example, an obese and lonely female whose main objective is to lose weight and thereby have more frequent social contacts. The therapist may feel that the primary determinant of her loneliness is a basic lack of social skills, and not her physical appearance. Another example is the inhibited child, whose current behavior pattern is being modeled after and reinforced by an unassertive parent, toward whom the focal behavior change program should be directed. Despite the potential conflict of opinion in each of these two cases, there is really no basic disagreement between client and therapist regarding goals. Should differences of opinion occur, they are more likely to involve *how* these goals might best be reached. In those instances where there is a need to have the client align himself with the therapist's objectives, care should be taken to specify how a given therapeutic course of action is more likely to provide the client with what he really wants to accomplish.

For the most part, the above considerations are a direct outgrowth of the assessment of those variables that maintain the presenting problem. A more difficult instance may arise when the therapist becomes aware of a problem functionally unrelated to those which brought the client to therapy. In deciding whether or not to raise and pursue a potential problem area with a client, the therapist should use as a rule of thumb the seriousness of the negative consequences of *not* changing the particular problem behavior. Ethical issues such as this one will be dealt with in Chapter 13.

Although we have discussed the need to determine goals at the outset of therapy, there will be numerous instances where goals are reformulated during the course of treatment, either because the therapist has reconceptualized problems in a different light or because the client has presented the therapist with new problems. In such situations, the same considerations regarding the determination of appropriate maintaining variables and priority ordering would apply.

Client's Expectations Regarding Treatment Procedures

The general question of client expectations regarding the actual treatment procedures to be used has received considerable attention in the psychotherapy literature (Goldstein, 1962; Hoehn-Saric, Frank, Imber, Nash, Battle, & Stone, 1964; Orne & Wender, 1968; Rotter, 1954). The consensus is that an accurate perception of what will take place in therapy can facilitate the course of treatment. Clearly, the client's expectations of what procedures will be employed will vary depending on past therapeutic experiences, level of sophistication, nature of the referral, and general image of psychotherapy in the current media.

It is often difficult to determine exactly the client's expectations of treatment. The frequent response, "I really don't know what to expect," may not accurately reflect the client's actual anticipation of the treatment procedure. It may be that the client feels the therapist is quizzing him, and he may want to avoid being "wrong." Assuming that everyone has some conception of what psychotherapy is like, careful probing may be required. From the point of view of the behavior therapist, the client's anticipation of insight versus relearning is particularly important to determine.

What does one do when the client's expectations are at odds with a behavioral approach to treatment? Interestingly enough, the answer to this question may be found in the writings of some psychoanalytically oriented therapists. For example, Sullivan (1954) suggests the following:

> I think that what society teaches one to expect is important. The person who comes to the interview expecting a certain pattern of events which does not materialize will probably not return; he will not say nice things about the interviewer if the latter, feeling that the things expected by his client are irrelevant or immaterial, ignores these expectations and presents the client with something much "better." In other words, what a client is taught to expect is the thing that he should get—or, at least, any variation should very clearly depart from it in a rather carefully arranged way (p. 28).

Alexander and French (1946), who were similarly attuned to the client's initial attitudes toward treatment, note:

> It follows that the therapist must first meet the patient on his own ground, tentatively accepting the patient's own view of the problem and seeking only secondarily, after orienting himself as to the patient's real motives, to utilize these actual motives to further such therapeutic aims as may then seem to be attainable (p. 113).

The question of just how far to go in meeting a client's expectations is frequently debated among behavior therapists (Lazarus, 1971). Should one make use of free association and dream analysis if the client feels this would be important? Should one delve deeply into the past history of a client who anticipated a historical analysis of his problem? Probably not. Instead, our therapeutic activities are guided by the belief that it is important for the behavior therapist initially to accept the client's expectations, to communicate that he can understand how the client might view the situation in that particular way (Erickson's utilization technique), and then gradually to persuade the client that a behavioral orientation represents an alternative and potentially more effective way of conceptualizing the change process.

In conveying what may be a totally novel conceptualization to some clients, the behavior therapist may draw on Ausubel's (1963) description of how clients can more readily assimilate new conceptual approaches. His concept of "advance organizers," in the form of general introductory concepts, allows the learner more easily to receive and retain new material that is being presented. In Ausubel's words:

> Since it is highly unlikely that at any given stage in the learner's differentiation of a particular sphere of knowledge we can depend on the spontaneous availability of the most relevant and proximate subsuming concepts, the most efficient way of facilitating retention is to introduce appropriate subsumers and make them part of cognitive structure prior to the actual presentation of the learning task. The introduced subsumers thus become advance "organizers" or anchoring foci for the reception of new material. In effect they provide an introductory overview at the appropriate level of conceptualization (p. 29).

Simply put, the use of advance organizers sets the stage for new ideas to make better sense. Clinically, it also allows the therapist to check the client's acceptance of certain basic assumptions before details of the procedure are presented.

Take, for example, a client who feels that the best way to approach his problem is to help him obtain some insight or understanding. The beginning behavior therapist may be tempted to expound on the irrelevance of insight in the behavior change process. This, however, may not be the best way to bring the client around to his point of view. Instead, the therapist can reconstrue the client's desire for understanding and insight in terms more amenable to behavior therapy. Some time can be spent reviewing past history as a means of disabusing the client of any notions that his problems are indicative of some "mental illness" or "neurosis" over which he has little control. Instead, the past may be construed as having provided various learning experiences that may have led to current problem behaviors. In the process of reviewing a client's past history, the therapist may introduce such advance organizers as "past learning," "learned fears," "models for imitation," and other similar social learning concepts. These concepts need not be introduced in a pedantic or formalized manner, but rather presented more subtly in the context of the material offered by the client. By utilizing techniques such as clarification and reflection of feeling to provide a "behavioral twist" to what is being said, the therapist may gradually lead the client to a different orientation toward his problems. In essence, the therapist can work within the client's frame of reference, showing concern and empathy, while subtly introducing him to a behavioral frame of reference. Such a tactic also allows the therapist to make periodic checks on whether or not the client is willing to accept this new conceptualization. The following transcript illustrates how this approach may be implemented.

Therapist: I'd like now to give you an idea of the problem as I see it, and then you can tell me whether or not I've missed anything, and whether or not it agrees with the situation as you see it. [*I think I've pretty much covered the major problem areas. It's time for me to present a summary statement (à la Sullivan) so that she can fill in any gaps or change any misconceptions I may have about the presenting problem. It can also help me communicate to her that I've been listening to what has been said thus far and that I'm trying to understand her.*] The primary problem that you want to have dealt with involves your nervousness and anxiety in social situations, primarily new situations, and particularly when you feel you are being evaluated by others. This may involve being at a party, presenting a talk, and other similar situations. Does that sound accurate?

Client: Yes, that's about it. The most important problem in my day-to-day life is really my anxiety when I'm with people, though being evaluated by others is also a problem.

Therapist: [*Based on what she said earlier, I think her problem reflects more of an inhibition than an actual behavioral or skill deficit. Of course, this has been based on her own verbal report, and I'm going to have to check it out further within the next session or so. I'll make some inquiries about instances in the past where she's been able to interact socially, try some role playing, and maybe even get reports from her friends.*] There was one other thing you had mentioned. You said that when you are in social situations, you know what to say, and you know what to do, but you feel too nervous to say or do it. Is that right? You become immobilized?

Client: Well, yes, but I wouldn't say I'm immobilized, though I think I should certainly be much better than I am. I do know what to do. I'm just too afraid.

Therapist: Right.

Client: There's also another thing, and this may be tied in with my other problems. I feel that I would like to be more open and more spontaneous with people than I am.

Therapist: Can you give me an idea when this occurs?

Client: Well, when I'm in a group. Especially if it's a group of people I don't know very well.

Therapist: I think you may be right. This may very well be a related difficulty. I would suspect that if we can get you to the point where you can learn to cope with nervousness in social situations this might very well help you to become more open and spontaneous. I think this is the direction which we should try to take—to work on problems in coping with the anxiety first, and then see what happens.

Client: OK. Fine.

Therapist: Before actually outlining what the treatment procedure will involve, I would find it very helpful if I could get an idea from you as to what *your* expectations are about what we're going to be doing. [*I can see by the blank look on her face that this question went over like a lead balloon. Maybe she thinks I'm testing her, and that she has to come up with the right answers. I'll have to remember to phrase this question differently in the future with other people. In any event, I should say something so that she doesn't feel bad about not being able to come up with an answer.*] I don't know if you've thought about this very much.

Client: Well, I've thought some about it, but I really don't know, because I've never been in any treatment before. I'm just not sure what it would involve.

Therapist: [*I can't accept her statement that she has no expectations. Everyone has some conception of what therapy will be like, even if it's only a vague one. It's probably not a good idea to push her too hard. I think I'll back off and take a different tack, acknowledging her lack of direct experience as a reason for not knowing precisely what would be involved, and drawing instead on more indirect sources of information.*] So, you haven't *directly* been involved, and you don't know specifically. But on the basis of contacts with other people who have been in therapy, or anything you've read about therapy, or seen in the movies or on TV, what is your view of therapy?

Client: Well, I have a couple of friends who are in therapy. In talking with one, the impression I get is that she talks a lot about her childhood, and what happened between her parents and herself.

Therapist: [*Hopefully, her psychodynamic orientation is not too strongly held. In any event, I should modify her expectations somewhat before I introduce a behavioral orientation.*] Well, what do you think of that?

Client: By understanding all of these things that happened in the past, she'll understand why she is what she is. So I imagine we'll talk a lot about what happened between my parents and myself.

Therapist: [*This is as good a time as any to find out a little bit about her relationship with her parents. In addition to finding out something about her social learning experiences, I might be able to get some clue as to how much she wants to talk about the past.*] Have you thought very much about your past —particularly about your family—as it relates to the difficulty you are having?

Client: Well, in a way I've been more fortunate than many people, because I get along very well with my parents. They're both school teachers. They're very nice people. What *I* thought about concerning the past is the attitude they had toward me. It has to do with the fact that they are teachers and see all kinds of different children and, well, many things happened that made me feel that I was being compared with the best of them. I know there are always some people who are better at some things than others, but I kind of had the feeling as a kid that I never could live up to these other kids.

Therapist: [*I don't want to pursue this area too much further, so I'll reflect and tie a few things together. Perhaps I can also use this as a chance to introduce some advance organizers that I might later use in conjunction with rational restructuring, emphasizing the terms "attitude" and "standards" as part of my clarification. I might be able to pick up on these later on,*

should I want to introduce rational restructuring as the thera-
peutic procedure.] So it sounds almost as if—because of the
circumstances in which you grew up, your parents being teachers and having been in contact with a large number of other
children—you developed an attitude toward yourself and
toward your own ability to live up to certain standards—a
certain uneasiness about the extent to which you could really
do things well.

Client: Um-hmm.

Therapist: And this is possibly related to the way your parents
reacted toward you—although they probably didn't do this
intentionally. There undoubtedly are other experiences in your
past that have contributed to some of the problems you currently have. It is kind of taken for granted that early learning
experiences determine current attitudes. The question I have
is how knowledge of everything that happened in the past can
help you in dealing with your current problems. My concern is
that if we spend a lot of time dealing with your past history,
after a year or two you may end up *knowing* what caused the
problem, but these problems might still exist.

Client: Um-hmm. It just seems to me that a lot of things can happen
when you are a young kid and can't figure things out. Although
you don't understand what's happening, you have an emotional reaction to it, you know. But you're not really aware of it.
If I could become aware of my emotional reactions, well,
maybe I wouldn't have to feel that way. It's the feelings that
are bothering me . . .

Therapist: . . . right . . .

Client: . . . and then *you* could understand how I feel.

Therapist: [*I'm not entirely certain what she's driving at. I have a*
feeling that she may be objecting to my emphasis on an intel-
lectual understanding of the past. What is clear is that she's
emphasizing emotional reactions. Perhaps I could just focus
on that. She's also saying that the past has been important in
creating her present difficulties. Rather than implicitly com-
municating to her that I think she's wrong, perhaps I can
build on this to convey a social learning orientation to her
problem; introducing the advance organizer "learning experi-
ence" would be appropriate here.] Um-hmm. So, in addition to
some of these attitudes you have learned from the past, there is

a whole set of emotional learning experiences you've gone through that have created certain emotional reactions to current situations.

Client: That's right.

Therapist: In many ways, learning to cope with your current emotions—learning to cope with situations without being overly emotional or anxious—is like a skill, and like learning a skill, it requires a good deal of practice. If you want to learn to drive a car, to ride a bicycle, to swim, or anything else, you usually don't spend a lot of time figuring out what in the past made you never learn this to begin with. Rather, you start from the situation here and now, and devise certain *new* learning experiences that will help you develop these skills. This is similar to the view I take toward your difficulties and to many other problems similar to your own. Granted that the past has been very significant in determining where you are now, more important in getting you to change between now and the future are the learning experiences that occur right now.

Client: I guess what you're saying makes sense; it's just that I never heard it before. The only experience that I've had was with this friend who was in therapy, where she spoke mostly of her past.

Therapist: In a sense, this is a relatively new approach—used only during the past ten or fifteen years or so. It's problem-oriented; it focuses on the here and now; and perhaps most important, it has as its goal helping the individual to overcome his problem as quickly as possible, without a long, drawn-out period of treatment. I assume that this is your goal as well—to overcome your problems in the fastest and best way possible.

Client: Certainly. And if this approach can do that, I think that would be great.

Therapist: [*It might be a good idea to have her read that recent magazine article that appeared on behavior therapy. Hopefully, any remaining skepticism can be overcome by the printed word.*] Fine. Along these lines, I have something you may be interested in reading. It can give you a better idea just what this orientation to therapy involves. This way, you can get an even clearer idea about the underlying philosophy of this approach to treatment.

Client: It seems to make sense. Yes. I'd be interested in looking at it.

Even after having been carefully prepared for a particular therapeutic procedure, clients may continue to be skeptical. We have attempted to deal with such clients by initially eschewing any direct attempt to change their attitude toward the treatment procedure, instead trying to determine which specific aspects of the therapeutic procedure bother them.

Having determined in greater detail what the client dislikes about the approach, the therapist can communicate that he understands and accepts the client's point of view, and that these initial reservations are not atypical. In other words, the therapist utilizes the resistance in much the same way as Erickson utilizes motoric and attitudinal features of subjects he is attempting to hypnotize. Take, for example, a client who feels that systematic desensitization is too simple and mechanical a procedure. We can honestly and readily agree with the client, acknowledging that, considering the complex and long-standing nature of his particular problem, it is not surprising for him to feel somewhat skeptical about the likelihood that such a simple procedure will help him. The therapist can emphasize, however, that despite the seemingly simplistic nature of the procedure, it has proven to be very effective in dealing with the problem behaviors in question.

We are moved to acknowledge here our awareness of the manipulative nature of the foregoing suggestions. To reiterate what is a truism in psychotherapy: All therapists influence their clients. Like other behavioral clinicians, we consider it preferable to deal as openly as possible with the control available to the therapist, rather than to pretend it does not exist.

Client's Expectations Regarding Likelihood of Change

It has long been recognized that a client's positive expectations for improvement provide an important motivation for behavior change (Goldstein, 1962). Commenting on this phenomenon, Frank (1961) has suggested ". . . part of the success of all forms of psychotherapy may be attributed to the therapist's ability to mobilize the patient's expectation of help . . ." (p.70–71). Almost no research has been done to determine how a client's positive expectations affect actual change; however, one may speculate that the client's greater attentiveness to therapeutic procedures and his conscientious between-session activities play a significant role (Rosen, 1974).

There are numerous ways to increase the client's optimism for behavior change. The therapist can allude to similar clients who have achieved success. He can also suggest or provide relevant reading material. If pessimism is due to ineffective therapy in the past, the therapist should emphasize the difference between past approaches and his own, with the clear implication that what is in store for the client is likely to be more effective. Special note can be taken of precisely what the client disliked about his previous therapy, so that such practices may be avoided, or at least presented in different forms. Some individuals may be skeptical about the likelihood of change because of seemingly similar attempts that have been unsuccessful in the past. If a client has read a book on relaxation techniques and found it to be ineffective, the therapist can emphasize that more closely supervised training procedures are needed in order for the method to work. It is not uncommon to find parents who, because of their own failures with the use of rewards, are skeptical about the likelihood of change in their child's behavior. To such parents, some of the subtleties involved in reinforcement programs, such as shaping, prompting, delay of reinforcement, and other related principles, should be delineated.

A procedure that has proven useful clinically is to have the client recognize that he may have been pessimistic in the past about changing, only to find that he could in fact change. The therapist can have the client relate instances in his recent past where he was pessimistic prior to learning some complicated skill (e.g., driving a car, learning a sport), and where practice and persistence resulted in positive consequences. The general objective here is to get the client to recognize that his current pessimistic attitude is perhaps unrealistic.

A similar tactic was used with a client who felt that change was unlikely in the absence of any insight into early childhood experiences or underlying conflicts. The therapist felt it was best not to push on this issue, deciding instead to attempt to win him over gradually. The therapist was able to make his point sooner than expected. During the same session that he conveyed pessimism, the client described an intimate relationship in his recent life and some of the profound effects it had on him personally. After spending some time discussing these personal changes with the client, the therapist smiled and questioned rhetorically: "Do you mean that all of this happened without any insight into the past?" The comment hit home, and the client became more positively inclined toward the therapy over the next few sessions.

Many of the above points are illustrated in the following transcript:

Therapist: I'd like to get some idea now of your attitude about the likelihood of seeing some change in yourself.

Client: Well, I don't know. Actually, I'm not too hopeful about seeing real change. There may be minor changes, but I'm sort of doubtful that there will be a major change.

Therapist: Why is that?

Client: Well, I guess it's just because I've had these problems as long as I can remember, and it's hard to conceive of myself as being a very different person. And also because I have friends who've been in therapy for a long time, and although there have been slight changes in them, there haven't been major ones; the basic problems will always be there.

Therapist: [*Hmm. I'm not quite sure where to take this. I don't think I want to directly refute any of these attitudes just yet. It might be a good idea to find out all the possible reasons for the pessimism first. I think I'll first reflect back what she said, which can give me a little more time to think.*] As you see it then, part of your skepticism is due to the long-term nature of your difficulties, and what you've seen in others. Has it also been because of any difficulty you may have had on your own in trying to make changes—trying to socialize more, to feel more comfortable with others?

Client: Not really. It's more that these difficulties are a major part of my personality; that's *me* and I can't conceive of myself as being different.

Therapist: So not having these problems is very foreign to what you are used to . . .

Client: Yes.

Therapist: . . . to the way you are right now.

Client: Right.

Therapist: [*She seems to be operating under the mistaken conception that because things were a certain way in the past, they always have to be that way in the future. If I can get her to describe an instance in her life where she was able to recognize that this attitude was unfounded, perhaps I can reduce her pessimism about behavior change with me. I'll have to do this with an abrupt transition.*] Have you, in recent years, ever been involved in any kind of new learning, involving a skill of some sort? Either an athletic skill, or learning how to drive, or something that is somewhat complicated—especially where you were doubtful in the beginning whether or not you actually could learn it but where you eventually did succeed?

Client: Well, learning to drive a car was very difficult for me. For most people who learn when they are teen-agers, it's nothing. But I only learned three years ago, and I can remember that for a long time I thought the world was divided into two types of people: those who could drive and those who could not. I was one of those who couldn't drive and I felt it would be such a fantastic thing if I were ever able to. I felt stupid because I knew that there were idiots who were driving. But somehow, on an emotional level, I felt I'd never be able to do it.

Therapist: And what happened?

Client: Well, I took lessons, and just kept at it. Eventually, I was able to drive.

Therapist: [*I couldn't have asked for a better example. Now to draw the parallel.*] It's very interesting, because it sounds as if your attitude toward driving—before you actually learned how to drive—was very similar to your attitude toward changing yourself, as far as your personal problems are concerned. I think in many ways, it's a very similar type of situation, because in order for you to eventually learn how to drive a car you had to overcome this initial pessimism. You had to persist, you had to learn it very gradually, and you had to practice. Slowly, after a period of time, it became more and more automatic, until you eventually reached the point where you may not have been consciously aware of everything you were doing while driving. For example, you could be talking to somebody else and not be aware that you were driving. So it *had* become part of you, a very natural thing with you. And I think the same thing can happen, as far as feeling comfortable socially is concerned. You can, indeed, learn the skill of coping with your anxieties, of feeling comfortable with other people. Although you may feel skeptical now, I feel confident that you can change.

Client: Well, I don't know.

Therapist: [*Perhaps relevant experiences of previous clients who have been initially skeptical might serve a useful modeling function.*] There have been a number of other people I've seen with problems very similar to yours, and they, too, were somewhat skeptical in the beginning—saying things like, "My problems have been around a long time," and "I can't see myself as being any different." I found that if they were willing to persist, and willing to go along with this new type of learning experience—learning a new way of approaching these situations, in a gradual way—they *did* start to change. Although I can't offer you any definite guarantee, I hope this will happen with you.

Client: And you've seen major changes occur in people?

Therapist: Major changes. And people often start to see themselves differently.

Client: Really? That sounds very good.

Therapist: [*I'm not sure how convinced she is. On the assumption that some doubt remains, it would be a good idea to invoke Erickson's utilization principle, and acknowledge that it is perfectly natural to have remaining doubts prior to actual behavior change. Of course, I can't be 100 percent sure I can help her!*] Now, I can sit here and talk to you about what I've seen, but you may never really be fully convinced until you start seeing some changes in yourself. So, I think what we should do is to begin, and then from time to time reflect back and see the extent to which you have, in fact, changed.

Client: Fine.

When the therapist senses that the client has some doubts, it is wise to single out a readily changeable behavior to focus on, to better convince the client that change is possible. With a highly anxious person, the use of a relaxation training session—even in those instances where desensitization may not have been planned— is likely to produce significant, even if only temporary, change. If a client is being prepared for systematic desensitization, work on hierarchy construction can be followed by a period of relaxation training. Discussion of anxiety-arousing situations will probably be somewhat upsetting, and the reduction of such anxiety with relaxation training can be used to illustrate the effectiveness of the desensitization procedure.

The Therapeutic Contract

A frequently neglected but important step in preparing a client for behavior therapy is making a therapeutic contract. Within any therapeutic interaction, certain implicit role demands are made on both therapist and client. To insure the success of the treatment procedure, the therapist should make certain that the client is aware of what is expected of him and is willing to comply with therapeutic requests. In addition to discussing issues such as the frequency of sessions, fees, cancellations, and other administrative details, the therapist should spell out the implicit two-way commitment. Thus, he can acknowledge that he will do all in his power to help the client change and to use any procedures that are likely to be most effective. In return, the client is expected to be candid in describing his problem behaviors and feelings, and to be willing to complete regularly any between-session assignments. The therapist should emphasize this latter point, adding that a limited amount can be accomplished during the relatively brief time allotted for the consultation sessions.

In discussing the therapeutic contract, the therapist may provide a summary statement of what has transpired in the clinical interaction thus far, including treatment priorities and general rationale for the behavior change process. The assumptions underlying the specific treatment procedures themselves may then be introduced gradually—generally at first and then in more specific terms —evaluating the client's acceptance of the procedure along the way. More detailed descriptions and actual illustrations of how this may be accomplished have been included in many of the following chapters.

● SUMMARY

Despite the strong emphasis behavior therapists place on specific techniques, the nature of the client-therapist relationship nonetheless remains an important dimension within the behavior change process. To begin with, the clinical interaction itself frequently can provide the opportunity to directly sample certain aspects of the client's problem behavior. The personal influence of the therapist can be important not only in enlisting the client's active cooperation within the consultation session, but also in instigating the client to try new behavioral alternatives in the real-life setting. The nature of the therapeutic relationship is also important in facilitating favorable client expectations for change and receptivity toward the behavioral approach. The chapter describes some of the potential difficulties encountered in preparing the client for the behavior change process, and illustrates how these may be overcome.

CURRENT BEHAVIOR THERAPY TECHNIQUES

Chapter 5

Relaxation Training

The use of relaxation has an extensive history in medicine, clinical psychology, and psychiatry. The pioneering work of Edmund Jacobson (1929) was concerned principally with the exploration of the Watsonian notion that thoughts and feelings were located in the peripheral musculature. Jacobson, a physician, also reported therapeutic benefits derived from relaxation when it was practiced by anxious people. In Europe, Schultz and Luthe (1959) were independently exploring the use of what they called "autogenic training" to reduce anxiety and foster well-being. In this country Haugen, Dixon, and Dickel (1963) outlined an entire therapy based on deep-muscle relaxation. Mothers who have gone through natural childbirth are also familiar with relaxation, not only to reduce anxiety but also to facilitate movement of the baby through the cervix (Lamaze, 1958). Of course, Wolpe's technique of systematic desensitization rests on the assumed need for the anxiety-inhibiting effects of striate muscle relaxation. More recently, psychologists and others interested in meditation and other eastern practices are drawing a connection between muscle relaxation and yoga exercises (e.g., Pfeiffer, 1967; Stoyva, 1968). The interest in transcendental meditation seems also to be part of the long-standing attempts of people to control their anxieties and generate feelings of well-being via relaxation or quiet contemplation.

● MUSCLE RELAXATION TRAINING

Data are plentiful demonstrating that relaxing one's muscles does markedly reduce anxiety (Jacobson, 1929; Lang, Melamed, & Hart, 1970; Paul, 1969b). Whether the anxiety-inhibiting effects of relaxation are truly necessary in the context of various behavior therapy procedures is very much an open research question (Wilson & Davison, 1971). For the clinician, however, available data do support the usefulness of teaching certain clients how to relax (see also Bernstein & Borkovec, 1973; Goldfried & Trier, 1974).

The mechanics of relaxation training are so straightforward that they can be put on tapes for at-home practice. Mainly this chapter will concentrate on pinpointing a number of potential pitfalls that await behavior therapists following through with any of several relaxation inductions. A failure to consider all or nearly all of the following details can preclude making full use of relaxation training procedures.

Preparations for Relaxation Training

Physical Setting

The noise level in the consulting room should be kept low, or at least constant. We have found it useful to use a white noise generator to minimize the disruption of outside noises, a consideration particularly important in these days of thin walls and flimsy construction. The illumination in the room should be kept dim, and particular attention should be paid to the amount of light that falls upon a client's closed eyelids inasmuch as the client usually relaxes in a reclining position. While a couch or bed is quite acceptable, we often make use of reclining chairs which can be placed in the upright position for other activities during therapy sessions. The client should be sitting or reclining comfortably in such a fashion as to keep any muscular tension to a minimum. The therapist should be positioned in such a way as to minimize embarrassment or discomfort to the client.

Preparation of the Client

Before embarking on a specific induction, the therapist should cover the following orientation points with the client.

1. The therapist tells the client that he is about to learn a *skill*, like driving a car or learning how to play a new sport. It is emphasized that people *learn* to be tense and anxious, and, in an analogous fashion, can be taught to relax. A corollary is the gradualness of the learning as well as the necessity for practice and for not expecting too much too soon.

2. The client is told that he may have unusual feelings, like tingling in the fingers or a floating sensation. Whatever the client experiences as different should be interpreted by him as signs that the muscles are beginning to loosen. This is important, for it is not uncommon for clients to react to the beginnings of relaxation in a fearful way because they are concerned that something bad is happening to them. On the contrary, such different sensations seem to be signposts of incipient relaxation.

3. It is suggested to the client that he adopt the set of "going with" the process, just letting things happen. If a client enjoys drinking now and then, reference can be made to the enjoyment one can have in relaxing with alcohol. Particularly with younger clients, passing reference can be made to previous drug experiences, where the phrase "Go with it" makes sense.

4. A very common pitfall is the sense of losing control. The clients whom one is likely to use relaxation with may well have fears of losing control. Periodic probes are therefore advisable, for example, "How do you feel about that?" With a client who might harbor such fears, one should present only a few minutes of relaxation induction at the first session, and *not* provide a tape to take home until the fears have been allayed.

5. It is emphasized to the client that he remains in *ultimate* control. The client can and should stop the proceedings any time they become aversive or uncomfortable. The therapist presents himself as a guide and teacher, but the client's own body remains his own to be in control of and to work with.

6. The therapist introduces the paradox that one learns to

gain control over oneself by letting go. A typical response of clients when they feel impending panic or tension is to tighten the reins of control rather than loosen them. An analogy of riding a horse may be mentioned to some clients. That is, by letting go of muscles and conscious control over the body, one is able gradually to learn to achieve a *greater* degree of more important and basic control over feelings and tensions. Furthermore, letting go and relaxing can facilitate planful thinking and attending to important activities. Indeed, the client can be told that relaxing one's muscles is a very active affair in a physiological sense: It is known that to relax a striate muscle, one sends particular kinds of efferent messages that inhibit the tension of specific muscles (Davison, 1966). An analogy that we have frequently used is floating in water; in order to float effectively a person must let go and allow the natural bouyancy of the body to interact with the specific gravity of the water.

7. It is occasionally necessary to allow clients to keep their eyes open for the initial sessions, especially when they seem concerned about what is in store for them. Clients have to build up trust in the therapist; by keeping the eyes open they can hold on to waking reality for as long as they feel is necessary. At the same time, one should point out that it is desirable ultimately to have the eyes closed so that visual distractions can be eliminated and more attention paid to the comforts of relaxing. This consideration seems particularly important with clients of the opposite sex, for it occasionally happens that people perceive this situation as sexually seductive.

8. The therapist structures all relaxation sessions in a low achievement fashion. That is, the client is told that he is about to begin to practice some exercises, and that usually people feel little difference the first few times, although some react very strongly the first time. Especially with clients who are concerned about how they are doing, it is important to point out that this is not a testing situation and not something that they have to work at in a dogged, grim fashion.

9. The client is told that his mind may wander during the induction, and is urged not to worry about this though he is asked to bring his thoughts back to the induction when

he can. As an example, the therapist can allude to every-day conversation, where it is not unusual for an individual's mind to wander for a moment or two but be easily brought back to the topic at hand.

10. The client is told that he is free to move around in the chair as much as he would like to maintain comfort. At the same time, he is encouraged not to engage in conversations with the therapist or to move around unnecessarily. Above all, it is important that the client not feel that he is in a straitjacket while relaxing in the chair.

11. A final, hopefully obvious point: The client should have a clear understanding of why he is about to learn relaxation. Unfortunately novice therapists, confident with their own assessment of a client's difficulties as being anxiety-related, may plunge ahead without appreciating the client's need to share the therapist's views of the problem(s) and to agree that relaxation training is necessary. We have dealt with this general aspect of behavior therapy in the preceding chapters.

Mechanics: General Considerations

There are a number of general procedural points important in most approaches to relaxation training.

For the training method that has clients tense muscles before letting go of them, clients are told not to strain the muscles by tensing as hard as possible, but rather to tense them only to ¾ of the potential tension. It is important to sense some tension in the muscles prior to letting go and relaxing them; however, there is no need for clients to exhaust or strain themselves.

It is also advisable for the therapist to demonstrate for the client how the various muscle groups are to be tensed. The therapist runs through the various exercises while the client sits and watches him. This should eliminate ambiguities and also help to relieve any inhibitions about making peculiar faces or assuming bodily postures that might be embarrassing for some clients. For this demonstration purpose, the therapist performs the exercises quickly, pointing out that this pace is deliberately faster than will be the case during the actual induction.

The therapist should encourage the client to ask questions so as to dispel ambiguities and to provide reassurance on any points that are troubling or unclear. This caveat is of course applicable in all therapeutic situations.

The therapist should check with the client for trick knees or sore backs so that tension-relaxation inductions can bypass areas of the body that are best left alone.

It is sometimes very uncomfortable for people who wear contact lenses to have their eyes closed for extended periods of time. It is important to determine if this is the case and to allow the client to remove contacts if he desires. The client is also encouraged to loosen any tight clothing and perhaps even to remove shoes if this will increase comfort.

In all relaxation inductions, the therapist's tone of voice should be low, soft, warm, melodic, and somewhat hypnotic; the pace should be much slower than conversational speech.

Relaxation via Tension-Relaxation

The following guidelines are especially appropriate for inductions that utilize alternate tensing and relaxing of muscles.

The therapist should allow about five to ten seconds of tension for each muscle group followed by approximately 20 seconds of suggestions to let go. Two tension-relaxation cycles for each muscle group are generally employed. In our own experience we have found it useful to intersperse some of the following aphorisms: "Just keep letting go, further and further," "Notice the contrast and enjoy the contrast," "Just think of loosening all those muscles, further and further, more and more," and so on. It is also useful to count from 1 to 10 occasionally, suggesting all the while that the person can let go more and more as each number is uttered by the therapist.

In accordance with the coping skill orientation suggested by Goldfried (1971), the client may be told that the tension phase will help him become more sensitive to those sensations associated with becoming anxious, and that these sensations will begin to serve as a cue or signal to relax away the tension.

Clients are instructed to release a tensed muscle group as suddenly as possible, as if to throw the tensions out of the body. This sudden release procedure, introduced independently by Arnold Lazarus and Gordon Paul, seems to shorten the time needed to acquire relaxation skills as compared to the more extended procedures of Jacobson.

Particularly for the beginning therapist, it is advisable to practice along with the client as he goes through at least the initial relaxation induction. We have found that the proprioceptive cues available to the therapist as he himself is relaxing helps mediate his own verbalizations so that they sound maximally relaxing and calming.[1]

Since we are working with highly subjective feelings, in those situations where polygraph recordings are not available it is useful to introduce some kind of shorthand communication system so that the client can indicate fairly readily and quickly how relaxed or tense he is feeling at any given time. We use a simple 0 to 100 scale, as diagrammed on page 88, where 0 represents complete relaxation and 100 represents maximum tension. It is important of course to determine the client's own construction of the points on this scale; clearly, a score of 30 for one client might indicate a considerably greater degree of subjectively perceived relaxation than for other clients. This scale can be introduced as follows:

To help us communicate about how relaxed or tensed you're feeling at various times during this training, I would like to introduce to you a little subjective rating scale. (*Therapist can hand client a card.*) You will notice that we conceive of this scale as being anchored at the zero end by feeling no tension whatsoever—perhaps how you might feel while relaxing at the beach on a warm summer's day—and at the 100 end by feeling as tense as you ever have felt—100 percent tension. Thus, scores in the area of 75 would indicate that you are feeling quite tense but not maximally tense, and scores in the area of 25 would indicate that you're feeling very relaxed, though not completely relaxed. Scores in the 50 area indicate naturally a midpoint between tension and relaxation. I do not of course expect you to be all that exact, but rather to give me only rough approximations of how tense or relaxed you're feeling at any given time. For example, where would you place yourself on the scale at the present time? . . .

OK, the score of 60 that you just gave me indicates that you're feeling somewhat more tense than you are relaxed but you're not feeling terribly tense, is that right? . . . Fine, you will get much better at using this scale as we go along, and I will come to be able to learn just how you are construing each of the points along this subjective rating scale.

---

[1] More than one behavior therapist we know has fallen asleep during his own relaxation induction. The desirability of this degree of therapist relaxation is questionable.

0	25	50	75	100
no tension, completely relaxed	very relaxed		very tense	maximum tension

The following is a transcript of a tension-relaxation induction, adapted from the clinical work of Arnold Lazarus.

Now, settle back as comfortably as you can, close your eyes, and listen to what I'm going to be telling you. I'm going to make you aware of certain sensations in your body and then show you how you can reduce these sensations. First direct your attention to your left arm, your left hand in particular. Clench your left fist. Clench it tightly and study the tension in the hand and in the forearm. Study those sensations of tension. And now let go. Relax the left hand and let it rest on the arm of the chair. And note the difference between the tension and the relaxation. (*10-second pause.*) Once again now, clench your left hand into a fist, tightly, noticing the tensions in the hand and in the forearm. Study those tensions, and now let go. Let your fingers spread out, relaxed, and note the difference once again between muscular tension and muscular relaxation. (*10-second pause.*)

Now let's do the same with the right hand. Clench the right fist. Study those tensions (*5-second pause*) and now relax. Relax the right fist. Note the difference once again between the tension and the relaxation. And enjoy the contrast (*10-second pause.*) Once again now, clench the right fist, clench it tight. Study the tensions. Study them. And now relax the right fist. Let the fingers spread out comfortably. See if you can keep letting go a little bit more. Even though it seems as if you've let go as much as you possibly can, there always seems to be that extra bit of relaxation. Note the difference once again between the tension and the relaxation. Note the looseness beginning to develop in the left and right arms and hands. Both your left and right arms and hands now are a little bit more relaxed.

Now bend both hands back at the wrists so that you tense the muscles in the back of the hand and in the forearm. Fingers pointing toward the ceiling. Study the tension, and now relax. Let your hands return to their resting positions, and note the difference between tension and relaxation. (*10-second pause.*)

Do that once again—fingers pointing to the ceiling, feeling that tension in the backs of the hands and in the forearms. And now relax. Let go. Further and further. (*10-second pause.*)

Now clench both your hands into fists and bring them towards your shoulders so as to tighten your biceps muscles, the large muscles in the upper part of the arm. Feel the tension in the biceps muscles. And now relax. Let your arms drop down again to your sides, and note the difference between the tension that was in your biceps and the relative relaxation you feel now. (*10-second pause.*) Let's do that once again now. Clench both biceps muscles, bringing both arms up, trying to touch with your fists the respective shoulders. Study that tension. Hold it, study it. And now relax. Once again, let the arms drop and study the feelings of relaxation, the contrast between tension and relaxation. Just keep letting go of those muscles, further and further. (*10-second pause.*)

Now we can direct our attention to the shoulder area. Shrug your shoulders, bringing both shoulders up towards your ears, as if you wanted to touch your ears with your shoulders. And note the tension in your shoulders and up in your neck. Study that tension. Hold it. And now relax. Let both shoulders return to a resting position. Just keep letting go, further and further. Once again, note the contrast between the tension and the relaxation that's now spreading into your shoulder areas. (*10-second pause.*) Do that once again. Bring both shoulders up as if to touch the ears. Feel the tension in the shoulders, in the upper back, in the neck. Study the tension in these muscles. And now relax. Loosen those muscles. Let your shoulders come down to a resting position, and study the contrast once again between the tension and the relaxation. (*10-second pause.*)

You can also learn to relax more completely the various muscles of the face. So, what I want you to do now is to wrinkle up your forehead and brow. Wrinkle it until you feel all your forehead very much wrinkled, the muscles tense, and skin furrowed. And now relax. Smooth out the forehead. Let those muscles become loose. (*10-second pause.*) Do that once again. Wrinkle up your forehead. Study those tensions in the muscles above the eyes, in the forehead region. And now, smooth out your forehead. Relax those muscles. And once again note the contrast between the tension and the relaxation. (*10-second pause.*)

Now close your eyes very tightly. Close them tightly so that you can feel tension all around your eyes and the many muscles that control the movements of the eyes. (*5-second pause.*) And now relax those muscles, let them relax, noting the difference between the tension and the relaxation. (*10-second pause.*) Do that once again now. Eyes tightly closed and study the tension. Hold it. (*5-second pause.*) And relax, let go, and let your eyes remain comfortably closed. (*10-second pause.*)

Now clench your jaws, bite your teeth together. Study the tension throughout the jaws. (*5-second pause.*) Relax your jaws now. Let your lips part slightly, and note the difference between tension and relaxation in your jaw area. (*10-second pause.*) Once again, jaws clenched. Study the tension. (*5-second pause.*) And now let go, further and further. Just continue to relax. (*10-second pause.*)

Now purse your lips, press your lips together. That's right, press them together very tightly and feel the tension all around the mouth. And now relax, relax those muscles around the mouth, and just let your chin rest comfortably. Once again now, press your lips together and study the tension around the mouth. Hold it. (*5-second pause.*) And now relax. Let go of those muscles, more and more, further and further. (*10-second pause.*) Note how much more loose the various muscles have perhaps become in those parts of the body that we have successively tensed and relaxed. Your hands, forearms, upper arms, your shoulders, the various facial muscles.

And now we'll turn our attention to the neck. Press your head back against the surface on which it's resting. Press it back so that you can feel the tension, primarily in the back of the neck and in the upper back. Hold it, study it. And now let go, let your head rest comfortably now, and enjoy the contrast between the tension you created before, and the greater relaxation you can feel now. Just keep letting go, further and further, more and more, to the best of your ability. Do that once again, head pressed back, study the tension, hold it, (*5-second pause*) and now let go, just relax, let go, further and further. (*10-second pause.*)

Now I'd like you to bring your head forward, and try to bury your chin into your chest. Feel the tension, especially in the front of your neck. And now relax, let go, further and further. (*10-second pause.*) Do that once again now. Chin buried in the chest, hold it. (*5-second pause.*) And now relax, just relax, further and further. (*10-second pause.*)

Now we can direct our attention to the muscles of the upper back. Arch your back, arch it, sticking out your chest and stomach so that you feel tension in your back, primarily in your upper back. Study that tension and now relax. Let the body once again rest against the back of the chair or the bed, and note the difference between the tension and the relaxation, letting those muscles get more and more loose. (*10-second pause.*) Once again now arch the back way up. Study the tensions. Hold it. (*5-second pause.*) And now relax the back once again, letting go of all the tensions in these muscles. (*10-second pause.*)

And now take a deep breath, filling your lungs, and hold it. Hold it and study the tension all through your chest and down into your stomach area. Study that tension, and now relax, let go. Exhale and continue breathing as you were. Note once again the difference between the tension and the relaxation. (*10-second pause.*) Let's do that once again. Take a deep breath and hold it. Hold it. Study those tensions. Study them. Note the muscles tensing. Note the sensations. And now exhale and continue breathing as you were, very comfortably breathing, letting those muscles of the chest and some of the stomach muscles relax, getting more and more relaxed, each time you exhale. (*10-second pause.*)

And now tighten up the muscles in your stomach. Tense those stomach muscles. Hold it. Make the stomach very hard. And now relax. Let those muscles become loose. Just let go and relax. (*10-second pause.*) Do that once again—tighten those stomach muscles—study the tension. (*5-second pause.*) And now relax, let go, further and further, more and more. Loosen the tensions. Get rid of the tensions and note the contrast between tension and relaxation. (*10-second pause.*)

I'd like you now to stretch both legs. Stretch them so that you can feel tension in the thighs. Stretch them way out, (*5-second pause*) and now relax. Let them relax and note the difference once again between tension in the thigh muscles and the relative relaxation you can feel now. (*10-second pause.*) Do that once again, locking your knees, stretch out both legs so that you can feel the muscles of your thighs getting very hard, very tense. (*5-second pause.*) And now relax, relax those muscles. Let them get loose. Get rid of all tensions in the muscles of your thighs. (*10-second pause.*)

Now tense both calf muscles by pointing your toes towards your head. If you point your toes upward towards your head, you can feel the pulling, the tension, the contraction in your calf muscles and in your shins as well. Study that tension. And now relax. Let the legs relax and note once again the difference between tension and relaxation. (*10-second pause.*) Once again now, bend your feet back at the ankles, toes pointing toward your head, and study the tension. Hold it, study it. And now let go, relax those muscles, further and further, more and more deeply relaxed. (*10-second pause.*)

Just as you have been directing your muscles to tense you've also been directing them to relax or to loosen. You've noted the difference between tension and muscular relaxation. You can notice whether there is any tension in your muscles, and if there is, you can try to concentrate on that part, send messages to that muscle to loosen, to relax. If you think of loosening that muscle, you will in fact be able to do so, even if only a little.

Now, as you sit there in the chair, I'm going to review the various muscle groups that we've covered. As I name each group, try to notice if there is any tension in those muscles. If there is any, try to concentrate on those muscles and send messages to them to relax, to loosen. (*5-second pause.*) Relax the muscles in your feet, ankles, and calves. (*5-second pause.*) Shins, knees, and thighs. (*5-second pause.*) Buttocks and hips. (*5-second pause.*) Loosen the muscles of your lower body. (*5-second pause.*) Relax your stomach, waist, lower back. (*5-second pause.*) Upper back, chest, and shoulders. (*5-second pause.*) Relax your upper arms, forearms, and hands, right to the tips of your fingers. (*5-second pause.*) Let the muscles of your throat and neck loosen. (*5-second pause.*) Relax your jaw and facial muscles. (*5-second pause.*) Let all the muscles of your body become loose. (*5-second pause.*) Now sit quietly with your eyes closed. (*5-second pause.*) Do nothing more than that. Just sit quietly with your eyes closed for a few minutes.[2] (*2-minute pause.*)

Now I'd like you to think of that zero to 100 scale, where zero is complete relaxation, and 100 maximum tension. Consider approximately where you would place yourself on that scale, and remember the number so that you can jot it down after you have opened your eyes. OK, I am going to count from

[2] At this point, the therapist can count from 1 to 10, suggesting deeper relaxation as per the instructions on pp. 96–97.

5 to 1. When I reach the count of 1, open your eyes, stretch, be wide awake, and then switch off the tape recorder. 5 . . . 4 . . . 3 . . . 2 . . . 1—eyes open, wide awake.

Practice of Exercises

As the client has already been told, the emphasis is on *practice*. In order to increase the number of sessions without increasing the expense to the client and the time spent by the therapist, we have made extensive use of tape-recorded relaxation instructions. We have found that simply telling a client to go home and practice relaxation exercises, even after a number of consulting room sessions, may not only do little good but may even be harmful, as the client is likely to have failure experiences and possibly grow to dislike the entire enterprise. Asking for between-session practice without tapes as guides often leads to complaints and despair or perhaps even worse, such as a tendency for the client to lie to the therapist about how well he is doing.

The outpatient client can be told to bring a cassette tape recorder with him to the consultation session, along with a blank tape. During the session, the therapist can then record the tape for the client (following all the precautions mentioned earlier in this chapter), thus tailor-making a tape for him, including or excluding certain elements as appropriate for a given individual. Even with a client of minimal means, urging the purchase of an inexpensive cassette tape recorder makes sense in the context of how much a given therapy session usually costs. As an alternative, we have made effective use of standard tape recordings particularly in our university clinic setting, where one of the consulting rooms can be set aside as a "tape room."

The home situation must be structured in an appropriate fashion for the client: He is asked to do his practice in a quiet place, preferably when he can look forward to privacy for up to half an hour, and to find a comfortable bed or chair in which to relax. The instruction is for practice once a day, usually not more. In spite of enthusiasm on the part of many clients, most people find it difficult to make time for more than one practice session per day. The importance of record-keeping is stressed to the client, including writing down any difficulties or other noteworthy events during training sessions. The 0 to 100 scale used before and after the session is particularly helpful in this regard. We have found the format below useful in keeping track of the client's practice sessions.

```
┌─────────────────────────────────────────────────────────────────────┐
│                     RELAXATION RECORD FORMAT                          │
│                                                                       │
│  ┌────────┬──────┬───────┬───────────────────────────────────────┐   │
│  │        │      │       │  Comments (Any difficulties?  Were    │   │
│  │  Date  │ Pre  │ Post  │  you interrupted?  Was today an       │   │
│  │        │      │       │  especially bad day?  Did you have    │   │
│  │        │      │       │  a headache?)                         │   │
│  ├────────┼──────┼───────┼───────────────────────────────────────┤   │
│  │        │      │       │                                       │   │
│  │        │      │       │                                       │   │
│  │        │      │       │                                       │   │
│  │        │      │       │                                       │   │
│  │        │      │       │                                       │   │
│  │        │      │       │                                       │   │
│  │        │      │       │                                       │   │
│  │        │      │       │                                       │   │
│  └────────┴──────┴───────┴───────────────────────────────────────┘   │
└─────────────────────────────────────────────────────────────────────┘
```

Since the client is going to engage in up to seven practice sessions without the direct supervision of the therapist, it is important to emphasize that he not expect too much from the tape, and that he not yet attempt to apply relaxation skills to *in vivo* situations. The reasons are obvious: Having experienced a deep state of relaxation, a client may feel that he can go out and face his problems with significantly less anxiety. He is likely to be disillusioned. Likewise, some clients expect the relaxation to carry over for hours after listening to a given tape. It is remarkable how many clients come to believe that they can learn to relax quickly and apply this in a life situation in spite of warnings by the therapist to the contrary. While any of these outcomes is possible, they are highly unlikely, and the therapist should take pains to point out that the benefits of relaxation are possible only with extended practice.

We have sometimes noticed a paradoxical worsening in the client's anxiety after listening to the tapes. While this may be part of the rare negative reaction to relaxation training (particularly in psychotic clients), it is much more often a function of the client beginning to become more aware of his tensions. The therapist can note that this increased awareness is a very good sign. It is emphasized that the tensions are ultimately to be used as cues for learned relaxation responses, and that the client must therefore learn to be sensitive to his body as to lay the foundation for later acquisition of relaxation to cues of internally felt anxiety (Goldfried, 1971).

As with all behavior therapy procedures, the therapist must gear subsequent intervention to the client's behavior. Thus, inquiries should be frequent and detailed about the client's use of the tapes, not only with respect to tension-ratings, but to more qualitative reactions, such as disliking a particular instruction, or liking another. In addition, a client may consistently report lightness rather than heaviness. Similar to what is advised in hypnosis (see pp. 106 ff.), the therapist would do well to utilize this disclosure and *suggest* such reactions in later tapes.

Relaxation via Letting Go

In Jacobsonian relaxation training, one wishes to move from letting go after initially tensing to the point where the client simply lets go without tensing. Clients begin to point out, perhaps after a couple of weeks of practice, that they have found themselves reluctant to tense muscles after a period of relaxation. For example, "I'm getting to the point where I wish the tape would just let me relax on my own"; or, "You know, I would have preferred just to be allowed to practice without any more tensing." Another cue seems to be when the client gets down to about 20 on the scale rather easily, that is, the client is getting "very relaxed" with nearly every relaxation session.

Letting go is the next logical phase, for at this point the client presumably has become more aware of minor tensions and more adept at eliminating them. The following transcript illustrates a letting-go induction.

> You are lying comfortably with your eyes closed, all parts of your body supported so that there is no need to tense any muscles. Just let go as best you can. (*3-second pause.*)
> Focus in on the feelings in your right hand and let go of whatever tensions might be there. (*3-second pause.*) Just relax. (*3-second pause.*) Relax all of those muscles to the best of your ability. (*3-second pause.*) Relax the muscles of the right forearm, just let go further and further. (*3-second pause.*) Just let go of those muscles more and more, deeper and deeper. Relax. (*3-second pause.*) Now relax the muscles of the upper right arm, just relax those muscles as best you're able. Continuing to let go further and further your entire right arm, forearm, and hand right down to the fingertips, just relax and let go. (*3-second pause.*) Relax. While you continue to let go of your right arm and hand, turn your attention to your left hand, and relax your left hand to the best of your ability.

(*3-second pause.*) Just let go further and further. Let go of the muscles in the left forearm, just relax. Further and further relaxed. (*3-second pause.*) Just feel the relaxation coming now into the upper left arm, those muscles also beginning to relax further and further, more and more. (*3-second pause.*) Just relaxing further and further, more and more relaxed. (*3-second pause.*) Relax now both your left and right shoulders, and feel the soft heaviness, the calm relaxation coming more and more into both your left and right arms, hands, fingertips. (*3-second pause.*) Just let go of those muscles further and further. (*3-second pause.*) Now we turn our attention to the muscles in the face. Smooth out your forehead, just relax those muscles. (*3-second pause.*) As you think of relaxing those muscles, you'll gradually become more and more able to feel the relaxation coming into them. Your eyes lightly and comfortably closed. (*3-second pause.*) Relaxation spreading warmly to your cheeks, these muscles looser and looser. (*3-second pause.*) Your jaws loosely relaxed, more and more, further and further. (*3-second pause.*) Feel the relaxation moving calmly into your neck, and down into your chest, as you relax further and further. (*3-second pause.*) As you think of letting go, you somehow are able to let go further, more and more than before. (*3-second pause.*) You're breathing slowly and regularly, letting go a little bit more each time you exhale. (*3-second pause.*) Relaxation coming down into your stomach now, more and more relaxed, just letting go further and further. (*3-second pause.*) Relax, just relax. Feel the relaxation in your hips and buttocks, as you are resting heavily and comfortably. Further and further relaxed. (*3-second pause.*) Relaxation spreading out into your thighs, more and more relaxed. (*3-second pause.*) Deeper and deeper. Just continuing to let go further and further, more and more. (*3-second pause.*) Relaxation spreading now to the calves of both your left and right legs, further and further relaxed. (*3-second pause.*) Relaxation down now into your feet, further and further relaxed. Just continuing to relax, further and further. (*3-second pause.*)

To help you relax even more, I am going to count slowly from 1 to 10. As I call out each number, see if you can relax a little bit more than before. Even when it seems impossible to relax any further, there is always that extra bit of calm and relaxation that you can enjoy, just by letting go further and further. (*3-second pause.*) 1, relaxing more and more.

(*3-second pause.*) 2, further and further relaxed. (*3-second pause.*) 3, more and more, further and further. (*3-second pause.*) 4, more and more relaxed. (*3-second pause.*) 5, relaxing your whole body, getting heavier and looser and more relaxed. (*3-second pause.*) 6, deeper and deeper, further and further relaxed. (*3-second pause.*) 7, your whole body further and further relaxed, heavier and looser, more and more calm. (*3-second pause.*) 8, further and further, more and more relaxed. (*3-second pause.*) 9, further and further relaxed. (*3-second pause.*) and 10, just continue relaxing like that. Continuing to relax further and further. (*3-second pause.*)

Now, as you relax like that, I want you to think of that scale that goes from zero to 100, where zero is complete relaxation and 100 is maximum tension. If you feel that you are at approximately 30 or below on that scale, in other words feeling quite relaxed, continue listening to this tape. If you are not that relaxed today, then remember your score and jot it down when you open your eyes. Switch off the tape recorder at this time if you are not at 30 or below. . . . (*10-second pause.*)

In a few minutes I am going to become silent so that you can practice the following exercise. I want you to think clearly to yourself of the word "calm" every time you exhale. I would like you to let go a little bit more each time you exhale and at the same time to think to yourself the word "calm." This will enable you to associate in your mind the word "calm" with the calm state you are now in. Each time you exhale I would like you to think silently to yourself the word "calm." Go ahead and do that until I return to talk to you once again. (*3-minute pause.*)

That's fine. Stop that exercise and listen to me once again please. I would like you to consider where you would place yourself on the zero to 100 scale, so that you can jot down that number on your record sheet when you awaken . . .

Now I'm going to count from 5 to 1 and at the count of 1 you will open your eyes and be alert and wide awake. 5 . . . 4 . . . 3 . . . 2 . . . 1—eyes wide open, awake, and switch off the tape recorder.

Weaning the Client from the Tapes

After the client is reporting consistently that the second tape (the letting-go induction) helps him to achieve fairly deep levels of relaxation (perhaps in the range of 10 to 20), the therapist should begin to lessen his dependence on the tape. This can be accomplished by instructing the client, prior to turning on the tape, to let go on his own for about 10 minutes. This enables the client to determine how much tension reduction he can achieve without the tape, while at the same time knowing that the tape ultimately will be used. In this fashion, three relaxation ratings are obtained— prior to relaxation, after relaxing for 10 minutes on one's own, and after listening to the tape. As the difference between the second and third rating diminishes, there is less need for the tape.

Differential Relaxation

Once the client has learned to relax with all parts of the body supported, it is often desirable to extend relaxation skills to stressful life situations in which it is impossible for the client to lie down and relax. The term "differential relaxation" refers to relaxing those muscles that are not essential to given activities. For example, when sitting and speaking with another person, one can inconspicuously relax many facial, back, stomach, and leg muscles. The transcript below illustrates procedures found clinically useful. The principle theme is to encourage the client to assess which muscles need not be tense at any given time, to note whether they are tense, and to let go of them selectively, analogous to the letting go that he has already learned. Other exercises can readily occur to the therapist, preferably ones that tend to simulate situations present in the client's current life situation (e.g., talking to someone).

The initial differential relaxation training session can begin with the client relaxing on his own for about ten minutes. When he signals that he has achieved a state of relaxation comparable to a score of 30 or below, the therapist may then proceed as follows:

> OK, would you open your eyes now, and I'll help you sit up in the chair. Now just sit there in the chair while I point out a few things to you. Please keep your eyes open; perhaps you'd like to look at the outlet on the wall. Just look at the outlet and notice that, while doing so, there is no need to tense many of your muscles. For example, there is no need to tense the muscles in your forehead, in your arms, shoulders, and legs. While you are doing something like looking at an object, it is still possible to keep many of your muscles very relaxed.
>
> You'll notice that you probably have to keep the muscles of your neck somewhat tense so that your head will remain upright, but there is really no need to tense your shoulders, or

your arms, or the various muscles of your chest and stomach, or your legs. Just notice how relaxed you can remain in many parts of your body and still continue looking at the outlet. Continue sitting there, and take note of any unnecessary tensions that may creep in now and then, and switch them off. Just as the tensing of a voluntary muscle is under your control, so also is the relaxation of that muscle. This will take some practice, but you can get a good idea of what it's like right now. Just relax more and more, and enjoy the pleasant feelings that accompany this relaxation. (*Let client just sit for about 15 seconds.*)

Now I'm going to show you something else. I'd like you to take this pad of paper in your hand and just twist it around. That's right, hold it in that hand and turn it about. Keep your eyes on it and practice using this hand while allowing your other muscles to remain relaxed. There is still no need to tense most of your facial muscles, or your other arm, or most of your stomach muscles, or your legs. These other muscles are not essential to what you're doing, so you can keep them quite relaxed and enjoy the calm that comes with the relaxation of even some of your muscles. (*Let client do this for a while.*) How does that feel? (*Client will undoubtedly report that it is quite nice, going along well. If he reports tensions, get him to relax those parts by concentrating on them; if he still reports tensions, tell him that he'll get better at it with practice.*)

OK, you can give me the pad. Now I'd like you to move over to that other chair. (*Direct client to sit in a straight-back chair.*) You'll notice that sitting in this chair involves more muscles than were needed to sit in the recliner. Since your neck is not supported by the chair, you have to keep those muscles active so that you can remain upright. But there is, once again, no need to tense your arms, chest, and stomach muscles, or your legs. These muscles can remain quite relaxed. See if you can reinstate the pleasant relaxation in all the nonessential muscles. . . . How does that feel?

Now would you please stand up and face me? . . . Notice that you must tense various muscles in your legs and stomach in order to remain standing, but there is really no need to have your arms and shoulders tense. Try to relax as many muscles as you can in the upper part of your body, especially in your face, shoulders, and arms. Many people find it helpful to exhale as much as they are able. (*Therapist demonstrates.*) This helps reinstate the relaxation and the general calm that accompanies it. Just stand as I am standing and relax as many muscles as you can. . . . Can you tell me which of your muscles are relaxed? (*Client will usually report relaxation in the upper part of the body. Acknowledge this and suggest other muscles which he can try to relax, if appropriate. All the while, therapist is assuming similar postures, in an effort to disinhibit the client.*)

This has been going very well, and between now and our next session I'd like you to practice differential relaxation a few times a day. This is a skill like any other, and the more you practice it, the better you'll get at it. Try to concentrate on any muscles that are particularly difficult to loosen. The main idea is for you to be able to relax as many muscles as you can and still do things.

The therapist should give at-home assignments that maximize success, only gradually moving to more problematical situations. For example, during a given week the client could try to relax nonessential muscles while watching TV quietly. Success here could be followed by attempts to relax while talking quietly with a friend. Only later on should efforts be made to relax when confronting truly challenging or frightening situations. Oftentimes the "calm" cue employed in practice with the letting-go tape is helpful.

Applications of Relaxation

Once the client has learned to relax in the way described thus far in this chapter, his newly acquired skill can be applied in a variety of ways.

1. Systematic desensitization to specific anxiety dimensions is perhaps the most obvious purpose to which relaxation training can be put (see Chapter 6).

2. Analogous to systematic desensitization is the way differential relaxation can be used in specifically programmed environmental situations. This is sometimes referred to as *in vivo* desensitization. The use of concrete charting of between-sessions assignments is strongly recommended. This kind of record-keeping can help clients focus on their homework, as well as assist the therapist in monitoring treatment. A suggested format appears below. In encouraging the client to relax in anxiety-provoking situations (starting of course with the easiest), the therapist does well to emphasize the coping nature of this newly

Date	Description of Situation	Tension level (0 to 100) before and after attempting to relax Before After	

acquired response or skill. Whether subsequent anxiety reduction is a result of counterconditioning (response substitution) or the acquisition of a coping skill is yet to be determined.

3. Newly acquired relaxation skills can help within therapy sessions by facilitating behavior rehearsal (see Chapter 7) if the request to engage in a particular kind of role playing elicits such levels of anxiety that the client is unable to attend to directions or to perform the overt role behavior.

4. The restructuring of cognitions is a relatively novel use for relaxation (see Chapter 8). For example, we have had occasion to convince clients that they are not suffering from heart attacks by pointing out to them that perceived palpitations can be controlled by relaxation. This suggests that what they previously thought was a heart attack was an anxiety reaction to a specific situation. Clearly, negative medical findings should precede this psychological interpretation of "heart attacks." In another setting, Davison (1966) was able to use differential relaxation to get a paranoid patient to restructure certain bodily sensations in a more naturalistic nonparanoid way.

5. In another application in the consulting room, relaxation can be used to reduce tensions to a low enough level so that the therapist can embark on a regimen of rational restructuring (see Chapter 8).

6. Like others (Tasto & Hinkle, 1973), we have been able to markedly reduce or even totally eliminate tension headaches by teaching clients to relax, particularly in the temple area. Weil and Goldfried (1973) have also reported the successful use of relaxation training with an eleven-year-old suffering from insomnia.

7. Clients with phobias and anxiety attacks are frequently "afraid of becoming anxious"—perhaps because of the unpleasant feelings, the inability to function, and the likelihood that other people will notice. With relaxation training, the person comes to construe himself as "someone who can control his tensions." The importance of a general change in self-concept should not be minimized in behavior therapy, particularly an increase in the feeling that one is in control (Geer, Davison, & Gatchel, 1970; Seligman, 1975).

8. Once the client has learned to relax, he can apply this newly acquired skill in a number of stressful situations that have not been dealt with in therapy, for example, going to the dentist. Again, emphasis is placed on the use of the skill for coping with a variety of anxiety-provoking situations.

● VARIATIONS IN RELAXATION TRAINING

The foregoing probably represent the relaxation procedures most widely used in behavior therapy. In recent years we have also used two variations: relaxation by sensory awareness and hypnosis. We turn our attention first to sensory awareness relaxation.

Relaxation by Sensory Awareness

In 1969 we learned from Dr. Bernard Weitzman of the New School for Social Research an induction that appeared to hold promise in teaching relaxation. The technique entails posing to the client a series of questions to be answered privately according to what the client can or cannot experience at any given time, for example, "Is it possible for you to imagine you are looking at something that is very far away from you?" It is emphasized to the client that the specific answers are not important, but only that he consider each question.

Having worked clinically with sensory awareness procedures since 1969, we only recently came upon a more extensive, theoretical/philosophical account of their origins in a book by Charles V. W. Brooks, *Sensory Awareness* (1974). The exercises stem from the work of Elsa Gindler in the early 1900s in Berlin; it was brought to this country just prior to World War II by Charlotte Selver. Among Selver's students in New York were Erich Fromm, Clara Thompson, and Fritz Perls. It should come as no surprise that these clinicians construe the exercises in ways quite different from the relaxation possibilities to which we restrict ourselves here.

Like muscle relaxation exercises, this induction can be put on a tape for at-home use. Clinically, we have found it effective to follow the tape with the letting-go induction already described. It should be noted that this procedure has not been investigated experimentally, but our favorable clinical experiences prompt us to include it here. A typical induction follows:

Just sit comfortably in the chair and listen very closely to what I am going to be saying to you. I'm going to try a series of experiments with you. Each experiment will be in the form of a question. Although each question is answerable by either "yes" or "no," it will not be necessary for you to say "yes" or "no" out loud or perhaps even to yourself, because the answer to each question will be your own particular reaction to the question. All this will become very clear as we proceed. Just remember to listen to the question that I pose to you, and do not be bothered by the unusual nature of some of them. Let yourself react to each question. However you react is fine. There really is no right or wrong way. Let your own reaction to each question be your own answer to each question. (*5-second pause.*)

Is it possible for you to *allow* your eyes to close? (*5-second pause.*)

If they are not yet closed you may close them now. (*5-second pause.*)

Is it possible for you to be aware of the point at which the back of your head comes into maximum contact with the chair? (*5-second pause.*)

Is it possible for you to imagine the space between your eyes? (*5-second pause.*)

Is it possible for you to imagine the distance between your ears? (*5-second pause.*)

Is it possible for you to be aware of how close your breath

comes to the back of your eyes every time you inhale?
(5-second pause.)
Is it possible for you to imagine that you are looking at something that is very far away? (*5-second pause.*)
Is it possible for you to be aware of where your arms are in contact with the chair (*5-second pause.*) and can you be aware of the points at which your arms lose contact with the chair? (*5-second pause.*)
Is either your left or right foot resting on the floor and if either or both of them are, can you feel the floor beneath your foot? (*5-second pause.*)
Is it possible for you to imagine in your mind's eye a beautiful flower suspended a few feet in front of you? (*5-second pause.*)
Is it possible for you to be aware of the space within your mouth? (*5-second pause.*) And can you be aware of the position of your tongue within your mouth? (*5-second pause.*)
Is it possible for you to feel even the slightest breeze against your cheek? (*5-second pause.*)
Is it possible for you to be aware of one of your arms being more relaxed than the other? (*5-second pause.*)
Is it possible for you to notice any change in the temperature of your body? (*5-second pause.*)
Is it possible for you to feel like a rag doll? (*5-second pause.*)
Is it possible for you to feel yourself floating as if on a cloud? (*5-second pause.*) Or are you feeling much too heavy for that? (*5-second pause.*)
Is it possible for you to imagine once again that you are looking at something that is very far away? (*5-second pause.*)
Is it possible to feel your face getting very soft? (*5-second pause.*)
(*Other questions can be repeated.*)
Can you allow your eyes to open (*5-second pause.*) and if they're not yet open you may open them now and be wide awake and very comfortable. Consider how relaxed you feel on the zero to 100 scale. (*5-second pause.*) Go over now and switch off the tape recorder.

Relaxation by Hypnotic Inductions

We take the position that an answer regarding hypnosis as a separate state is not necessary in order to effectively utilize hypnotic training procedures in behavior therapy. Whether state theories as

favored by Hilgard (1965) and Orne (1959) or nonstate conceptualizations as proposed by Barber (1969) and Sarbin (1950) have
more or less validity is irrelevant for clinical purposes. The evidence
indicates that suggestions of relaxation during an hypnotic induction
can help many people relax.[1]

Preparing the Client for Hypnosis

Many of the preparatory comments reviewed above for muscle
relaxation training are appropriate in preparing clients for hypnosis.
We will highlight some considerations that are peculiarly important
for hypnosis.

The therapist is well advised not to exhibit uncertainty about
what he is doing; nor, indeed, should he *be* uncertain. For one thing,
clients are probably going to be apprehensive when they are about to
be hypnotized, and any signs that the therapist is less than well-
versed in these procedures is probably going to be detrimental.

Since many hypnotic clients fear losing control, the therapist
would do well to point out that the client always remains in ultimate
control. This means that the client can and should wake himself if
he feels that he does not want to proceed any further.

The client is urged to let himself become a part of the process
rather than remain an analytical observer. It is of course assumed
that the client agrees to be hypnotized and is desirous of experiencing such a state. This motivation can be used to persuade the client,
as far as he is capable, to adopt a rather passive, lackadaisical attitude. The client can be assured that there will be ample time afterwards for discussion and analysis.

Some clients are concerned about what their hypnotizability
implies about their personality. Thus, it is good to emphasize that
research has failed to show any important correlations between
hypnotizability and such traits as intelligence or strength of character. Like the suggestions already reviewed, this can serve to reduce
the client's concern about what is going to happen.

The therapist should point out that there will be no untoward

---

[1] In spite of the rarity of negative reactions to hypnosis, we nonetheless
recommend that the clinician be prepared to use his general clinical
skills and sensitivities to reassure clients, should they become frightened
during or following an induction. No therapy procedure should be used
casually; this caveat is particularly appropriate for hypnotic inductions,
and we are moved to recommend supervised practice with hypnosis before using it clinically.

sequelae from the hypnotic induction. Thus, the client will be able to remember everything, will not have any headaches afterwards, and in general will have an enjoyable experience.

General Guidelines for Hypnotic Inductions

There are countless hypnotic inductions, most of which are described in Weitzenhoffer (1957). The therapist can suggest eye closure after fixating on a target, or he can suggest arm lowering, or arm levitation. We have found it very useful to think in terms of Erickson's (1959) *utilization* procedures. As we have noted in Chapter 4, Erickson's basic thesis is that the hypnotist should very carefully observe what the client is doing at any given time and then make it appear that it is precisely what the therapist *wanted to happen*. Thereby, he presumably achieves more and more control over what the client is going to do next. For example, in suggesting heaviness of an extended arm, the therapist may notice that after 10 minutes the arm has not moved downward at all. At this juncture, it is possible to tell the client that the arm in fact seems to be too light to come downward; the therapist would then do well to suggest arm *lightness*. Another example would be to suggest that the eyes will close at some unspecified future point in time; by not stating exactly when the eyes will close, the therapist avoids the unhappy situation of having predicted eye closure with none occurring.

A corollary of this utilization approach is that the client never does anything wrong, unless of course he refuses to abide by some basic rules, like extending his right arm when the therapist instructs him to. Thus, if a client fails to respond to a suggestion, it is important that he not worry that he has failed. It is similarly important for the therapist to make it appear that the client's response was not at all unexpected, that, indeed, the therapist prescribed it. This can be done in many ways. For example, the hypnotist may suggest a magnetic force drawing two outstretched hands towards each other. If the hands are not moving together, the therapist changes the suggestion to indicate that the hands are being repelled from each other. Above all, the client should not gain the impression that the induction is proceeding poorly.

Another corollary is that suggestions should be hedged to minimize the chances of the hypnotist being wrong. Thus, rather than saying "Your body is getting heavier and heavier" (for, in fact, the client at that time may be experiencing lightness), the therapist is advised to say something like: "You may have noticed a change in the weight of your body, perhaps it feels heavy or perhaps it feels light." In this way the therapist minimizes the risk of suggesting something that may not be happening or that may not happen in the future.

Suggestions Following the Hypnotic Induction

Whether or not the client would be judged as being in a trance, the therapist can suggest that the client's body is getting more and more relaxed. If the therapist's voice is soothing, the pace slow and measured, and if distractions are at a minimum, chances are that the client will begin to relax even though he may not enter a hypnotic state. It is important, in other words, to keep one's purposes clearly in mind. Since we make use of hypnosis primarily to facilitate relaxation, it is relatively unimportant to achieve an actual hypnotic state (assuming, again, that such a state exists). Thus, there can be extensive suggestions of calm and relaxation, not unlike those during the relaxation training described above.

Sample Hypnotic Induction

(*Therapist is seated beside the client so that, as the client looks straight ahead, the therapist is out of his view.*) Would you please extend your right arm in front of you with the palm facing down? That's fine. I would like you to find a spot on the back of your hand that you can look at. We will call this the target. I would like you to simply stare as long as you can at the target, and just allow to happen whatever you feel is happening. Just try to relax and involve yourself as best you can in what is going to follow.

As you stare at the target you may become gradually aware of the weight in that outstretched hand and arm. You may even begin to feel a sensation of tightness in your shoulder as you are supporting the outstretched hand and arm that are gradually becoming heavier. More and more heavy. As you continue to stare at the target I would like you to imagine that there is around the wrist of your outstretched hand a large water bucket. This bucket is empty right now, but perhaps you can already feel the extra heaviness as your outstretched arm is supporting that bucket. Continue staring at the target and become aware of the feeling of heaviness becoming more and more noticeable in your outstretched hand and arm.

As you continue to stare at the target you can imagine

something very interesting is happening to the bucket. I am gradually filling the bucket with water. I am pouring about a quart of water into that empty bucket. The bucket becomes somewhat heavier from the weight of the water. More and more heavy. (*As the client apparently experiences difficulty holding up the outstretched hand and arm, the therapist makes certain to comment on whatever movements are taking place.*) That's right, you can feel the weight of the bucket gradually pushing the hand and arm down, more and more down. (*Therapist's voice becomes quieter; pace slows.*) The weight of the bucket becoming more and more pronounced. Another quart of water going into the bucket. The hand and arm getting heavier and heavier, oh so heavy. The eyes perhaps getting somewhat tired from staring at the target. (*As the client blinks his eyes, the therapist should comment on this.*) As you continue to stare at the target, you notice that every time your eyes blink, they somehow seem heavier, more difficult to open once again, but you continue to stare at the target as long as you can. Another quart of water pouring into the bucket. The hand and arm getting heavier and heavier. (*By this point some clients have lowered their arm right down to the side of the chair, and perhaps have even closed their eyes. If this happens, the therapist should move to the paragraph below that begins with "After eyes have closed."*)

The bucket getting heavier and heavier, more and more heavy. The eyes more and more tired from staring. Perhaps you're becoming aware already of a feeling of heaviness and relaxation coming into your entire body. The eyelids getting tired from staring. More and more tired. Heavy. Loose and relaxed. More and more tired and drowsy and sleepy. Another quart of water being poured into the bucket, and the weight of the bucket becoming almost too much to withstand. The eyes becoming tired from staring, more and more drowsy and sleepy.

(*After eyes have closed.*) That's fine, you can allow your eyes to remain comfortably closed. The arm down by your side now.

(*If eyes still open.*) Fine, you can close your eyes now. No more need to imagine the heavy bucket filled with water.

You're settled comfortably into the chair, and with your eyes closed you now find it even easier to concentrate on my words. Just let go and let yourself listen to my words.

You can get more and more relaxed. And perhaps a little

drowsy as well, but you will always be able to hear my voice and respond to my suggestions.

Your body is getting more and more heavy. (*Notice here that the induction talks little if at all about hypnosis, and that from this point onward it greatly resembles the letting-go induction described above.*) Just let go of your muscles. Your body getting heavier and heavier. Each time you exhale, letting go further and further. More and more relaxed. Drowsy and sleepy. The arms heavy, loose, and relaxed. The shoulders loose and relaxed. The facial muscles soft and relaxed. Just let the relaxation flow down from your forehead, through your face, into your neck, and now flowing peacefully to your chest and stomach. More and more relaxed. Deeper and deeper. Letting go further and further. Continuing to relax more and more. Relaxation flowing into your hips, your thighs, down through your calves into your feet. More and more relaxed.

To help you get even more relaxed, I am going to count from 1 to 10. With each count, you may find yourself getting even drowsier, heavier, and more deeply relaxed. 1, more and more relaxed. 2, your whole body getting deeper and deeper relaxed. 3, further and further. 4, 5, 6, further and further. 7, 8, deeper and deeper relaxed. 9, and 10. (*From this point onward, the therapist can carry on as if he had engaged in the letting-go induction.*)

Applications of Hypnosis in Behavior Therapy

The most frequent use of hypnotic procedures is in facilitating relaxation. Clients who respond favorably to a hypnotic induction seem to be able to relax comfortably with such an induction in a relatively short time as compared to the more extended training in Jacobsonian relaxation. When we employ hypnotic inductions, a heavier emphasis is placed on suggestions of relaxation than on any specific characteristics of the trance state.

Although there is no good experimental evidence that shows heightened clarity of imagery following hypnotic inductions, it is possible that a reduction of distraction as well as specific suggestions can help certain clients generate clear, lifelike images. This has obvious application in desensitization, where, regardless of theoretical persuasion, there is agreement that clear images are important.

Another use of hypnotic inductions is to help people talk about aspects of their lives that they may be reluctant to discuss while awake. Thus, many clients *request* to be hypnotized because they believe they can come up with information that is not available to them while awake. We avoid the issue of whether such memories are "unconscious" and prefer to view this as the client telling the therapist he will feel more comfortable talking under one set of circumstances than under another. Some clients may wish initially to disown what they are telling the therapist by virtue of being hypnotized, and only later take responsibility for the information they are providing. Once again it must be emphasized that we are neither accepting nor rejecting a state theory of hypnosis; what is important is that the use of such inductions can be helpful in achieving specific goals, in this case the gathering of relevant assessment data.

Hypnosis Versus Relaxation

Assuming that a client can be relaxed more quickly via a hypnotic induction than by muscle relaxation training, might not muscle relaxation training contribute to transfer of skills more readily than hypnosis and more than the sensory awareness procedures outlined above? This is a crucial question. Bernstein and Borkovec (1973) have indicated that relaxation training is more generalizable to the nontherapy setting because it is a learned skill, whereas hypnosis is imposed on a passive client. While this proposal is plausible, there are thus far no data to support it. Moreover, as indicated above, our preferred way of carrying out an hypnotic induction leaves ultimate control with the client. In addition, we frequently move from hypnotic relaxation either to the use of the "calm" cue or to a letting-go induction. This has a client end up procedurally in the same place regardless of whether he went through the tension-release exercise phase or not.

Given the state of the field, we are thrown back on our clinical experiences. In Chapter 4, we proposed that a crucial—and often overlooked—facet of behavior therapy is enlisting the client's cooperation and raising his hopes for improvement. For many clients, especially those in desperate straits, the impressive changes that may result from a successful hypnotic induction, sometimes in the first session, can give the necessary impression that something is going to happen in therapy. (Hopefully the therapist can come through on this promissory note!) If research shows that certain combinations of hypnotic and muscle relaxation can be more effective than muscle relaxation alone, we shall have a firmer base on which to make a decision.

● SUMMARY

Discussion centered in this chapter on diverse procedures for teaching anxious clients how to relax. The preferred inductions entail a modified form of Jacobsonian relaxation training, according to which a client is first taught to become aware of muscle tensions and then to release them; with supervised practice, most clients appear able to learn this skill. Relaxation via sensory awareness and via hypnotic inductions were also described, though question was raised as to how readily clients might be able to transfer such training to the real-life situation. Special attention was paid to preparing clients for relaxation training. The newness of such procedures for the average client, along with occasional fears of losing control, warrant caution by the clinical behavior therapist. A number of specific suggestions were offered to avoid most of the problems likely to occur in clinical practice.

Chapter

Systematic Desensitization

Systematic desensitization, an anxiety reduction procedure developed by Salter (1949) and by Wolpe (1958), has proven itself markedly effective in reducing unrealistic anxiety. When an individual is capable of responding effectively to a given situation and yet continues to react with neurotic fear and avoidance, direct attention to anxiety reduction is appropriate. The technique of systematic desensitization itself entails having a deeply relaxed person imagine a graded series of increasingly aversive situations. Thus, a person who has been judged to be unduly anxious about speaking in public, would, in collaboration with his therapist, draw up a series of circumstances that represent his sensitivity to speech-giving situations. In a fashion to be described below, the person imagines each situation under conditions of deep-muscle relaxation, so that he is able to tolerate greater and greater levels of anxiety. Considerable clinical (Paul, 1969a) and experimental (e.g., Bandura,

1969; Davison & Wilson, 1973b) evidence supports the conclusion that this procedure can significantly reduce unrealistic tensions.

There are numerous theoretical explanations for the efficacy of systematic desensitization (see reviews by Wilson & Davison, 1971; Davison & Wilson, 1973b; Wilkins, 1971): the substitution of relaxation for anxiety (basically Wolpe's counterconditioning hypothesis), the gradual exposure to anxiety-eliciting stimuli (the so-called extinction hypothesis, Wilson & Davison, 1971), the contingent reinforcement of increasingly bold approach responses (Leitenberg, Agras, Barlow, & Oliveau, 1969), the self-control hypothesis of Goldfried (1971), the cognitive relabeling view (Valins & Ray, 1967), and the "maximal habituation" hypothesis of Mathews (1971). The issue is far from settled. In fact, in our opinion greater confusion reigns today than ten years ago.

The challenge to the practicing clinician, then, is to justify the procedure, or any variation, to take into account as many explanations as possible. In other words, the behavior therapist should conduct desensitization in such a way as to minimize the chances of his violating the procedural consequences of any explanation that has substantial experimental support. In what follows, we attempt to do just that.

It is worth emphasizing that this behavior therapy technique relies heavily on the client's imagery. In a sense, whatever relearning or reconditioning is taking place occurs while the client is silently visualizing scenes. The assumption is that an imaginary aversive scene is a functional equivalent of the real situation; enabling a person to confront a fantasized representation of what he is afraid of is assumed to be analogous to his learning to face the situation in real life (Grossberg & Wilson, 1968).

● PROCEDURAL CONSIDERATIONS

The initial decision is, of course, whether to employ desensitization at all. The mere presence of disruptive anxiety is not, in itself, sufficient justification. Consider the following example from our clinical supervision.

An intern had been desensitizing a college sophomore for several weeks for test anxiety. The client had already completed most of the hierarchy, but no clinical improvement was discernible. In fact, the client had begun "forgetting" appointments. When we were assigned the supervisee, the question naturally arose as to whether an adequate assessment had been made. In a somewhat offhand way, we asked her during the initial supervisory session: "How are the client's study habits?" To the chagrin of all, the supervisee had not made this kind of inquiry. When she did, it turned out that the client's dormitory situation made studying next to impossible, and the client had not taken steps either to alter the dorm setting or find a quieter place to work. Thus, what had been conceptualized as test anxiety was reconstrued as a behavioral deficit which the client was—appropriately, we felt—reacting to with anxiety. Desensitization was, therefore, dropped; and the therapist began working with the student on problem solving (see Chapter 9), which in this instance took the form of working out more effective study conditions.

The above example illustrates an erroneous decision to desensitize. One can also err in *overlooking the opportunity* to desensitize. For example, a thirty-five-year-old construction foreman came to us from an internist with the diagnosis "depression." He was having trouble getting out of bed in the morning, exhibited the usual features of a severely depressed person (Beck, 1967), and was in danger of losing his job. A behavioral assessment revealed that the man—in spite of his overtly gruff appearance and demeanor—was overly concerned about being disliked by the workers responsible to him. The depression began shortly after the client had been promoted to his position of authority, where he often found it necessary to order men around, criticize their work, and, more often than he liked, be the object of baleful stares and disgruntled shrugs. Therefore, a hierarchy on social criticism was drawn up, and, in conjunction with therapist suggestions of how to phrase his orders, the man's underlying social sensitivities were markedly reduced and, most importantly, his depression alleviated.

Assessment of Themes

Perhaps the greatest challenge to the clinician contemplating desensitization is to decide *what* to desensitize. The task is to isolate the most important dimension or dimensions to which the person should become less anxious. This is not an easy matter. Consider, for example, a person who is fearful of leaving the home. Should one assume that his interests would best be served using a hierarchy of situations depicting his going further and further from his home? As indicated in Chapter 2, we caution against such a simpleminded approach, for it may well be that the primary concerns of the person relate to situations that he is heading towards *after* leaving the house. For example, a man might be fearful of leaving his home only during the week but not on the weekends; the observant clinician would use this information to explore whether difficulties on his job might be underlying his reluctance to leave the home. Thus, a person who initially appears agoraphobic might eventually be viewed as unduly sensitive to criticism.

Even when a basic dimension has been settled upon, there are numerous parametric considerations. Consider the individual who has excessive fears of speaking in front of groups. The choice of items might have to reflect the facial expressions of certain people in the audience, while at the same time not include the time of day or the weather conditions outside the fantasized room. But none of this should be assumed, and only by careful observation and interviewing is it possible for the skilled clinician to decide on the most relevant parameters of fear.

Another aspect to the assessment situation is the notion of a basic theme as a *conceptualization* of the therapist. We have long ago stopped asking ourselves whether we have "truly" isolated a basic anxiety dimension of our clients. Rather, we ask ourselves how best to construe a person's difficulty so as to maximize his gains. In other words, rather than looking for the "real hierarchy," we look for the *most useful* hierarchy. This has important implications, not the least of which is the freedom to attempt to reconceptualize various client problems in terms amenable to desensitization. An earlier example demonstrated how one might fruitfully construe a problem of depression in terms of an anxiety/avoidance gradient, where desensitization would be appropriate. The clinician must ask himself what the implications are likely to be should a particular desensitization actually succeed. For instance, will a person depressed about her lack of meaningful social contacts be happier if her inhibitions about talking to people are reduced by desensitization? Looked at in this way, the clinician would seem to have both greater freedom and greater challenge in isolating anxiety dimensions.

Item Construction

What will the items actually look like on an anxiety hierarchy? In addition to the parametric considerations mentioned above, one should attempt to adequately sample the problem. A metaphor we have found useful in our clinical work is to have the client regard his total anxiety as a large balloon full of an infinite number of stimulus elements, each of which is associated with a given amount of anxiety. The task is to sample from this balloon in such a way that one has a good representation of all the elements in it. In addition, one wishes to sample items of varying degrees of aversiveness so that the presentation can be graduated. Generally speaking, one aims for about one to two dozen stimulus situations to be extracted from this conceptual balloon.

Another consideration in the choice of items is to make them as concrete as possible, keeping in mind that the ultimate task will be for the client later to imagine a situation as it is described by the therapist. Thus, the various important parameters of each situation must be included in each item so that maximally vivid and constant imagery is facilitated. An item such as "giving a talk" would therefore not be as desirable for someone being desensitized for speech anxiety as an item like "You approach the podium, place your notes on top of it, and look out at the audience."

The following transcript illustrates some of the ways the therapist can move from the general to the specific in constructing hierarchy items from complaints that are often vaguely stated by the client.

Therapist: OK, so it seems that you're having trouble talking to people.

Client: Yes. I just can't seem to get off the ground with them.

Therapist: Well, let's see if we can get more specific. Do you find yourself at a loss for words?

Client: At times.

Therapist: [*I wonder if he is capable of carrying off a conversation. At least he's not saying very much to me. Let's try an open-ended question.*] Tell me more about that.

Client: Well, it's not so much that I don't think of what it would be nice to say. It's more that I'm uptight about saying what's on my mind.

Therapist: [*He seems to have answered my question sooner than I expected. There doesn't seem to be a deficit of instrumental behaviors. Rather, he seems blocked by anxiety.*] I see. What you're saying is that you feel inhibited, or nervous, about expressing what's on your mind, and you sometimes don't say anything at all.

Client: Right, the words flash through my mind, but I get so tense when I think about saying them, that I end up not saying much of anything at all. And that, for a salesman, is a bad state of affairs.

Therapist: Right. So do you think you'd get on better with people, especially your customers, if you felt less tense or anxious when you had to talk with them?

Client: Yes, I really think that could help. If only I could relax a little when it's time to talk, I think the words would come out, and that'd help a whole lot.

Therapist: Fine. So what we have to try to do now, and in the next couple of sessions, is to identify the kinds of situations in which you'd like to say what's on your mind but in which you're currently inhibited from doing so. What we will be doing together over the next couple of sessions is identifying one or two dozen situations that have caused you needless distress in the past, do so now, or might conceivably do so in the future. What these situations will have in common is that they will all relate to your difficulty talking to others, especially in business situations. [*It's always a good idea to check that the client understands and agrees with the direction I'm taking, particularly when the procedure will take up as much time and effort as desensitization.*] Are you with me?

Client: Yup, I'm with you.

Therapist: OK, let's start with your telling me, if you can, what the last situation was like where you had something to tell someone but just couldn't.

Client: Well, I don't know if this is what you're after, but last Sunday —hell, this is going to sound crazy—but last Sunday, after the service station man had filled my tank with gas, I had difficulty asking him to do my windshield, even though there's a big sign in the window saying that the station prides itself on service. I did finally get it out, but I was almost in a cold sweat.

Therapist: [*That sounds like more of an assertion problem to me. I'll wait a bit and collect more items before following up that lead.*] Right, I can see that gave you trouble, though maybe not as much trouble as other situations might, since you did manage to get the words out. But we need relatively easy items as well as really tough ones—where you can't speak at all—so let's get down on this little (3x5) card a good enough description of that situation so that, later on, you can generate a clear image. How does this sound: "The station attendant has just finished filling your tank; he comes to the car window and says 'That'll be $9.00' and you say, 'Right, would you please get the windshield?'" How's that?

Client: That's pretty good, but what I said was: "My windshield is pretty dirty—do you mind cleaning it?"

Therapist: If that's more natural for you, sure. (*Pause*) But I wonder if you're not being a bit apologetic when you say "... *mind*"?

Client: You're right, I did have the feeling that I was apologizing. In fact, as I think about it now, I have the sense that I was ashamed of having a dirty windshield! (*Laughs sheepishly.*)

Therapist: (*Trying to set client at ease.*) That can happen in the best of families. (*Laughs at own attempt at humor.*) OK, how would you *like* to be able to express yourself there?

Client: I'd like best of all to say simply: "Please clean the windshield."

Therapist: (*Correcting item description on card.*) OK.

Client: What happens now?

Therapist: Well, since we're at the end of the hour, I'd like to suggest that you take along with you a few of these little cards and see what you can come up with. [*Based on the conscientiousness I've seen in him over the past few sessions, I would guess he can come up with at least some material for the hierarchy— not all clients can.*] Just jot down a description of any situations that occur to you between now and our next session. You might find it useful just to attend to problems you have this week—if you're going to suffer, let's get some mileage out of it. [*I intentionally want to inject a light note into what has been a heavy session—also focusing on one's "weaknesses," as a client must do during hierarchy construction, is not an easy thing, and this particular client has a good sense of humor.*]

Client: (*Smiling a bit ruefully.*) Fine with me.

In choosing items the clinician relies on his familiarity with the person's life space. Moreover, we do not restrict ourselves to situations that the person has actually been anxious in, for a truly phobic individual is likely to have successfully avoided maximally anxiety-provoking situations. Thus, particularly when trying to fill out the upper end of an anxiety hierarchy one might very well wish to construct items which *could* and are *likely to* elicit maladaptive levels of anxiety. For example, a male client who was having difficulty with his father-in-law arranged his encounters with the man in such a way as to preclude the following situation: "You are sitting down to dinner in your father-in-law's home and he turns to you and asks 'Isn't it about time you got a better job?'" It is likely that the client had never been in the situation, but might acknowledge "That's what I live in dread of happening." This would seem to make such an item particularly appropriate for his hierarchy.

If it is at all possible, one should try to construct some of the hierarchy items so that the likelihood of occurrence in real life is under control of the client. For example, if a client becomes anxious when meeting somebody for the first time, rather than having all hierarchy items describe situations where another person approaches the client, it would be preferable to include instances where the client himself approaches a stranger. In this way, subsequent *in vivo* exposures can more closely match what has been worked on in imagination.

A useful strategy in collecting items, in addition to relying on one's own familiarity with the kinds of situations the client is troubled by, is to have the client self-observe his anxiety reactions between sessions. The client is urged to make his feeling of anxiety a cue for stopping and asking himself "Now what is happening here that could possibly be making me tense?" In this fashion the client's own difficulties in living become an important aid in collecting items for the reduction of his anxiety. The therapist might also seek assistance from observations by significant others in the person's life. For example, a person's spouse or friend might be invited to a session to provide hints about situations causing anxiety. Yet another aid is questions like the following: "Do you remember the last time you got upset, perhaps earlier today or on your way to this session?" These and other questions get the client to focus on his feelings of uneasiness as tied to specific stimulus situations. Further, the therapist can also use the client's reactions in the interview itself for clues in selecting hierarchy items. A client who is having difficulty speaking to the therapist or looking him in the eye might very well be anxious in front of authority figures, or possibly with people in general. The interpersonal framework of Harry Stack Sullivan again appears useful for the behavior therapist.

In the process of discussing potential hierarchy items during the consultation session, the therapist might inquire about the client's emotional reactions resulting from talking and even thinking about such situations. If the client indicates that he indeed is getting upset, the therapist can suggest that this is a good sign. What it means, in essence, is that it is possible to create within the session those events that are causing difficulty for the individual. In fact, the therapist may utilize such emotional upset to good advantage by following hierarchy construction with a period of relaxation training during the same session. Assuming that the client reports the positive effects of the relaxation, the therapist may then point out that what has occurred during this session is a living demonstration of how the procedure works, namely, simulating during a session situations that elicit anxiety, and then having the client's deep state of muscular relaxation reduce the tension.

Multiple Hierarchies

In the early desensitization literature (e.g., Wolpe, 1958), it was recognized that a client might well have more than one anxiety dimension to which he is being desensitized. This being the case, it was prescribed that the clinician construct multiple hierarchies in a way that would insure each one being "pure" on a given dimension. Thus, someone who is fearful both of social evaluation and of flying would have two separate hierarchies, perhaps with each hierarchy sampled alternately during a desensitization session. Thus, the least difficult item from the evaluation hierarchy would be followed by the least difficult item from the flying hierarchy, and then back to the evaluation hierarchy. An examination of what is happening here indicates that the client is being presented with a single hierarchy. What this has meant for us procedurally is that we do not hesitate to mix dimensions in a particular anxiety hierarchy.

Ordering Items

Assuming that the therapist has collected promising items for an anxiety hierarchy, he is then faced with the task of ordering these in terms of increasing aversiveness. This can be done in a number of ways, one of which is to employ the same 0 to 100 scale used in relaxation training. We generally begin by reading aloud each item—one to a small file card—and having the client rate it either as low, medium, or high in terms of its anxiety-provoking qualities. Having made this tripartite division, the client can then be asked to assign a numerical rating to each item whereby the easy items are rated between 0 and 33, the moderate ones 34 to 66, and highest ones 67 to 100. This, of course, is simply an ordinal scale, and both clinician and client would do well not to become unduly obsessed with any higher level of mathematical sophistication. By assigning these numbers, though, it is often possible to find gaps between items that should be filled. Such undesirably large spaces can be lessened by increasing the length of time to an anticipated aversive event, reducing the aversiveness of the event itself, introducing fearless models into the situation, and so forth. For example:

(Original item, rated 50)	You're being introduced by the chairperson of your symposium, and you're looking out over the small, smiling crowd.
(Original item, rated 65)	You're being introduced by the chairperson of your symposium, and you're looking out over the large, basically hostile audience.
(Inserted item, rated 60)	You're being introduced by the chairperson of your symposium, and you're looking out over the large, smiling crowd.

As a rule, we avoid gaps between items exceeding 10 units on the 0 to 100 scale. A small procedural point: Write each hierarchy rating in pencil rather than pen in the upper right-hand corner of each card. This makes clear to the client that the ordering of items can be readily changed when necessary.

Below is a hierarchy adapted from a client who was phobic about flying; the items are arranged in order of increasing aversiveness.

1. Your boss tells you that, in 6 months, you'll have to fly out to the coast for a new account [rated 10].
2. You're sitting in your living room, watching a football game on TV, and you hear a plane overhead [rated 20].
3. A colleague at work tells you of the great plane trip he had to Florida [rated 25].
4. Your wife asks you, a week before your trip, whether you'll be needing any formal clothes to take along [rated 30].
5. You're up in the attic, looking for your two-suiter to take along on your trip to the coast [rated 35].
6. As you look through your desk diary, you're reminded that the coast plane trip is coming up in two weeks [rated 45].
7. The evening before the trip, you're folding socks and underwear into your suitcase [rated 50].
8. The taxi is pulling off the expressway at the exit marked "Airport," on the way to your trip [rated 60].

9. There are five people ahead of you in line at the Pan Am ticket counter, having their baggage checked and tickets validated [rated 70].
10. You're walking down the ramp onto the plane, and the flight attendant asks for your boarding pass [rated 75].
11. As you look out the window, you observe the plane just getting airborne, and you can see the Bay Bridge in the distance [rated 85].
12. You've been flying for a couple of hours, the air gets choppy, and the captain has just put on the fasten-seat-belt sign [rated 90].
13. The ride is quite bumpy, and you check to see that your seat belt is fastened [rated 95].
14. You wake up the morning of your trip to the coast and say to yourself, "Today's the day I leave for the coast." [rated 100].

Testing and Training in Imagery

Recall that a crucial assumption of desensitization is that an image can be a functional representation of the real-life situation, that is, an imaginal item can stand in the place of what actually bothers the person. This basic assumption of desensitization has been supported in a number of experimental studies (e.g., Grossberg & Wilson, 1968). Regardless of the interpretation one places on the behavior change process, all theoreticians and researchers agree on the common point that a person must be able to become anxious from imagining a situation in order to be an appropriate candidate for desensitization. If, for example, a client can imagine the most upsetting situation and yet not become anxious by the fantasy, it does not make sense to go through the extensive exercises necessary to eventually reach this top item. It is therefore essential that one check whether a client can become anxious from an image before even considering this procedure.

This can be done in a number of ways. We have found it beneficial, perhaps even during the first session, to have the person close his eyes and to imagine a situation which, on the basis of the assessment data collected so far, would be anxiety-provoking in real life. If the client reports a relatively clear image and yet does not report anxiety (fortunately a rare occurrence), then the therapist has to question seriously whether for this client an image can be a functional equivalent of a real situation. In those unusual instances where the person fails to report tension, the therapist would not want to give up immediately but would rather embellish the situation and urge clearer imagery in hopes of eliciting an emotional reaction. In the absence of more objective measures of clarity in imagery, the clinician is necessarily limited to self-report and observation. In a way, finding out whether a person has a clear image and whether he becomes anxious from it is a process of persuasion: The client in essence has to convince the therapist that he has a good enough image and that he is anxious from it. Our clinical impression is that those rare individuals who do not get anxious from images seem to suffer less from anticipatory anxiety.

It is also worth noting that one should test for imagery when the client is not deliberately relaxing. The reason is straightforward. A client already skilled in relaxation might be able to use this skill to inhibit whatever anxiety would otherwise be elicited by an imaginary situation. This can result in false negatives, that is, people would be excluded as appropriate for desensitization when they should be included.

Though few techniques have been fully worked out for training in imagery, there are several procedures we can suggest. For example, the clinician can present to a plane phobic a situation where he is in his seat as the engines are turned on in a jet airplane. From his own familiarity with flying, the therapist could then ask the person to try to visualize the fasten-seat-belt sign on the display area above him; it might also be suggested that a tall flight attendant is approaching him and telling him that his seat belt should be made tighter. By verbally providing additional details of the situation, and of course, by encouraging the person simply to try to conjure up the event, the therapist stands a greater chance of concluding that a client can in fact generate vivid images. Regarding the question of whether the situation is anxiety provoking, some clients—again not the typical instance—have difficulty reporting their feelings. Here the clinician might have to ask the person a general question such as "Do you feel good or do you feel bad?" and only subsequently get into details of whether a bad feeling means anxiety.

Another way to train a client to create an image is to capitalize on his current sensations and immediate memory. In asking a client to imagine himself in a given situation, the therapist wants him to cognitively place himself *in* the situation—in other words, not to see himself as an outside onlooker would, but actually to experience what is going on. The client can thus be asked to sit back comfortably in his chair, close his eyes, and be instructed as follows:

> Imagine sitting in a chair, in this room. Try to feel the chair under you. Feel your back against the chair. Now, in your imagination, I'd like you to try to visualize your knee (*pause*).

Just try to see your knee. Now I'd like you to try to see your shoe. (*Therapist describes details of the shoe.*) Now look around the room. Look at me. Try to see my face. (*Therapist describes details of his face.*) Now look toward the door. The door is slowly opening and someone whom you know well is standing at the threshold.

If the client continues to have difficulty creating an image, he can be instructed to verbalize those aspects that he *can* see, as it frequently happens that the verbalization helps to clarify the image. Should difficulties continue to persist, the client can be given a homework assignment, where this entire procedure is practiced between sessions.

Relaxation Training

The therapist should have the client practice relaxation on his own between sessions while anxiety items are being collected. The two crucial aspects of desensitization—relaxation training and constructing a hierarchy of aversive imaginal situations—go along in tandem over a number of sessions. In what follows procedurally we make the assumptions that a client has learned relaxation sufficiently well to achieve a state of quiescence while lying on the therapist's couch or lounging chair, and that an adequate hierarchy has been composed.

● TRADITIONAL DESENSITIZATION

According to Wolpe's original formulations, it is absolutely essential that a client being desensitized maximize the amount of time that he is imagining a situation without becoming anxious, and that he minimize the amount of time he is confronted with an imaginal situation that elicits anxiety. The concern about resensitizing a client compels the clinician following Wolpe's original procedures to present items in such a way that the person experiences as little anxiety as possible when imagining a situation. The following transcript contains the instructions given to a client being desensitized in this traditional fashion:

(*The client has been relaxing on his own in the reclining chair.*) OK, now just keep relaxing like that, nice and calm and comfortable. You may find it helpful to imagine a scene that is personally calm and relaxing, something we'll refer to as your pleasant scene. . . . Fine. Now, you recall that 0 to 100 scale we've been using in your relaxation practice, where 0 indicates complete relaxation and 100 maximum tension. Tell me approximately where you'd place yourself now on that scale. . . . (*Therapist is advised to look for a rating that reflects considerable calm and relaxation, often in the range of 15 to 25.*)

Fine. Soon I shall ask you to imagine a scene. After you hear the description of the situation, please imagine it as vividly as you can, through your own eyes, as if you were actually there. Try to include all the details in the scene. While you're visualizing the situation, you may continue feeling as relaxed as you are now. If so, that's good. After 5, 10, or 15 seconds, I'll ask you to stop imagining the scene and return to your pleasant image and to just relax. But if you begin to feel even the slightest increase in anxiety or tension, please signal this to me by raising your left forefinger. When you do this, I'll step in and ask you to stop imagining the situation and then will help you get relaxed once more. It's important that you indicate tension to me in this way, as we want to maximize your being exposed to fearful situations without feeling anxious. OK? Do you have any questions? . . . Fine, we'll have ample opportunity afterwards to discuss things in full.

What happens here is a give-and-take between therapist and client. The client is told, while relaxed, to imagine a given situation. If the client does not signal anxiety, the therapist withdraws the item after 5, 10, or 15 seconds. If the client does feel anxious, he is to signal, at which point the therapist withdraws the item and attempts to relax the person once again for a minute or two before the next item is presented. The hierarchy card might very well look like the figure below. The numbers refer to seconds, and the plus signs indicate visualizations that did not elicit anxiety, the minus signs, situations that did.

SAMPLE HIERARCHY CARD IN
TRADITIONAL DESENSITIZATION

	10
You are sitting at your desk, preparing some notes for a speech you will be giving in three weeks.	
-3 +5 -7 -8 +10 +15	1/13/76

In most cases, anywhere from two to five items can be covered in a given session. It must be kept in mind, of course, that the clinician is unlikely to spend an entire session doing just desensitization. In clinical practice one *seldom* is dealing with a single problem or employing a single technique.

● SELF-CONTROL VARIATION OF DESENSITIZATION

In 1971, Goldfried presented a conceptualization of desensitization that has important procedural implications. His hypothesis is that desensitization is best construed as training in coping skills. According to this view, a fearful individual learns to relax when tense. In this fashion, desensitization sessions provide practice in coping with anxiety.

Although there are similarities to traditional systematic desensitization, the self-control variation involves certain procedural changes, including the rationale presented to the client, the focus placed on relaxation training, the guidelines for hierarchy construction, the way scenes are presented during desensitization proper, and the emphasis placed on the use of relaxation as a coping skill.

Rationale Given to Client

The client is presented with a view of desensitization as training in coping with anxiety. As suggested by Goldfried (1971), the rationale can be stated as follows:

> There are various situations where, on the basis of your past experience, you have learned to react by becoming tense (anxious, nervous, fearful). What I plan to do is help you to learn how to cope with these situations more successfully, so that they do not make you as upset. This will be done by taking note of a number of those situations which upset you to varying degrees, and then having you learn to cope with the less stressful situations before moving on to the more difficult ones. Part of the treatment involves learning how to relax, so that in situations where you feel yourself getting nervous you will be better able to eliminate this tenseness. Learning to relax is much like learning any other skill. When a person learns to drive, he initially has difficulty in coordinating everything, and often finds himself very much aware of what he is doing. With more and more practice, however, the procedures involved in driving become easier and more automatic. You may find the same thing occurring to you when you try to relax in those

situations where you feel yourself starting to become tense. You will find that as you persist, however, it will become easier and easier (p. 231).

In elaborating on the specific nature of the desensitization, it can be indicated that the training during the consultation sessions not only provides the client with a behavior rehearsal for coping with specific situations, but also offers the opportunity to learn the skill of relaxing away tensions in general.

Relaxation Training

The muscle relaxation training consists of those procedures outlined in Chapter 5. In line with the coping orientation, the client is also informed that the tension phase during the early period of training should allow him to become more sensitive to those muscular cues associated with anxiety, and that these sensations will eventually become a signal for him to relax away this tension. Thus, emphasis is placed not only on learning how to relax, but also on recognizing those proprioceptive cues associated with tension.

Hierarchy Construction

We have already questioned the necessity of using hierarchies reflecting "pure" themes. In using the self-control variation of systematic desensitization, the nature of the specific situations eliciting anxiety is less important than the client's awareness of what it feels like to be tense. In other words, *The client is being taught to cope with his proprioceptive anxiety responses and cues rather than with situations which elicit the tension*" (Goldfried, 1971, p. 232). For example, Goldfried (1973) reported the use of self-control desensitization in the case of a pervasively anxious client, where the multithematic hierarchy contained such diverse items as driving in a car, skiing, riding an elevator, being alone, taking a test, and listening to arguments.

Desensitization Proper

The work carried out during the consultation sessions is viewed as providing the client with a behavior rehearsal of what he is eventually to do in a real-life situation. Consequently, rather than switching off the scene, which would be analogous to escape from the aversive situation, the client instead is instructed to maintain the image, all the while attempting to relax away whatever tensions may arise. Inasmuch as the client is being asked to do two things at once —to imagine himself in a situation and to attempt to relax away tension—it helps to suggest that he imagine himself relaxing in the situation itself. Thus, if he feels anxiety while sitting at his desk preparing for a speech, he should imagine sitting at the desk and attempting to relax away the tension.

Variations are possible in the self-control procedure. We came to realize this while collaborating on this book. One of us was having clients maintain the image until they were successful in relaxing away the anxiety; while the other was providing clients with a fixed exposure time, regardless of whether or not they were successful in relaxing away their anxiety at the end of that time period. With both of these procedures, however, the client would not move on to the next hierarchy item until he had been reasonably successful in coping with the easier one. Although there are no data to indicate which of these variations is superior, there are case reports and supporting data for the effectiveness of this general approach to desensitization (D'Zurilla, 1969; Goldfried, 1973; Jacks, 1972; Meichenbaum, 1973; Zemore, 1975).

Use of Coping Relaxation *in Vivo*

Inasmuch as self-control desensitization is construed as providing a client with the use of relaxation as a coping skill, a crucial component of the procedure is to have the client use differential relaxation to cope with stress in real-life situations. In addition to instructing the client to use relaxation to cope with his everyday anxieties, the therapist can encourage the client to record his experiences. In fact, the more conscientious client will at times happily interfere with the systematic completion of the hierarchy items within the consultation session by desensitizing himself *in vivo* to certain items that have yet to be covered during the session.

• TAPED SYSTEMATIC DESENSITIZATION

On the basis of a series of experiments by Nawas and his students (Nawas, Fishman, & Pucel, 1970), we have been experimenting clinically with the use of the Goldfried variation on audio tape. The apparent implications of the Nawas research are that clients are not resensitized when forced to imagine difficult situations. This being the case, we have had occasion to tape-record for a client a series of presentations of perhaps three to five items so that the person can practice these visualizations at home between sessions. A typical tape would begin with 5 or 10 minutes of relaxation suggestions, followed by instructions along self-control desensitization lines. The only difference is that the therapist is not present to insure that a person is coping relatively well with a given item before moving on. This possible difficulty is easily handled by instructing the client (and most clients seem capable of following these instructions) to turn off the tape recorder if he finds himself confronted with a more difficult item before he feels comfortable with the one immediately preceding. The most obvious advantage of employing tapes in this way is the greater amount of between-session practice, with concomitant facilitation of therapy and saving of client expense. It is likely that as many as half a dozen 30-minute tapes have to be made for a given client to practice with for a period of two to three months.

The following transcript illustrates the taped desensitization procedure:

OK, now, you're settled back in your bed at home. Just close your eyes. I'm going to spend the next few minutes getting you nice and loose and relaxed. Just let go of your body, let go of your arms, just relax, further and further. (*5-second pause.*) That's fine. Further and further relaxed. (*5-second pause.*) Just let go a little more as I count from 1 to 10. Let yourself go a little more with each count. 1, get more and more relaxed. (*5-second pause.*) 2, deeper and deeper. (*5-second pause.*) 3, 4, just let go. (*5-second pause.*) 5, more and more relaxed. (*5-second pause.*) 6, 7, deeper and deeper. (*5-second pause.*) 8, 9, and 10, loose and relaxed. Further and further. (*Therapist can continue with relaxation suggestions if necessary.*)

Now I'll review the procedure with you. I'll present a situation to you. I'd like you to imagine the situation as vividly as you can, as if you were actually there. And imagine it for as long as I give you time to imagine it. Should any tension arise while you are in that imaginary situation, see if you can relax it away. See if you can let go of the tension, at least some of it. If the item creates no anxiety, that is fine also. Just remain in the scene and continue relaxing.

OK now, if you are feeling quite comfortably relaxed, let the tape continue running. If you're still feeling a little tense, I would like you to turn off the tape recorder and relax on your own for a few minutes.

OK, you're relaxing very comfortably. Imagine that you're passing your boss in the hall first thing in the morning and he nods hello to you. (*15-second pause.*) OK, stop imagining that and return to your relaxation or to your pleasant scene if you like, and just relax. Perhaps that item did not make you in the slightest bit tense. But perhaps it made you a little bit tense. If it did, you tried to relax away those tensions to the best of your ability. Just continue relaxing. Imagine once again now, it's first thing in the morning, you're passing your boss in the hall and he nods hello to you. (*30-second pause.*) OK, stop imagining that, and return to the relaxation once again, just continue relaxing, further and further relaxed. All right, if you're feeling comfortably relaxed, just let the tape recorder continue running. If not, turn it off for a few minutes until you're feeling relaxed once again.

OK, relaxing comfortably, imagine that you're entering the employee's cafeteria and as you pass by Mildred's table you hear a snicker. (*15-second pause.*) OK, stop imagining that and relax once again, just let go, further and further, deeper and deeper relaxed, more and more. That's fine. Let's imagine that once again: entering the employee cafeteria, you pass by Mildred's table and as you do so you hear a snicker. (*30-second pause.*) OK, turn off that situation and go back to your relaxation, back to your pleasant scene if you like. Just let go, just let go a little more as I count from 1 to 5, let's see if you can relax even more deeply. 1, just let go, 2, 3, 4, and 5. If you're feeling quite relaxed continue on; if not, turn off the tape recorder for a few minutes until you're feeling relaxed once again.

Just relaxing further and further, more and more. Imagine that the woman behind the counter is making a roast beef sandwich for you, and she is beginning to put mustard on instead of mayonnaise and you say: "Excuse me, but I would rather have mayonnaise than mustard." (*15-second pause.*) OK, stop imagining that and relax once again, further and further relaxed. More and more relaxed. Remember to relax away whatever tensions may arise during a given visualization. OK, again you're in the line, the woman is about to put mustard instead of mayonnaise on the roast beef sandwich, you say: "I would rather have mayonnaise than mustard on my sandwich." (*30-second pause.*) OK, stop imagining that and relax once again.

Remember, if you have time, imagine a scene over and over again. Letting go further and further. If you're feeling quite relaxed, continue on. If not, switch off the recorder for a few minutes and relax on your own for a while. OK, just relax further and further. More and more relaxed.

You're sitting at your desk and the phone rings. You lift up the receiver and the boss's secretary says that the chief would like to talk to you for a few minutes. (*15-second pause.*) OK, stop imagining that and relax once again; just relax, further and further relaxed. Letting go, deeper and deeper relaxed. Imagine once again now, at your desk and the phone rings and the boss's secretary says the chief would like to speak to you for a few minutes. (*30-second pause.*) OK, switch that scene off and listen to me once again.

Shortly, I am going to count from 5 to 1 and at the count of 1, you'll open your eyes, be alert and wide awake. Jot down your notes on this particular session, as you've listened to these past four items on your hierarchy. 5, 4, 3, 2, and 1. Eyes opened, wide awake, and jot down your comments.

● DIFFICULTIES IN DESENSITIZATION

It might be helpful to review some of the problems the therapist must be attentive to in doing any of the variations of desensitization.

Generation of Clear Images

As already stated, it appears essential from all theoretical perspectives for clients to create and maintain clear anxiety images. The reader has only to experiment with himself in generating a particular image and trying to hold it without undue shifts to become aware of the problems confronted by a client. Considerable practice and encouragement are necessary to ensure that the client visualizes his hierarchy scenes as vividly as possible.

Restlessness

It is understandable that clients might become restless if a desensitization session lasts for more than half an hour at a time. As is always the case in therapy, an intervention has to be tailored to the client's own needs and capacities. With some clients a therapist may have to settle for a 15-minute series of presentations, while for others he might be able to extend it to a full hour.

Relaxation

Assuming the importance of relaxation either as a counter-conditioning response or as a coping skill, the clinician has to continually ensure that the client is proficient in this skill. This would seem to be particularly important if the therapist is doing traditional Wolpean desensitization, where relaxation must be paired with anxiety stimuli and as little anxiety as possible associated with hierarchy items.

Nonaversiveness of Items

Should a client begin to report that more difficult items do not seem as difficult as he originally thought, it should not necessarily be assumed that the hierarchy is faulty or that desensitization is not proceeding well. On the contrary, the therapist might well attribute this to forward generalization of extinction (Lang, Melamed, & Hart, 1970), or to the possibility that the client has been "getting ahead" by using his relaxation skills to cope with such situations (Goldfried, 1971). In effect, he has been chipping away at the lower end of a ladder so that by the time an item originally rated as 70 is reached during desensitization, its anxiety-provoking properties may have been reduced to 30 or 40.

● *IN VIVO* EXPOSURES

The person should be explicitly encouraged to expose himself gradually to situations analogous to those successfully covered in imaginal desensitization. Thus, an acrophobic client who has imagined himself standing on top of a stepladder without feeling tension would be encouraged to attempt the same thing at home. Instructions to relax away the tensions at home should facilitate such graduated *in vivo* exposures. Of course, clients must be forewarned that setbacks or failures are likely to occur, and that these should be regarded as challenges for continued behavior of increasing boldness.

In vivo desensitization plays a particularly important role in those situations where the client may be having difficulty creating an image or where he may not experience anxiety during visualizations. In such instances, the therapist may construct a series of graded situations for *in vivo* exposure. Depending on the particular target behavior, this might even be arranged within the consultation session itself. For example, one client who became excessively anxious in the presence of extraneous noises was unable to "hear" such sounds when the situations were presented in imagination. Inasmuch as one such noise was the sound of loud gum-chewing, the therapist brought a package of gum to the session and chewed vigorously while the client relaxed for increasingly long periods of time. The *in vivo* desensitization eventually reached the point where the client was deliberately offering gum to friends and associates, so that he would have the opportunity to desensitize himself in a variety of real-life situations.

There may be instances where systematic desensitization with imaginal exposure is possible, but where *in vivo* desensitization would be preferable. Consider the case of a concert pianist who was too anxious to perform in an upcoming recital. Since the therapy was taking place at a training clinic, the therapist could enlist the aid of several interns, and was able to arrange for a therapeutic recital. The client went through a mock recital, with the therapist sitting by his side, instructing him in the use of differential relaxation. Consistent with the evidence that indicates that real-life exposure plays an extremely important role in anxiety reduction (Agras, 1967; Sherman, 1972), the treatment procedure turned out to be highly effective. Indeed it took considerably fewer sessions than probably would have been required if systematic desensitization had been used. In fact, considering that imaginal presentation of situations represents a pragmatic compromise of what might be achieved by means of real-life exposure, the therapist should always be mindful of the greater desirability of using *in vivo* desensitization.

A serendipitous use of *in vivo* desensitization occurred with a client of ours who was extremely fearful of dogs. After the initial session, a friend of his phoned to say that his dog just had puppies, and asked, jokingly, if he would like to have one. Rather than declining in horror, the client recalled our preliminary discussion of graded exposure as a means for reducing his phobia, so he asked his friend to set one puppy aside for a week. At the following therapy session, the decision was made to have his family accept the puppy, for two reasons: He felt he was relatively capable of tolerating a baby dog in his home; and we both agreed that he might be desensitized to dogs as this pup slowly matured. The therapy, therefore, entailed his having his pup grow up in the home, in the context of gleeful and frolicky interactions involving the client's children, his wife, and what turned out to be a gentle and playful cocker spaniel. Telephone contacts revealed that, after six months, the man was no longer fearful of dogs.

● GROUP DESENSITIZATION

Following Lazarus (1961) and Paul and Shannon (1966), it is possible to conduct any of the variations of desensitization with several clients simultaneously. Adhering to Wolpe's procedural requirements, Lazarus, as well as Paul and Shannon, ran both homogeneous and heterogeneous groups of phobics, moving up hierarchies at the pace of the slowest group member. Others, in published analog experiments (Nawas, Fishman, & Pucel, 1970), have followed the procedures outlined above as taped systematic desensitization. It is readily apparent how much easier it is to work with more than one client at a time if scenes do not have to be withdrawn as soon as any one person experiences anxiety.

Applications of Desensitization

The range of anxiety-related problems that have been shown amenable to desensitization seems to run the entire gamit of neurotic disorders (Bandura, 1969; Paul, 1969b; Meyer & Chesser, 1970), including interpersonal anxiety and the whole range of "classic phobias" (such as heights and enclosed spaces). In addition, problems traditionally classified as psychophysiological disorders have also responded well: asthma, hives, headaches, impotence. The limits, we may assume, are set mainly by the ingenuity of the behavior therapist in construing client difficulties in terms appropriate for desensitization.

● SUMMARY

This chapter has dealt with several variations of systematic desensitization, a procedure entailing graduated exposure to imaginal aversive stimuli, typically under conditions of muscle relaxation. Both clinical and experimental data attest to the usefulness of these procedures for reducing unrealistic fears, although the learning mechanisms underlying the efficacy of any of the procedural variations remain to be elucidated. The techniques detailed in this chapter do not, in any event, directly contradict any current hypotheses and, indeed, are consistent with most of them. Special attention has been paid to the decisions of whether to desensitize and to what. Desensitization, in the hands of a skilled, creative clinician, can apparently be useful over a broad range of neurotic and psychophysiological disorders, even when anxiety is not a salient component of the presenting complaint.

Chapter  7

Behavior Rehearsal

The idea of simulating interpersonal situations within the consultation room is hardly an invention of behavior therapists. In the early 1800s Reil (Zilboorg & Henry, 1941) recognized the therapeutic importance of having mental patients "act out" their interpersonal problems. During the early part of the twentieth century, Moreno (1947) incorporated role playing into a psychodramatic school of group therapy. Although there are certain points of similarity between psychodrama and the rehearsal procedures used by behavior therapists, the primary goal in the psychodramatic use of role playing has been to uncover the individual's blocked affect and to trace current problems back to their historical origins. As viewed from within a behavioral frame of reference, behavior rehearsal is used primarily in helping the client to learn new ways of responding to specific life situations.

We have used the terms "behavior rehearsal" and "role playing" interchangeably. Although both refer to the simulation of real-life situations within the consultation room, the function of behavior rehearsal is less ambiguous. This chapter deals with behavior rehearsal as a way to train new response patterns. Although role playing may be used for such purposes, it has also been employed as an assessment device (Goldfried & Sprafkin, 1974), as a means of achieving catharsis (Moreno, 1947), as a procedure for bringing about attitude change (Rosenberg, 1952), and to provide the client with insight into the developmental origin of his problems (Moreno, 1947).

The early work on the effectiveness of behavior rehearsal procedures seemed to indicate that it had the potential for training individuals in assuming a new behavioral role (Haskell, 1957; Kelly, Blake, & Stromberg, 1957). On the basis of uncontrolled clinical observations, Lazarus (1966) provided some initial evidence to suggest that behavior rehearsal is more effective than either advice or nondirective procedures in resolving interpersonal difficulties. More recent controlled analog research (e.g., Eisler, Hersen, & Agras, 1973; Hersen, Eisler, Miller, Johnson, & Pinkston, 1973; McFall & Lillesand, 1971; McFall & Marston, 1970; McFall & Twentyman, 1973) has demonstrated that behavior rehearsal procedures provide an effective means for facilitating assertive behavior.

The concept of "role" is important in the therapeutic uses of rehearsal procedures, and generally refers to those socially defined behaviors associated with a given position (e.g., husband, wife, father, mother, supervisor). In terms of role theory (Sarbin & Allen, 1968), problems arise when a discrepancy exists between the role behaviors available to a person and the expectations held by others in the immediate environment. Such discordance may be due to a number of different factors, such as a change in role status, a shifting in role definitions resulting from cultural changes, or an inappropriate social learning history. To state that a person's behavior is congruent or discrepant with certain role expectations is not to say that he is deliberately and consciously playing or avoiding a role. Although a certain amount of self-conscious effort may be associated with the initial stages of learning a role, as in the "make believe" activities readily observed among children (Mead, 1934), a well-learned behavior pattern eventually reaches the point where it occurs automatically.

In their discussion of role theory, Sarbin and Allen (1968) have described the procedure by which an actor goes about learning his theatrical role. The general learning sequence is as follows:

The actor has available some information which he must learn in the form of a script. He must learn not only the verbal responses, but also the actions and gestures appropriate to the part. . . . For the actor simply to study the requirements of the role is not enough; before the role is completely learned, the actor must *practice* in order to perfect his part. . . .

Another feature of the dramaturgic model of role learning is the presence of a coach. . . . Because of his own special skills and prior training, the coach can guide and advise the novice. Often the coach has played the role that the actor is trying to learn or has observed frequent performances of the role by experts. He detects mistakes, he suggests a regime of training, and in a variety of other ways aids the actor in mastering his role. He is in a position to regulate the pace of learning, because he knows whether the actor's progress is rapid enough for him to meet the expected standard within the time available; he may speed up or slow down the learner's pace as required.

An important function of the coach is to provide social reinforcement to the learner. Praise and criticism provide incentives for the learner, and at the same time furnish feedback which can be used to improve performance. After a scene the coach may give the actors an evaluation and critique of the performance, much in the manner of parents who praise their child for acting like a "big boy" all day.

The coach frequently serves as a model for the learner. Sometimes the coach enacts the role for the novice, explicitly instructing him to imitate (Sarbin & Allen, 1968, p. 548).

Sarbin and Allen here illustrate the similarities between the way actors learn their parts and the manner in which social roles are learned. The similarity between the above description and behavior rehearsal procedures as used within the clinical context is even more striking. By rereading the above paragraph and simply paraphrasing Sarbin and Allen's description—replacing "client" for "actor," and "therapist" for "coach"—one ends up with an excellent overview of the way in which behavior rehearsal is used in clinical practice.

● IMPLEMENTATION OF BEHAVIOR REHEARSAL

The behavior rehearsal treatment package may be broken down into four general stages: (1) preparation of the client, (2) selection of target situations, (3) behavior rehearsal proper, and (4) carrying out of new role behaviors in real-life situations.

Preparing the Client for Behavior Rehearsal

The major goals during this initial phase are to have the client recognize the need for learning a new behavior pattern, accept the idea that behavior rehearsal would be an appropriate way to develop this new social role, and overcome any initial uneasiness regarding the notion of playacting in the consulting room.

Even though it may be fairly clear to the therapist that the client's problems stem from a deficiency in certain social skills, the client himself may not be construing his difficulties along these lines. Using many of the procedures outlined in Chapter 4, it is incumbent on the therapist to persuade the client to accept this orientation.

Assuming that the client is willing to accept a behavioral interpretation, the next step is to convince him that behavior rehearsal can help him to overcome these deficiencies. Although there are clearly a number of ways the therapist might outline behavior rehearsal, our own preference is to present the method in general terms, outlining the more specific details only when it is apparent that the client seems receptive to the approach. It has been our experience that some clients react negatively to behavior rehearsal when it is described to them, partly because they feel that this technique would not help them to *really* change, and partly because they feel generally awkward about playacting. By gradually introducing a description of behavior rehearsal, the therapist stands a better chance of having the client eventually accept the approach. The following clinical interaction with an unassertive female client illustrates how this might be carried out:

Client: The basic problem is that I have the tendency to let people step all over me. I don't know why, but I just have difficulty in speaking my mind.

Therapist: [*My immediate tendency here is to reflect and clarify what the client said, adding a "behavioral twist." In paraphrasing what she has already said, I can cast it within a behavioral framework by introducing such terms as "situation," "respond," and "learn."*] So you find yourself in a number of different situations where you don't respond the way you would really like to. And if I understand correctly, you would like to learn how to behave differently.

Client: Yes. But you know, I *have* tried to handle certain situations differently, but I just don't seem to be able to do so.

Therapist: [*Not a complete acceptance of my conceptualization, seemingly because she has tried to behave differently in the past and nothing has happened. What I should do, then, is somehow provide some explanation of why previous attempts may have failed, and use this to draw a contrast with a potentially more effective treatment strategy that we'll be using in our sessions.*] It's almost as if there is a big gap between the way you react and the way you would *like* to react.

Client: It seems that way, and I don't know how to overcome it.

Therapist: Well, maybe you've tried to do too much too fast in the past, and consequently weren't very successful. Maybe a good way to look at the situation is to imagine yourself at the bottom of a staircase, wanting to get to the top. It's probably too much to ask to get there in one gigantic leap. Perhaps a better way to go about changing your reaction in these situations is to take it one step at a time.

Client: That would seem to make sense, but I'm not sure if I see how that could be done.

Therapist: Well, there are probably certain situations in which it ✓ would be less difficult for you to assert yourself, such as telling your boss that he forgot to pay you for the past four weeks.

Client: (*Laughing.*) I guess in that situation, I *would* say something. Although I must admit, I would feel uneasy about it.

Therapist: But not as uneasy as if you went in and asked him for a raise.

Client: No. Certainly not.

Therapist: So, the first situation would be low on the staircase, whereas the second would be higher up. If you can learn to handle easier situations, then the more difficult ones would present less of a problem. And the only way you can really learn to change your reactions is through practice.

Client: In other words, I really have to go out and actually force myself to speak up more, but taking it a little bit at a time?

Therapist: [*This seems like an appropriate time to introduce the function of behavior rehearsal. I won't say anything about the specific procedure yet, but instead will talk about it in general terms, and maybe increase its appeal by explaining that any failures will not really "count." If the client goes along with the general description of the treatment strategy, she should be more likely to accept the details as I spell them out.]* Exactly. And as a way of helping you carry it off in the real-life situation, I think it would be helpful if we reviewed some of these situations and your reactions to them beforehand. In a sense, going through a dry run. It's safer to run through some of these situations here, in that it really doesn't "count" if you don't handle them exactly as you would like to. Also, it can provide you an excellent opportunity to practice different ways of reacting to these situations, until you finally hit on one which you think would be best.

Client: That seems to make sense.

Therapist: In fact, we could arrange things so that you can actually rehearse exactly what you would say, and how you would say it.

Client: That sounds like a good idea.

Although some clients acknowledge that behavior rehearsal might be helpful, they often are concerned that they would be simply learning to "play a role," and that they would not be *really* changing. The therapist can certainly agree with this, and might in fact raise the issue if he senses that this is a concern for any particular client. The client should be made aware, however, that in the process of learning any new role, there is apt to be some feeling of artificiality during the early phases of the learning process. This point can be made most convincingly by pointing to any new roles the client has recently assumed, such as becoming a spouse, parent, student, and so forth.

There seems to be something about the role-playing process itself that creates some uneasiness. The client may feel a bit shy, or perhaps may not think that he is very good at acting. The client may verbalize this feeling of awkwardness at this point in the behavior rehearsal procedure, or he may state it during behavior rehearsal proper. It may be possible to overcome this uneasiness by gradually lapsing into role playing via a discussion of a hypothetical situation, having the client give a detailed verbal description of what he would say and do in this situation, and perhaps by the therapist casually demonstrating how this response might be role-played. The therapist might say something such as: "Perhaps instead of *telling* me what you would do (did) in that situation, I think I would get a better understanding if you *showed* me what would (did) happen." Even with all these efforts, certain clients will flatly refuse to participate in behavior rehearsal. An acceptable compromise would be to have the client work his way up a hierarchy *in vivo*, with the in-session preparation consisting of a rehearsal in imagination and/or a detailed discussion of how the situation might best be handled.

Selecting Target Situations

Except when clients are having difficulty handling only a few specific situations, the therapist can draw up a hierarchy along which the training will take place. Many of the same guidelines used in hierarchy construction for systematic desensitization are relevant here (see Chapter 6). The items should provide a good sample of those situations where the client's behavioral deficit is likely to manifest itself. If at all possible, it is preferable to use situations that the client himself could instigate, so that there is greater likelihood of him being in that situation in the future. In the case of a male who feels uncomfortable in heterosexual interactions, for example, it would be better to include the situation where *he* goes over and says "hello" to a female, rather than one in which the woman approaches him.

The arrangement of the items into hierarchial order for behavior rehearsal may pose certain problems not found in desensitization. The basic question here is how to rank order the items. In the case of a desensitization hierarchy, the client's subjective anxiety level is sufficient. In behavior rehearsal, on the other hand, items should be arranged according to the complexity of the behavioral skills required. While there is bound to be some rough correlation between complexity of social skills and amount of anxiety experienced, the therapist should also rely on his own knowledge of the behavioral requirements associated with certain situations. The following hierarchy focuses on interpersonal skills for a socially deficient male client.

1. You stop at a gas station and ask the attendant for a map.
2. A man, whom you do not know, is standing next to a bulletin board in the post office. You go over and start small talk.
3. A woman, whom you do not know, is standing next to a bulletin board in the post office. You go over and start making small talk.

4. You are in a crowded cafeteria, and you sit down next to a man you do not know and strike up a conversation.
5. You are being interviewed for a job by a man.
6. You are having a conversation with a male friend whom you know casually.
7. You go to speak with your supervisor about a report you are writing; he seems to be receptive and friendly.
8. You go to speak with your supervisor about a report you are writing; he seems to be very cold and aloof.
9. You go over to a female coworker at the end of the day, and ask her a question about some job she's currently working on.
10. You are in a crowded cafeteria, and you sit down next to a woman whom you do not know and start to strike up a conversation.
11. You are having a conversation with a female acquaintance that you have just met for the first time.
12. You ask a female coworker if she would be interested in having a drink with you after work.
13. While having a conversation with a female acquaintance whom you know casually, you ask her whether she would be interested in going to a movie with you.

There are several ways relevant situations may be obtained. One of the most frequent methods is simply asking the client during the clinical interview, with the questioning being guided both by the therapist's clinical inferences as well as his knowledge of the client's environment and particular problem. All too frequently, however, clients find it very difficult to come up with specific examples. Here we face once again many of the assessment issues discussed earlier in Chapters 2 and 3. At times a significant other in the client's life, such as a spouse, relative, or friend, can offer the perspective that the client lacks. A particularly useful assessment device in dealing with various behavior deficits consists of self-monitoring, which also provides an ongoing evaluation of progress as behavior rehearsal proceeds.

Behavior Rehearsal Proper

In many respects, behavior rehearsal may be construed as a gradual shaping process. This is true not only because a hierarchy is employed, but also because complex social interactions entail a number of component skills. In order for the client to interact appropriately with another individual, more than just knowing *what* to say is required. The tone of voice, the pace of his speech, gestures, eye contact, general posture, and a host of other factors can all play a significant part in achieving competent social skills. Rather than attempting to change the client in all of the components at once, the therapist would be wise to select only a few at a time, and then focus on these during the rehearsal of any given situation. Particularly when clients show severe deficits, it is probably unrealistic to put together all of these subskills until the later phases of training.

As is the case with the psychodramatic procedures outlined by Moreno, some sort of initial "warm-up" is useful—and at times essential—for actually carrying out the behavior rehearsal procedure. In addition to helping the client get into the mood for role playing, the warm-up period also helps to specify in some detail the nature of the situation to be enacted. Up until this point, the description of the hierarchy item is likely to involve one or two sentences. To recreate the situation within the consultation room, information is needed regarding the nature of the physical environment (e.g., doors, chair, table), the other people involved, and the precise nature of the interaction to be simulated. The therapist serves very much the function of a director, where, with information provided by the client, he helps to set the stage and contributes to the realism required for the behavior rehearsal procedure. The physical arrangements within the consultation room might have to be altered, with furniture moved around to assist in creating a more realistic simulation. In addition, the use of ancillary therapeutic aides (e.g., clinical trainees) can be helpful as a means for introducing other relevant characters in the situation.

In actually initiating the behavior rehearsal procedure, it is also useful to begin with a situation that offers little difficulty to the client. This, too, can contribute to the warm-up process, for the therapist as well as the client. It can also help the therapist see how well the client can stay in role, for some individuals do not fully understand the task requirements of behavior rehearsal. If, for example, a client responds by stating, "I would ask the clerk to please wait on me," the therapist should encourage him to backtrack and respond as if he were actually in the situation.

Once it is apparent that the client can stay in role, the actual training situations may be enacted. Starting from the bottom of the hierarchy, each situation is role-played, with the client receiving some feedback about the adequacy of his performance. There are many ways of providing this feedback, including therapist's comments and the client's own subjective evaluation—both of which can be aided considerably by either audio- or video-taped instant replay. If at all possible, it is preferable for the client to evaluate the adequacy of his own performance; this can help him learn to become more sensitive toward his behavior and facilitate the self-monitoring and corrective actions taken between sessions. If the client is accurate in evaluating his performance, the therapist can simply concur, perhaps adding some observations of his own.

As mentioned earlier, care should be taken not to demand too much of the client during the early phases of training. Thus, focus might be placed on eye contact and smiling during one series of enactments, with feedback being provided on additional components of the interaction once the client becomes adept at adequately performing these earlier behaviors. In the case of behavioral deficiencies where nonverbal cues play a salient role, it is evident that video-tape procedures could be most helpful.

If it appears that the client's performance in any given situation is extremely deficient, or not readily corrected by feedback, *modeling* procedures would be in order. This can be easily accomplished by using a therapeutic aide, or by having the therapist reverse roles with the client and demonstrate the more appropriate response. Inasmuch as modeling procedures have been found to be most effective when the discrepancy between the observer and model is minimal (Bandura, 1969), the therapist should not provide too competent a model. To some extent, however, this danger is minimized by the use of hierarchically arranged situations.

In addition to the use of modeling procedures, the client may at times require *coaching*. One of the principal uses of coaching is to provide the client with information about the appropriateness of his behavior. With clients having difficulty in social interactions, for example, we have found it most profitable to make use of therapeutic assistants. Not only is this helpful in creating a more realistic simulation of the real-life situation, but it also provides the client with "expert" advice about people's expectations in certain situations. The utility of coaching is attested to by a series of studies on assertion training (McFall & Twentyman, 1973), where it was found that the therapeutic effectiveness of behavior rehearsal was enhanced by coaching. When used together with rehearsal procedures, coaching appears to provide the client with information as to *what* he should say or do in any given situation, whereas rehearsal provides actual practice in *how* to do it.

Almost every client experiences anxiety when placed in social situations that he is unable to handle effectively. This can frequently present a dilemma for the therapist, for it may not be clear whether the anxiety is antecedent or consequent to the behavioral deficiency. Is the client unable to respond because he is anxious, or is he anxious because he is unable to respond? Case history information regarding the duration and pervasiveness of the target behavior can be helpful in shedding light on this question. Also, some clients are able to state outright that they know what to say or do, but are just too nervous to do it. Where a behavioral deficiency does exist, the client's excessive anxiety may interfere with the retraining process. A hierarchy of graded tasks can clearly help minimize the anxiety. The use of coping relaxation during the behavior rehearsal sessions can reduce the interference from anxiety. We have also observed clinically that many clients who manifest behavioral deficits also have rather unrealistic expectations about the outcome of their actions. For example, it is not uncommon for an unassertive client to fear that if he stands up for his rights, other people will dislike him. Rational restructuring can encourage the client to give up his unassertive behavior. This might simply involve pointing out the self-defeating aspects of his expectations—if you want to earn the respect of others, then you *should* stand up for your own rights—or it might entail some of the more detailed procedures described in Chapter 8. In the final analysis, however, these inappropriate cognitions are likely to change once the client reaches the point where he is able to respond appropriately *in vivo*.

Although our discussion of behavior rehearsal has involved the use of overt, role-playing procedures, there may be times when *cognitive rehearsal* is called for. With some clinical problems, realistic or ethical limitations may rule out the feasibility of overt behavior rehearsal. For example, if the client's problems occur when he is in a large group setting, or over extended periods of time, it may not be possible to simulate such situations within the consultation room. Overt behavior rehearsal might also be ruled out in the case of behavioral deficiencies of a primarily sexual nature. Also, as we mentioned earlier, some clients are simply too embarrassed to act through their problems. In such instances, the client can be asked to imagine himself in each of the target situations, and then to attempt to imagine himself responding appropriately. Although this procedure may be viewed as a watered-down behavior rehearsal, some data show that covert rehearsal is just as effective as overt role playing in the facilitation of assertive behavior (McFall & Lillesand, 1971; McFall & Twentyman, 1973). So that the therapist can assess the adequacy of the response and provide appropriate feedback, the client should concurrently verbalize what is going on as he is "doing it" in imagination.

Once the client achieves some criterion of acceptability on any particular item, he is then ready to move to the next more difficult situation. Although the similarities here to the desensitization process are obvious, some added complications exist in the case of behavior rehearsal. With desensitization, successful completion of an item is determined primarily by the client's subjective estimate of anxiety. With the more complex social response patterns typically involved in most behavior rehearsal procedures, the therapist must take a more active role in deciding what, in fact, is adequate. This is not to imply that the client does not contribute to this decision. It should be kept in mind, however, that the client's inability to evaluate the appropriateness of various actions may be part of his problem. In arriving at a standard for social adequacy, the therapist should take great care to base his estimate on the likelihood of the client receiving positive feedback in his own particular environment, rather than making a judgment which stems solely from what the therapist personally feels the client should do.[1] Therapeutic aides or cotherapists can be most useful at this point to provide the needed consensual validation of the therapist's judgments.

The following transcript with a socially inadequate male client illustrates many of the above-mentioned points.

Therapist: Let's take the situation where you see a woman standing in front of the bulletin board, and you go over to strike up a conversation. Ms. Phillips can play the part of the woman. [*This situation involves being in the post office, which in no way resembles this consulting room. I'll have to spend some time setting the stage, so we can more realistically simulate the actual situation.*] Tell me more about the physical set-up. Where would the bulletin board be?

Client: Right about here (*pointing toward the wall*).

Therapist: What else?

Client: Well, it would be in the post office, right near the window where they sell the stamps.

Therapist: And where would that be?

---

[1] Assertion training for women requires special consideration, for their new way of responding may also meet with *negative* consequences. This issue is discussed in Chapter 13.

Client: (*Pointing*) Right about here.

Therapist: Where would you enter?

Client: The corridor is down along here (*pointing*).

Therapist: Do you have any questions before we begin?

Client: No, I don't think so.

Therapist: All right, then why don't you go down to the other end of the corridor, and come in.

Client: (*In role*) Hello. My name is Bob. What's yours?

Cotherapist: (*In role*) Ann.

Client: (*Pause*) Umm . . . what are you doing?

Cotherapist: Looking at this bulletin board.

Therapist: [*He's obviously having difficulty handling this situation. His social deficiency seems to be greater than I originally anticipated. I think I'll stop the interaction at this point, and let him hear himself on tape; I hope he'll be able to hear where he's having trouble.*] (*Rewinding tape recorder*) Let's stop here and listen to it. (*After reviewing tape*) What do you think of it?

Client: I sounded very awkward.

Therapist: In what way?

Client: I couldn't think of anything to say.

Therapist: All right, let's discuss that for a moment. [*Giving him feedback from the cotherapist would probably be helpful. It's unlikely that anyone in a real-life interaction would tell him what they thought of his comment.*] (*Turning to cotherapist*). What was your reaction in that situation?

Cotherapist: Well, I really didn't know how to take it when he came over to speak to me. I had never seen him before, and I thought it was strange that he should introduce himself so suddenly. I guess many other women would probably feel the same way in my situation.

Therapist: [*Time for some information on what might be a more socially appropriate alternative.*] What do you think might be more appropriate to this particular situation?

Cotherapist: I guess if he came over and started reading the bulletin board, he might be able to make some comment about the notice itself.

Therapist: (*Turning to client*) What's your reaction to that?

Client: That probably would have been easier.

Therapist: [*Good. It's always helpful when the client seems receptive to your suggestion of a new way to respond. In light of the initial problems he had, though, I think it would be a good idea for me to model both the appropriate content and style of responding.*] Let me be you for a moment, and go through this situation again. (*In role, reading notice on bulletin board*). They keep increasing the cost of stamps.

Cotherapist: (*In role*) I know. It's really outrageous.

Therapist: (*In role*) I wonder why the cost keeps going up?

Cotherapist: Undoubtedly because of the incredible waste and inefficiency that goes on.

Therapist: (*Out of role*) What did you notice in that situation?

Client: (*Smiling*) It seemed to work better that time. You also seemed more sure of yourself.

Therapist: [*I feel flattered—a completely inappropriate reaction in this situation! Back to being a therapist. Let's see if he's able to identify some of the specific behavioral components associated with how I was interacting.*] How could you tell?

Client: Well, you started by saying something about what was on the bulletin board. Also, you didn't hesitate when you spoke, the way I did.

Therapist: Okay. Why don't you go through that situation again, this time trying to react in much the same way as I did.

Carrying Out the New Role in Real-Life Situations

Once the client has been successful in performing a given pattern within the consultation session, he should be ready to try out this behavior *in vivo*. The client should be made to clearly understand that application in the real-life situation is part and parcel of the therapy procedure. This can be accomplished by periodically reminding the client what he is to do between sessions, and routinely beginning each session by checking on his homework.

If the rehearsed items have been constructed so that the interaction can be initiated by the client (e.g., going over to speak to someone, as opposed to waiting for the person to come to him), the client has a better chance of actually placing himself in the situation he has rehearsed in therapy. Written self-observations are extremely useful in this regard, in that they can provide a day-to-day account of target situations and the client's response. Written records also provide a subtle reminder for the client to actually try out his new response *in vivo*. We have made a practice of asking clients to keep a daily record of their behavior in target situations, specifying the antecedents, their own actual behavior, and the resulting consequences. In fact, we often instruct clients to keep a separate page in their book for each day, whether or not any relevant social interaction has occurred. The demand characteristics of a blank page are such that clients frequently feel compelled to do something to fill it! Another helpful device is to divide a page in half, with accounts of inappropriate behavior on one side, and appropriate behavior on the other. Not only does this provide a clear account of the client's progress, but it also serves as an additional motivation to balance the ledger. The client should be cautioned, however, not to attempt too much at once, but rather to proceed in a more or less hierarchical fashion.

In discussing the client's experiences during the week, considerable emphasis should be placed on the consequences of his newly acquired behavior pattern. This is particularly true in those cases where the client has previously held unrealistic expectations about the reactions of others; new experiences can provide reality checks on his beliefs. As the client begins to recognize that positive consequences do result from his new way of responding, he should make a deliberate effort to remind himself when entering new situations in the future (e.g., "People will *not* think badly of me if I assert myself; in fact, they're likely to respect me more!"). In addition to focusing on the external consequences of the client's appropriate responses, his own attitude toward his behavior should be determined. Hopefully, it will be positive. If not, perhaps he is expecting too much of himself too soon. In addition to reinforcing the client's accomplishments, the therapist should make it a point to elicit some self-reinforcements from the client (e.g., "I really felt good about being able to say what was on my mind in that situation.").

If practical limitations are not too great, it can also be helpful if the therapist, or a therapeutic aide, actually accompanies the client in a real-life situation to observe his new response pattern. In addition to insuring that the client will be making attempts to practice *in vivo*, it also adds some security to the interaction.

Except when the therapist is an agent of social change, as is discussed in Chapter 13, a decision on the appropriate behavior for the client to learn is based on what is most likely to pay off in the individual's particular environment. Thus, an ongoing assessment of the consequences of the client's actions is needed to determine whether this judgment has been accurate or not. How, in fact, are the client's parents, teacher, spouse, roommate, or friend responding to this new behavior? In some instances, significant others may have to be asked to be patient with the client until he is able to arrive at the socially appropriate way of responding. This is particularly true in the case of children during the early phases of assertion training, where they may not as yet have fully learned to discriminate between assertiveness and aggressiveness.

● RELATED PROCEDURES

A technique closely related to behavior rehearsal is Kelly's (1955) fixed-role therapy. Fixed-role therapy, which dates back to the late 1930s, is based on the general assumption that individuals can change their behavior as a function of tentatively "trying out" certain behavior patterns. Both therapist and client construct an actual role sketch, which provides a thematic description of the behavior pattern the client is to follow (e.g., sensitivity to the feelings of others, openness in the expression of feelings). The client is asked to assume this new role over a period of several weeks. Role playing during the consultation sessions facilitates this enactment process. Even though the client is being asked to try out new behaviors in his day-to-day life, the therapy is structured in such a way so that none of it is "for real." Thus, although there is no hierarchy to insure the gradualness of behavior change, the "make believe" and "experimental" nature of the task is designed to prevent the client from feeling that too much is being demanded of him too fast.

Similar to Kelly's fixed-role therapy is the technique that Lazarus (1971; Wolpe & Lazarus, 1966) has called "exaggerated role-taking." Instead of writing a behavioral sketch, the client is asked to think of a specific individual who possesses those characteristics he lacks. Film stars, royalty and other similarly well-known individuals are employed, as their behavior pattern is likely to be fairly well-known to both client and therapist. The client practices this exaggerated role in the consultation sessions, and is also encouraged to behave similarly *in vivo*. Presumably, by enacting the new behavior pattern in extreme form, the less extreme, appropriate way of responding is more readily learned.

● APPLICATIONS

As indicated above, behavior rehearsal procedures are relevant when the client manifests some behavior deficiency. Thus, rehearsal techniques are useful as a means of providing training in assertive behavior and social skills. We would hasten to add, however, that increased assertiveness and improved social skills may be achieved by means other than behavior rehearsal. We have seen several instances where rational restructuring accompanied by self-monitoring served to facilitate assertive behavior. Such a therapeutic strategy is particularly relevant when the client's unassertiveness is due primarily to an inhibition stemming from an unrealistic anticipation of negative consequences. Further, when clients manifest difficulties in social interaction, the main problem may not be so much a function of any behavioral deficit, but rather the result of simply not knowing *what* to say or do. In making this distinction between the information and skills associated with a social role, Ryle (1949) has observed:

> Learning *how* or improving an ability is not like learning *that* or acquiring information. Truths can be imparted, procedures can only be inculcated, and while inculcation is a gradual process, imparting is relatively sudden. . . . (p. 59)

Thus, some clients can be helped by simply providing them with information on what they might say or do in various situations. The factors associated with the selection of the appropriate therapeutic procedure for such target behaviors are discussed in Chapter 11.

Assertion Training

Behavior rehearsal has been used most frequently with clients who have trouble asserting themselves. In fact, the terms "assertion training" and "behavior rehearsal" have often been used interchangeably. Unfortunately, this equation is inaccurate conceptually, and can frequently lead to communication problems. To begin with, behavior rehearsal denotes a specific therapeutic procedure (i.e., enactment of real-life situations in the consultation room), whereas assertion training deals more with the *objective* of the technique (i.e., increased assertiveness). Further, to state that a client has received assertion training says little about the specific procedures employed. Although behavior rehearsal might be used, increased assertiveness might be accomplished by means of *in vivo* relaxation, rational restructuring, self-monitoring, desensitization, or some combination thereof.

Early recognition of the problem of unassertive behavior was provided by Salter (1949). In his book *Conditioned Reflex Therapy,* Salter described the characteristics of the "inhibitory personality," which he attempted to explain in Pavlovian terms. Wolpe and Lazarus (1966) construed assertion training in much the same way as relaxation, in that it provided another means for "reciprocally inhibiting" anxiety. We prefer to view unassertive behavior as reflecting a specific skill deficit and/or behavioral inhibition, presumably resulting from faulty social learning experiences.

In contrast to a number of other behavior problems, unassertiveness is relatively easy to assess. Unassertive individuals typically *know* that they do not stand up for their rights, and can frequently report their temptations to speak up, as well as their subsequent regrets about not having done so. In the most general terms, assertiveness refers to socially appropriate behavior that is likely to be effective in eliminating obstacles interfering with the individual's goals. The implications of such a definition are that the truly assertive individual is capable of expressing positive as well as negative feelings, which Lazarus (1971) has aptly referred to as "emotional freedom."

Something might be said at this point on the distinction between assertiveness and aggressiveness. Although one might think that the two typically go together, this is not necessarily so. For example, it is not uncommon to come across the otherwise shy and unassuming client who displays periodic temper outbursts. In such instances, the expression of anger often reflects the release of pent-up feelings resulting from situations where the individual may have found it difficult to speak his mind. Conversely, the sheer volume or magnitude of the individual's response should not be taken as a defining characteristic of assertive behavior. An appropriately assertive individual may quietly, yet most effectively, be able to work toward the goal of making his position clear to others, and be successful in removing any obstacles that interfere with his own personal goals. The individual who copes with an unreasonable clerk by quietly insisting on speaking with his supervisor may be seen as more appropriately assertive than the individual who responds with a fit of rage. Numerous illustrations of the distinction between assertiveness and aggressiveness can be provided to clients by assigning Alberti and Emmons' (1974) *Your Perfect Right,* a paperback book that also nicely outlines the rationale behind and the methods involved in assertion training.

Behavior rehearsal may also be used as a means of assertion training with children. Gittelman (1965) has described the use of such a procedure with a thirteen-year-old boy whose explosive temper was endangering his academic status. Behavior rehearsal was carried out in a group setting, which essentially involved provoking the client in a series of simulated situations, and shaping up a more appropriate response. With younger children, behavior rehearsal might well be placed within the context of a game. The following transcript illustrates how this was done with a shy and unexpressive seven-year-old girl.

Therapist: Let's play a game with these blocks; we'll build a house. I'll be the worker, and you be the person in charge. (*Role playing*) OK now, where shall I put these blocks?

Client: (*Softly*) Uh . . . they can go over there.

Therapist: [*Although her response is somewhat tentative, I'll go along with it so as to provide some initial positive reinforcement for what is an approximation to an assertive response.*] (*Placing blocks where indicated*) OK, I'll put them right here then. How about these?

Client: (*Softly*) You can put them there also.

Therapist: [*Let's see if I can get her to show some initiative by deciding what we should be doing next.*] What shall I do now?

Client: (*Pause*) Get some more blocks and put them in the same pile.

Therapist: OK. Now what?

Client: Put more there.

Therapist: [*She seems to be handling that fairly well. Let's see what she can do if I throw a mild obstacle in her path.*] (*Softly*) No, I want to put them in a different pile.

Client: All right.

Therapist: [*She needs some encouragement. Perhaps I can coach her on a more appropriate way of responding.*] (*Stepping out of role*) Wait a minute. Remember that *you* are the one that's in charge, and you have to tell *me* what to do, even if I don't want to do it. (*Back in role*) I want to put these blocks in a new pile.

Client: No, I'm sorry, but you can't. We have to build up that section first.

Therapist: All right. But can I knock over the blocks and start again?

Client: (*Hesitantly*) No. Let's finish it first.

Therapist: [*She seems to be holding her ground fairly well. Some reinforcement is in order at this point. Also, I'd like to change the situation somewhat so as to focus on how softly she's been speaking. Let's see if I can come up with a game that's more likely to elicit a louder response.*] (*Stepping out of role and putting his arm around client*) That was real good. Let's make believe now that you're on top of this high building, and I'm working below. You can stand up on the chair and make believe you're at the top of the building. (*Back in role*) How many more blocks do we need here?

Client: (*Standing on chair*) Five more.

Therapist: What? I can't hear you. I'm all the way down here.

Client: (*A little louder*) Five more.

Therapist: What was that?

Client: (*Much louder*) I SAID WE NEED FIVE MORE!

Social Skills Training

Behavior rehearsal can also be employed in training more general social skills, such as how to handle oneself with a parent, with a close friend, and in other similar interpersonal situations.

A problem frequently encountered in college clinics and counseling services, for example, is that of the student who is uncomfortable in social interactions, particularly of a heterosexual nature. With these and other social skill deficits, behavior rehearsal can be most effective when combined with a discussion of what is and what is not appropriate in given social interactions. Opposite-sexed cotherapists or therapeutic aides are useful here, not only for the implementation of behavior rehearsal, but also as information sources for appropriate social behavior. Training in social skills also seems to lend itself to group settings, particularly if the group is composed of clients with similar problems. The advantages of behavior rehearsal in group settings are many: social interactions can be more realistically simulated; each client's progress can serve a modeling function for the other members of the group; and the social pressures inherent in such settings can encourage each individual to try out his new responses *in vivo*.

Other Applications

In addition to assisting the client in overcoming a more general deficit, behavior rehearsal may also be used to help individuals in handling specific forthcoming crises. These situations, which are likely to be both novel and important to the individual, may involve being interviewed for a job, asking the boss for a raise, or trying to convince a professor to postpone the due date for a term paper. Such uses of rehearsal procedures in clinical settings are typically tangential to a more comprehensive treatment program. Another ancillary use of behavior rehearsal during the course of therapy may be to "instigate" an otherwise difficult-to-implement behavior. For example, the procrastinating office worker may be asked to cognitively rehearse the act of gathering the information necessary for completing a monthly report.

In viewing behavior rehearsal procedures as a means of skill training, it should be kept in mind that many self-control procedures are taught to clients via behavior rehearsal. Thus, procedures for training a client in the self-control of anxiety by means of coping relaxation or rational restructuring can be done by having clients rehearse (cognitively or overtly) this skill in hierarchically arranged situations.

Outside of the formal therapy situation, there are almost no limits to the possible applications of behavior rehearsal. Simulation procedures have been used extensively in business and industry (Corsini, Shaw, & Blake, 1961). Bard and Berkowitz (1967) have also described the use of behavior rehearsal in police training, particularly as a way of enhancing effectiveness in family crisis intervention. In the case of costly and potentially dangerous projects—such as the training of astronauts for space travel—it is hard to conceive of such programs without the use of simulation and behavior rehearsal procedures.

● SUMMARY

Behavior rehearsal consists of a simulation of real-life situations within the consultation room. The general purpose is to train the client in new and more effective behavior. Preparatory to behavior rehearsal proper, the client might have to overcome any initial uneasiness associated with playacting. If the particular target behavior consists of a deficit involving a number of different situations, the use of a hierarchy is recommended. Role playing, modeling, coaching, and feedback are all used in changing both the content and style of the client's behavior patterns. In addition to the overt enactment of responses, cognitive rehearsal procedures may be called for at times. Behavior rehearsal should most appropriately be viewed as providing an intermediate step in changing behavior, with the eventual behavior change occurring as the client tries out the new role *in vivo*. Rehearsal procedures are appropriate for dealing with behavioral deficits, such as unassertiveness or poor social skills. In addition, it is also useful for preparing individuals for certain novel situations, where it may be either impossible or inadvisable to allow the individual to obtain "on the job" experience.

Chapter

Cognitive Relabeling

As we have suggested in preceding chapters, the search for the most important controlling variables often leads us to a consideration of cognitive factors, among which are the client's expectations, attitudes, and beliefs. The purpose of this chapter is to outline procedures for modifying aspects of an individual's cognitive processes that are likely to have implications for behavior change. One such cognitive relabeling procedure is based on the assumption that certain maladaptive emotions and behaviors are mediated by unrealistic expectations. Drawing on Ellis' (1962) work, we describe procedures by which individuals may learn to rationally restructure their irrational beliefs, thereby breaking what may be construed as well-learned, but maladaptive, sets. The second aspect of cognitive relabeling is based on the social psychological literature, and deals with the potential effect of the client's attribution on the change and maintenance of behavior.

● RATIONAL RESTRUCTURING

One of the primary assumptions underlying the rational-emotive approach to therapy as described by Ellis (1962) is the belief that many of the maladaptive emotional reactions and behaviors that we see clinically are mediated by the individual's attitudes toward, and assumptions about, the world around him. In the theoretical writings of Kelly (1955) and Rotter (1954), expectations were also said to play a major role in determining behavior. In referring to maladaptive reactions, for example, Rotter has stated the following:

> Relatively high expectancy for punishment . . . is the closest one comes in social learning theory to a term at least partially overlapping the concept of anxiety, emotional disturbance, or frustration state as used in other systematic frameworks (Rotter, 1954, p. 237).

Perhaps an even more basic theoretical context in which rational restructuring may be understood is to be found in Dollard and Miller's (1950) discussion of man's "higher mental processes." Recognizing the unique ability of human beings to utilize language and to reason symbolically, Dollard and Miller suggest that the individual's overt response to many situations is mediated by cue-producing responses. These cue-producing responses function, in essence, as labels. Consequently, emotional reactions may be viewed as responses to the way a person labels a situation, and not necessarily to the situation itself. The relationship between Dollard and Miller's theorizing and rational restructuring is apparent in the following quote from Ellis:

> It would appear, then, that positive human emotions, such as feelings of love or elation, are often associated with or result from internalized sentences, stated in some form or variation of the phrase "This is good for me!" and that negative human emotions, such as feelings of anger or depression, are associated with or result from sentences stated in some form or variation of the phrase "This is bad for me!" (Ellis, 1962, p. 51).

In addition to suggesting that emotional reactions are mediated by internal sentences, Ellis assumes that an individual's maladaptive emotional response reflects his indiscriminate and automatic labeling of a situation. Thus, although the emotional reaction may be appropriate to the label one attaches to a situation, the label itself may be basically inaccurate. For example, a person may become anxious in a situation he has mistakenly labeled as dangerous. In such instances, it is the label, not his reaction per se, that is inappropriate.

Ellis maintains that in the process of being socialized within our culture, many people develop a set of ideas or attitudes that are, in fact, *irrational.* These assumptions are classified as irrational because they are not likely to be supported (i.e., confirmed) by one's environment. According to Ellis (1962), these commonly held, but irrational, beliefs are as follows:

1. The idea that it is a dire necessity for an adult human being to be loved or approved by virtually every significant other person in his community (p.61).

2. The idea that one should be thoroughly competent, adequate, and achieving in all possible respects if one is to consider oneself worthwhile (p. 63).

3. The idea that certain people are bad, wicked, or villainous and that they should be severely blamed and punished for their villainy (p. 65).

4. The idea that it is awful and catastrophic when things are not the way one would very much like them to be (p. 69).

5. The idea that human unhappiness is externally caused and that people have little or no ability to control their sorrows and disturbances (p. 72).

6. The idea that if something is or may be dangerous or fearsome one should be terribly concerned about it and should keep dwelling on the possibility of its occurring (p. 75).

7. The idea that it is easier to avoid than to face certain life difficulties and self-responsibilities (p. 78).

8. The idea that one should be dependent on others and needs someone stronger than oneself on whom to rely (p. 80).

9. The idea that one's past history is an all-important determinant of one's present behavior and that because something once strongly affected one's life, it should indefinitely have a similar effect (p. 82).

10. The idea that one should become quite upset over other people's problems and disturbances (p. 85).

11. The idea that there is invariably a right, precise, and perfect solution to human problems and that it is catastrophic if this correct solution is not found (p. 87).

According to the theory behind rational restructuring, the extent to which a person tends to label situations in accord with one or more irrational beliefs will strongly determine his maladaptive emotional responses and ineffective behavior. It should be stressed, however, that it is unlikely that someone consciously or deliberately "tells himself" any of these statements when he is actually in a situation. Presumably because of the overlearned nature of the beliefs, they become as automatic and seemingly involuntary as a well-learned set (Woodworth & Schlosberg, 1954).

Empirical Support

Before turning to a description of the way rational restructuring may be implemented, we might note something about the empirical status of theoretical assumptions underlying the approach. In an investigation of the effect of self-statements on mood states, Velten (1968) had subjects read self-referent statements which varied in content. Some of these statements reflected elation ("This is great —I really do feel good—I *am* elated about things"), others were depressive in quality ("I have too many bad things in my life"), and still others were neutral ("Utah is the Beehive State"). Using verbal report as well as various indirect indicators (e.g., writing speed, reaction time) as measures of mood state, Velten found mood to change with the type of statements read. Subsequent studies have similarly supported the conclusion that one's self-verbalizations can significantly affect emotional arousal (May & Johnson, 1973; Rimm & Litvak, 1969; Russell & Brandsma, 1974).

Some empirical support exists for the contention that irrational self-statements, although not necessarily the eleven specified by Ellis, are associated with maladaptive emotional reactions. For example, Goldfried and Sobocinski (1975) found that the tendency to hold irrational beliefs was positively correlated with social, speech, and test anxiety. In addition, they found that individuals who expected approval from others experienced greater emotional upset when imagining themselves in social situations that might be interpreted as involving rejection by others. Further indirect support for the contention that irrational self-statements underlie maladaptive emotional arousal comes from several outcome studies, showing that anxiety in public speaking situations (Karst & Trexler, 1970; Meichenbaum, Gilmore & Fedoravicius, 1971; Trexler & Karst, 1972), interpersonal anxiety (DiLoreto, 1971; Kanter, 1975), and test anxiety (Meichenbaum, 1972) can be significantly reduced by teaching the clients to modify their irrational self-statements.

Implementation of Rational Restructuring

Within the Dollard and Miller (1950) framework, the primary objective in utilizing rational restructuring is to train the client to perceive environmental cues more accurately, so that realistically dangerous situations are clearly differentiated from those where the source of harm is purely imaginary. Or as Ellis (1962) has put it:

> If . . . people essentially become emotionally disturbed because they unthinkingly accept certain illogical premises or irrational ideas, then there is a good reason to believe that they can be somehow persuaded or taught to think more logically and rationally and thereby to undermine their own disturbances (p. 191).

The crucial question is how best to "persuade" or "teach" the client to label situations more rationally.

Other than the detailed and relatively explicit rationale provided by Ellis, comparatively little has been done to outline specific procedures for implementing the attitude change and relearning process. A typical strategy has been to verbally attack the client's irrational beliefs and cajole him into thinking more logically. But this approach, we suggest, may backfire in some cases. The research literature in social psychology has shown that certain individuals may actively resist change when coerced into changing their beliefs or behavior (Brehm, 1966; Davison, 1973). The practicing clinician with a knowledge of basic principles of behavior change and a good creative imagination can undoubtedly devise a number of ways for clients to learn to label situations more rationally. Although there is as yet no empirical evidence that singles out *the* best procedure, we offer the following guidelines that we have found useful in teaching clients to think more rationally, thereby reducing their emotional difficulties.

Presentation of Rationale

The basic assumptions underlying rational restructuring are explained to the client in nontechnical terms. Examples are offered to illustrate how our feelings can be affected by what we tell ourselves. The therapist can point out, for example, that there is nothing intrinsically anxiety-provoking about the size and shape of a gun being aimed at you, but the concern that it might hurt you does cause anxiety. If someone had never seen or heard of a gun before, his reaction to it would probably be one of curiosity rather than anxiety.

A more interpersonally meaningful example might then be offered. One that we have employed successfully is to describe two hypothetical individuals getting ready to attend the same discussion group. The first person is feeling calm about the prospect, and, in fact, is looking forward to the evening ahead. His thoughts about the situation may run as follows: "It should be an interesting discussion tonight. There'll probably be several people there that I don't know, which can give me the opportunity to make some new friends. There'll also be some people there I know and whom I like very much, so I'll be able to renew some friendships." The second person, by contrast, is nervous and fearful. His thoughts are, "I don't know how well I'll do tonight. There are going to be many people there I don't know, and I'm not sure if I will be able to say the right thing. I don't want to look foolish, especially since there will be many people there that I like." The clinician can then suggest that these different emotional reactions are due to the different self-statements.

Clearly we are unable to offer hard data to support the assumption that negative self-statements *always* precede and cause emotional upset. It may be that certain, or even all, anxieties are classically conditioned (Wolpe, 1958) and that self-statements are secondary to these fears. Our purposes here, however, are clinical and pragmatic, and it may be that *believing* that one's negative self-statements cause emotional turmoil can be useful in helping people change their feelings.

In describing and illustrating the basic rationale, it is often helpful for the therapist to point out that in many situations we may not *literally* "tell ourselves" things which lead to emotional upset. Because of the well-learned nature of our associations in many situations, we may have reached the point where the labeling process is quite automatic—as in the example with the gun.

The following transcript illustrates this initial step:

Client: My primary difficulty is that I become very uptight when I have to speak in front of a group of people. I guess it's just my own inferiority complex.

Therapist: [*I don't want to get sidetracked at this point by talking about that conceptualization of his problem. I'll just try to finesse it and make a smooth transition to something else.*] I don't know if I would call it an inferiority complex but I do believe that people can, in a sense, bring on their own upset and anxiety in certain kinds of situations. When you're in a particular situation, your anxiety is often not the result of the situation itself, but rather the way in which you *interpret* the situation—what you tell yourself about the situation. For example, look at this pen. Does this pen make you nervous?

Client: No.

Therapist: Why not?

Client: It's just an object. It's just a pen.

Therapist: It can't hurt you?

Client: No.

Therapist: If, instead, I were holding a gun or a knife, would that make you nervous?

Client: Yes.

Therapist: But a gun or a knife is also just an object. Unlike a pen, however, a gun or a knife *can* actually hurt you. It's really not the object that creates emotional upset in people, but rather what you *think* about the object. [*Hopefully, this Socratic-like dialogue will eventually bring him to the conclusion that self-statements can mediate emotional arousal.*] If you had never seen a gun or a knife, do you think you would be upset?

Client: Probably not.

Therapist: [*Now to move on to a more interpersonally relevant example, but not yet one that samples the presenting problem.*] Now this holds true for a number of other kinds of situations where emotional upset is caused by what a person tells himself about the situation. Take, for example, two people who are about to attend the same social gathering. Both of them may know exactly the same number of people at the party, but one person can be optimistic and relaxed about the situation, whereas the other one can be worried about how he will appear, and consequently very anxious. [*I'll try to get him to verbalize the basic assumption that attitude or perception is most important here.*] So, when these two people walk into the place where the party is given, are their emotional reactions at all associated with the physical arrangements at the party?

Client: No, obviously not.

Therapist: What determines their reactions, then?

Client: They obviously have different attitudes toward the party.

Therapist: Exactly, and their attitudes—the ways in which they approach the situation—greatly influence their emotional reactions.

As illustrated above, the therapist has been describing the significance of self-statements in a fairly general way, not yet relating the labeling to the client's particular problems. It is important to have the client agree to what has been described thus far before carrying the procedure any further. Applying this analysis to the client's own problems is likely to be considerably more complicated than the simple examples described above. The client's acceptance of the basic rationale will minimize complications as the procedure progresses.

Overview of Irrational Assumptions

Before analyzing the client's specific problem in rational terms, it is a good idea to present the various irrational assumptions to determine to what extent he concurs with these beliefs. Since the ideas outlined on pages 160–161 are stated in extreme form, it is not unusual for clients to disagree with most of them. Although the therapist himself can present these irrational beliefs for the client's evaluation, we have also found it helpful to ask him to read Ellis and Harper's (1962) *A Guide to Rational Living*, which offers a down-to-earth discussion of each of these commonly held irrational ideas, together with many illustrations of how each interferes with day-to-day living.

The primary objective at this point is to help the client recognize clearly that these beliefs are untenable. Although he may acknowledge that it would be *nice* if each of these expectations could be met, he should recognize that holding a belief that each of these *should* or *must* occur is bound to lead to disappointment and frustration. The world simply does not satisfy our demands all the time; much of our emotional turmoil is self-produced when we tell ourselves that a horrible state of affairs will result if certain of these expectations are not fulfilled. Rather than arguing with the client and trying to convince him how foolish he is for accepting any of these beliefs, it would be far more effective for the client *himself* to offer arguments to refute these expectations. The social psychological literature suggests that this method is more effective in creating attitude change (Brehm & Cohen, 1962).

The transcript presented earlier continues, this time reflecting how the therapist, by playing devil's advocate, gets the client to openly refute a particular irrational expectation.

Therapist: I would like to do something with you. I'm going to describe a certain attitude or belief to you, and I'd like you to assume for a moment that I actually hold this belief. What I would like you to do is to offer me as many reasons as you can why it may be irrational or unreasonable for me to hold on to such a belief. OK?

Client: All right.

Therapist: Assume that I believe the following: Everybody must approve of me, and if this doesn't happen, it means that I am really a worthless person. What do you think of that?

Client: I don't think it makes much sense.

Therapist: [*We're off to a relatively good start. A certain percentage of clients—fortunately a small percentage—will initially acknowledge that the belief does not seem irrational to them. But now he has to be more specific.*] But why doesn't it make much sense?

Client: You really can't expect that people are going to do that.

Therapist: (*Naively*) Why not?

Client: It just seems unreasonable for you to expect that they would.

Therapist: [*We don't seem to be getting anywhere. I can prompt him indirectly by being a bit more extreme in my belief, hopefully making counterarguments a bit more obvious.*] I feel that every single person that I run into during the course of the day is going to have to smile and say nice things to me. And if this doesn't happen, I really feel down.

Client: But the world is simply not set up that way. There may be people who don't react to you positively because of things that are going on with themselves.

Therapist: [*That's a good reason, but it needs some elaboration.*] What other reasons could there be? I tend to think that everything is somehow caused by me.

Client: But that's ridiculous. It's possible that someone you meet may have had a bad night's sleep, or may have had an argument with his wife, and is in no mood to deal with you.

Therapist: [*I'll reinforce him by accepting this explanation, but then present another example of my irrationality.*] So you think that some of the day-to-day variations in the way people react to me can be due to things completely apart from my own adequacy?

Client: Of course.

Therapist: OK, that certainly is a possibility. But what about when someone is really disapproving of *me*? For example, a close friend may disagree with something I say. Now in that case, I usually feel that I am wrong, and I must be worthless for him to have disagreed with me.

Client: But you can't expect him to agree with everything you say.

Therapist: Why not?

Client: If you did, you would really be dishonest.

Therapist: But I feel that it is more important for me to get everyone to approve of me and like everything I say and do, than it is for me to really express the way I feel. In fact, I sometimes feel like a weather vane, shifting whichever way the wind might be blowing.

Client: But that's ridiculous! What happens to *you* as a person?

Therapist: [*He seems fairly strong on this point, so I think I'll back off a little.*] That seems to be a big problem with me; I often don't know who I am as a person. I seem to be so concerned about defining my own worth in terms of what everyone else's reactions are toward me. But how else can I think?

Client: Maybe you should consider how *you yourself* feel about certain things you do. Provided you're not really hurting anybody else, if you feel that what you are doing is right, perhaps you should be satisfied with that and realize that not everyone is going to agree.

Therapist: [*I'm satisfied that he sees the irrationality in that belief.*] That seems to make some sense. If I can only really accept it.

Client: You'll have to, because the other way is not at all reasonable.

Therapist: (*Stepping out of role*) OK. You seem to have a very good perspective on the rationality of that belief. Why don't we move on to another notion?

In most cases, it probably would not be necessary to systematically review all of the eleven irrational ideas, since many of them may not be at all relevant to a particular client's problems. Although there is no hard and fast rule about which irrational idea is relevant to which target behavior, we have found the first two notions— "Everybody must love me," and "I must be perfect in everything I do—" to be appropriate for a large percentage of clients. In the final analysis, however, the therapist must use his own clinical judgment in deciding which of these irrational ideas are relevant.

Analysis of Client's Problems in Rational Terms

The client thus far presumably agrees with the assumption that emotional upset is mediated by internal sentences—however automatic—and that there are certain specific irrational beliefs that may be responsible for creating this upset. At this point, the client should focus on his *own* problems and try to determine what he may be telling himself when he experiences emotional upset. A review of specific upsetting situations can be most useful at this point.

An analysis of the irrationality of the client's self-statements may be approached at two levels: (1) the *likelihood* that the client is correctly interpreting the situation, and (2) the *ultimate implications* of the way the client has labeled the event. Consider the male client who reacts with disproportionate emotional upset when he is unsuccessful in obtaining a date with a particular woman. The most readily accessible interpretation of this situation that is probably mediating his upset may be: "She does not like me." The extent to which this belief is rational may be examined by discussing any other possible reason which might have determined her refusal (e.g., other commitments, timing of the request for a date). The second-level analysis of the rationality of his attitude toward this refusal can take the following form: "Let's assume for a moment that she really doesn't like you. Why should this make you so upset? I wonder whether or not there may be certain other things you are implicitly telling yourself about her not liking you?" This discussion may lead the client to recognize that his overreaction in this situation is being mediated by one or more of the irrational beliefs that he has already personally disavowed (e.g., "Everybody must love me").

There are times when a client may insist that he is not telling himself anything while in an anxiety-provoking situation. At this point, one can return to the example given earlier about a gun being pointed at the client, whereby the reaction is immediate and the mediating self-statements are overlearned and automatic. Although some clients are unable to report what they may be telling themselves while actually in a situation, they frequently have ruminative concerns either before or after the event. Even if a client has difficulty acknowledging the existence of any irrational self-statements, he may be willing to accept the interpretation that, in light of his emotional overreaction to a particular situation, it is *as if* he did believe something catastrophic might occur.

It is not uncommon at this stage for a client to react as follows: "I can accept everything you say, and I'll agree that I am causing my own upset in many of these situations. The thing is, I don't know how I can change!" The client is now ready for the next phase of rational restructuring.

Teaching the Client to Modify His Internal Sentences

The therapist should acknowledge that the client's knowledge alone may be insufficient to produce any real change. What is needed is for him to apply what he knows in theory. To teach the client this skill, the therapist may begin by describing a typical learning sequence. When feeling upset, the client will stop and attempt to ferret out what he is telling himself about the situation that may be responsible for this upset. In essence, the client's emotional reaction now acts as a *signal* or *cue* to stop and think, "What am I telling myself that may be irrational?" Any thought or statement including "should" or "must" might also be a cue, for these words are likely to indicate irrational demands. By breaking up what heretofore might have been an automatic reaction, the client now becomes more aware of his inappropriate self-statement, and can proceed to reevaluate this belief more rationally. Then the client replaces the irrational self-statement with a more realistic appraisal of the situation, noting any subsequent decrement in emotional upset. The client should be told that this procedure may be deliberate and tedious at first. With practice, however, he can expect to find each step easier to carry out, with the latter portions of the chain moving forward in time. Clients have reported that what previously was an anxiety-provoking situation eventually is deliberately approached with a more realistic attitude, and the initial upset is thereby eliminated. Further, as the learning process continues, the rational self-statements that the client uses can be expected to become less deliberate and more automatic.

There are a number of aids that may be used in implementing the relearning process—including imaginal presentation of emotionally arousing situations, overt behavior rehearsal, *in vivo* homework assignments, modeling, group interaction, and bibliographic material.

Imaginal Presentation

As in systematic desensitization, the client's real-life problem situations may be replicated in imagery within the consultation room, thereby providing the client with the opportunity to reevaluate rationally any self-statements which mediate his emotional upset. In carrying out *systematic rational restructuring* (Goldfried, Decenteceo, & Weinberg, 1974), a hierarchy of increasingly difficult situations is constructed, with successful coping at one level determining progression to the next, more difficult, situation. In many respects, systematic rational restructuring parallels the self-control variation of systematic desensitization (Goldfried, 1971) outlined in Chapter 6, except that rational reevaluation replaces relaxation as the active coping skill.

In using an imaginal presentation of hierarchy items, many of the points we have made in Chapter 6 on systematic desensitization are relevant here as well. Since the client's rational reevaluation involves an active coping attempt on his part, the client should be instructed to "stay in the situation" until he has successfully reduced his upset. If the reaction is one of anxiety, then the method of classifying levels of anxiety may be employed (see page 87). Similar methods of classifying levels of upset may be used with other emotional reactions, such as depression and anger.

As with systematic desensitization, the client can be instructed to imagine that he is in a situation while it is described by the therapist. He is then told to note how anxious (depressed, angry) he feels. If he finds that his emotional reaction is above a certain level (e.g., 25), he is to stop and think, "What am I telling myself that is making me upset?" The client then "thinks aloud" and attempts to determine the irrational ideas producing his reaction. The therapist's role is to prompt the client in such attempts to reevaluate the situation in more rational terms. Following this rational reevaluation, the client can note his presumably decreased anxiety (depression, anger) level.

Before actually implementing this rational restructuring technique, the therapist can serve as a model, demonstrating exactly how it is done. The item at the bottom of the hierarchy may be used for this purpose. With anxiety in public speaking situations, for example, the scene may involve the client sitting at his desk two weeks before giving his speech, preparing some notes. The therapist can then think aloud along the following lines:

> I'm sitting here, looking over some of my notes, and I feel myself getting tense. I'm up to a level of about 35. So I stop what I'm doing and think, "What must I be telling myself that is creating this anxiety?" Well, I think I'm worried that I won't do a good job in giving the talk. But why does that upset me? People will probably react negatively to me. But why does that upset me? Maybe they'll think badly of me and perhaps even make fun of me. But wait a minute. That's a pretty stupid idea. It's unlikely that people are going to laugh at me, or really think that badly of me on the basis of one speech. After all, I'm not a professional speaker. Even if they did think badly of me—which is probably just an outside chance—it really wouldn't be all that terrible. I would still be me. I still have other things that I can do fairly well. In thinking about the situation a little bit more rationally, it doesn't seem to upset me so much. I don't feel so nervous as I did before; perhaps now I'm only at a level of about 20.

Even when the therapist clearly spells out the procedure and models the way it may be implemented, some clients have initial difficulty in following through as directed. Quite often, considerable clinical sensitivity is required to assist a client in ferreting out the irrational beliefs that may be operating, thus leading him to a more rational reevaluation. The following transcript illustrates this.

Therapist: I'm going to ask you to imagine yourself in a given situation, and to tell me how nervous you may feel. I'd then like you to think aloud about what you might be telling yourself that is creating this anxiety, and then go about trying to put your expectations into a more realistic perspective. From time to time, I will make certain comments, and I'd like you to treat these comments as if they were your own thoughts. OK?

Client: All right.

Therapist: I'd like you to close your eyes now and imagine yourself in the following situation: You are sitting on stage in the auditorium, together with the other school board members. It's a few minutes before you have to get up and give your report to the people in the audience. Between 0 and 100 percent tension, tell me how nervous you feel.

Client: About 50.

Therapist: [*Now to get into his head.*] So I'm feeling fairly tense. Let me think. What might I be telling myself that's making me upset?

Client: I'm nervous about reading my report in front of all these people.

Therapist: But why does that bother me?

Client: Well, I don't know if I'm going to come across all right. . . .

Therapist: [*He seems to be having trouble. More prompting on my part may be needed than I originally anticipated.*] But why should that upset me? That upsets me because . . .

Client: . . . because I want to make a good impression.

Therapist: And if I don't . . .

Client: . . . well, I don't know. I don't want people to think that I'm incompetent. I guess I'm afraid that I'll lose the respect of the people who thought I knew what I was doing.

Therapist: [*He seems to be getting closer.*] But why should that make me so upset?

Client: I don't know. I guess it shouldn't. Maybe I'm being *overly* concerned about other people's reactions to me.

Therapist: How might I be overly concerned?

Client: I think this may be one of those situations where I have to please everybody, and there are an awful lot of people in the audience. Chances are I'm not going to get everybody's approval, and maybe that's upsetting me. I want everyone to think I'm doing a good job.

Therapist: Now let me think for a moment to see how rational that is.

Client: To begin with, I don't think it really is likely that I'm going to completely blow it. After all, I have prepared in advance, and have thought through what I want to say fairly clearly. I think I may be reacting as if I already have failed, even though it's very unlikely that I will.

Therapist: And even if I did mess up, how bad would that be?

Client: Well, I guess that really wouldn't be so terrible after all.

Therapist: [*I don't believe him for one moment. There is a definite hollow ring to his voice. He arrived at that conclusion much too quickly and presents it without much conviction.*] I say I don't think it'll upset me, but I don't really believe that.

Client: That's true. I would be upset if I failed. But actually, I really shouldn't be looking at this situation as being a failure.

Therapist: What would be a better way for me to look at the situation?

Client: Well, it's certainly not a do-or-die kind of thing. It's only a ridiculous committee report. A lot of the people in the audience know who I am and what I'm capable of doing. And even if I don't give a sterling performance, I don't think they're going to change their opinion of me on the basis of a five-minute presentation.

Therapist: But what if some of them do?

Client: Even if some of them do think differently of me, that doesn't mean that I *would* be different. I would still be me no matter what they thought. It's ridiculous of me to base my self-worth on what other people think.

Therapist: [*I think he's come around as much as he can. We can terminate this scene now.*] With this new attitude toward the situation, how do you feel in percentage of anxiety?

Client: Oh, about 25 percent.

Therapist: OK, let's talk a little about some of the thoughts you had during that situation before trying it again.

In the above transcript, the therapist assumes a fairly active role in the rational restructuring procedure. In any given instance, the therapist must use his clinical judgment to determine just how active a role to play. Once the client appears to be capable of identifying certain irrational beliefs and is able to put them into more reasonable perspective, the therapist gradually fades the prompts he offers, thereby allowing the client to follow through more autonomously with the reevaluation procedure.

It may happen that the emotional upset will *not* diminish after a period of rational reevaluation. This situation can be handled in a number of ways. One procedure would be to move down to a less difficult item on the hierarchy. Another approach might be to prolong the exposure time, instructing the client to continue the reevaluation process. Sometimes a client may also require relaxation training. It might also be appropriate to review with the client the specific irrational self-statements that he has been attempting to reevaluate, for they might not be the ones which are mediating the upset. Finally, the therapist should also consider the possibility that his assessment has been inaccurate, and that there are, in fact, no internal sentences which are functionally tied to this particular client's problem.

Behavior Rehearsal

In carrying out rational restructuring via *overt* behavior rehearsal, the guidelines outlined in Chapter 7 may be followed, except that hierarchy items should be constructed so that they lend themselves to enactment in the consultation room. The same procedure described for imaginal presentation of items (e.g., having the client think aloud, using therapeutic prompts) can be employed here as well.

In Vivo Assignments

In addition to practice during consultation sessions, the client should be encouraged to utilize this same procedure *in vivo* whenever he experiences emotional upset. The format provided on page 175 can be used to keep a record of his success in carrying out the homework assignments. Because of the relatively unsystematic

RECORD OF ATTEMPTS TO USE RATIONAL REEVALUATION IN OVERCOMING ANXIETY

Description of Situation	Initial Anxiety Level (0 to 100)	Irrational Thoughts	Rational Reevaluation	Subsequent Anxiety Level (0 to 100)

occurrence of situations in which he is to utilize this rational reevaluation *in vivo*, the client should be cautioned that he cannot expect to be successful in all of his attempts. Even if he is not initially successful, however, these *in vivo* trials will serve the function of providing him with the set to cope.

We have often found it appropriate to utilize relaxation procedures along with the client's attempt at rational restructuring, particularly with a client who is generally anxious or one who is attempting to rationally restructure his internal sentences in situations eliciting high levels of anxiety. Ample experimental evidence suggests the difficulties people typically have in thinking clearly when experiencing high levels of anxiety (Gaudry & Spielberger, 1971; Lazarus, 1966; Spielberger, 1966). Thus, once the client has been thoroughly trained in relaxation, he is instructed to use this relaxation skill to calm himself, and then to examine rationally any unrealistic evaluations that may have created the initial emotional upset. Self-relaxation is interspersed between the client's recognition that he is experiencing upset and the ferreting out of his irrational beliefs. This may be done in conjunction with imaginal rehearsal, as well as during *in vivo* homework assignments.

Modeling

In addition to demonstrating to the client the exact process of rational reevaluation, the therapist also presumably serves as a model—at least implicitly—when he conveys his belief that there are more appropriate ways to view the world. Considering the evidence indicating that modeling procedures are an effective way to modify someone's standards for self-evaluation (Bandura & Kupers, 1964; Liebert & Allen, 1967; Mischel & Liebert, 1966), or what someone tells himself about a situation (Meichenbaum, 1971), it would seem appropriate for the therapist to make explicit use of modeling procedures in the implementation of rational restructuring. The therapist might relate any of his own personal experiences that are likely to be beneficial therapeutically. For example, to a forty-five-year-old male executive who tended to become unduly anxious and angry when things did not go according to plan, one of us related a potentially upsetting experience he himself had recently had. The therapist and his family were returning from vacation when they were informed at the airport that their flight would probably be delayed for several hours. The airport waiting room was noisy and uncomfortable, and many of the inconvenienced passengers were becoming increasingly upset. After determining that no alternate arrangements could be made, the therapist endeavored to maintain a sense of calm by viewing this situation in a realistic perspective. In describing this situation to the client, the therapist emphasized his initial upset—to minimize the discrepancy between therapist and client, and also to demonstrate how this upset might serve as a cue for coping—and then related exactly what he told himself in reevaluating the situation more rationally. Although the therapist described his personal experience only to demonstrate how rational reevaluation might be used, the client happened to find himself in a similar situation a few weeks later. In marked contrast to what previously would have occurred, the client used rational reevaluation to maintain a sense of calm throughout the entire ordeal. An additional reinforcement was his traveling companion's admiration of the client's ability to cope with the frustrating situation!

Group Settings

Rational restructuring can also be carried out in group settings, where modeling effects may be expected as other group members report their success experiences (Goldfried & Goldfried, 1975).

Further, a group setting is convenient for utilizing behavior rehearsal procedures, particularly with clients experiencing social-evaluative anxiety.

Bibliotherapy

One final procedure to which many clients respond favorably is bibliotherapy. As already mentioned, the book we find to be most helpful is Ellis and Harper's *A Guide to Rational Living* (1962), which describes and illustrates how unrealistic thinking leads to a wide variety of problem behaviors. More often than not, clients report finding case illustrations relevant to themselves in this book. A further advantage is that reading this inexpensive paperback can save considerable therapeutic time.[1]

Applications of Rational Restructuring

Considering the basic assumptions underlying rational restructuring, it would seem to be applicable to many forms of maladaptive affect (e.g., anxiety, depression, anger). Ellis (1962) has presented case reports in which rational-emotive therapy was successful with problems such as frigidity, impotence, marital difficulties, and psychopathy. Controlled experimental evidence of the procedure's efficacy involves such social-evaluative targets as speech anxiety (Karst & Trexler, 1970; Meichenbaum et al., 1971; Trexler & Karst, 1972), test anxiety (Meichenbaum, 1972), and interpersonal anxiety (DiLoreto, 1971; Kanter, 1975).

We have also found rational restructuring to be particularly useful when the client's problems seem to be functionally tied to his unrealistically high criteria for self-reinforcement. Although a person may be functioning at an objectively competent level, he may be upset because he falls short of the high expectations he holds for himself. Bandura (1969) has written extensively on this issue, and suggests the following:

> Undoubtedly many competent people do experience a great deal of self-generated distress and many self-imposed constraints as the result of adherence to ill-advised or excessively high standards of self-reinforcement. To the extent that a change agent differentially

---

[1] A revision of this guide has recently been published by Prentice-Hall (1975). Among other things, Ellis and Harper make even clearer their emphasis on integrating cognitive change procedures within the kind of broad-based behavior therapy described in this book.

reinforces realistic standard-setting behavior and elicits emulation of more lenient self-evaluative standards as conveyed through his comments and actions, the client's habitual self-attitudes are likely to undergo change (p. 614).

In addition to being a primary focus in therapy, rational restructuring may help modify a client's unrealistically high standards when they interfere with the implementation of other behavior change procedures. For example, a client in the process of being desensitized may feel that he *should* be progressing faster than he is, and consequently may become discouraged and even reluctant to continue. In such instances, rational restructuring may be the only way to salvage the therapist's attempt to modify some other problematic aspect of the client's behavior.

Although the absence of assertive behavior has been typically construed within the behavior therapy literature as a reflection of a behavior deficit (i.e., the appropriate behaviors do not exist within the individual's response repertoire), we have observed clinically that clients frequently show dramatic increases in assertive behavior following rational restructuring. Specifically, clients may apply rational restructuring in situations where they have previously been unassertive. In such cases, the clients' assertiveness was apparently inhibited by unrealistic concerns about possible reactions of others (e.g., not receiving approval), and not by an inability to emit the assertive response.

It is frequently difficult for the therapist to know when rational restructuring is likely to be the most appropriate treatment to use, particularly when the problem involves anxiety. A useful theoretical guideline has been suggested by Bandura (1969), who notes:

> The overall evidence would seem to indicate that emotional behavior may be controlled by two different stimulus sources. One is the emotional arousal self-generated by symbolic activities in the form of emotion-provoking thoughts about frightening or pleasurable events. The second is the response evoked directly by conditioned aversive stimuli. The former component would be readily susceptible to extinction through cognitive restructuring of probable response consequences, whereas elimination of the latter component may require repeated nonreinforced exposure to threatening events either directly or vicariously (p. 364).

The following case study illustrates a situation where rational restructuring was found to be more useful than systematic desensitization.

Case Illustration

The client was a twenty-seven-year-old college student whose primary problem was test anxiety; he was also anxious in other academic evaluative situations. He had previously been enrolled in three other colleges, but in each instance had dropped out after only a semester or two. The client had been seen by another behavior therapist, who attempted to alleviate the client's evaluative anxiety using systematic desensitization. Upon returning to college for the fourth time, however, the client found his problems to persist; it was at this point that he contacted the present therapist.

Knowing beforehand the client's presenting problems, the therapist anticipated that he would appear to be shy and retiring; this was not at all the case. The client was a tall, well-built, good-looking young man, who behaved in an assertive and self-confident way during the initial therapeutic contact. He related his current difficulties in academic situations, reporting that his anxiety in the classroom had become so severe that he was unable to tell one instructor his name when asked. Although desensitization had appeared to be successful at the termination of his previous treatment (i.e., he was eventually able to visualize scenes without experiencing anxiety), for some unknown reason, the effects of treatment did not continue over time. Perhaps the hierarchy used was not relevant to the current academic situation, or maybe his not being in school at the time of the desensitization contributed to minimal carry-over. At any rate, the new therapist began by drawing up a revised hierarchy.

Before systematic desensitization could be implemented, however, a number of incidents suggested that rational restructuring might be preferable. There were times when the client reported the *complete absence* of anxiety in testing situations. An example of this occurred when one instructor presented the class with a surprise quiz, for which no one was prepared, including the client. Although his performance on this quiz counted toward his final grade, he took a very casual and relaxed attitude toward it; as far as he was concerned, the quiz "didn't count." The client also related an example where he had no difficulty participating verbally in class. This occurred during a flu epidemic; because the client had been out sick for a while, the instructor inquired about his health prior to the beginning of class. The client consequently approached this class with the feeling that the instructor was concerned about his welfare and therefore must like him.

The client reported being very anxious as he sat and studied for his exams; although *in vivo* relaxation was helpful in calming him down, the benefits were short-lived. When asked to specify exactly how he went about studying for his exams, the client indicated that he typically used six or seven textbooks other than the one assigned for the particular course. In fact, because he felt that the assigned text was too basic, he never bothered to use it in his studying! As his studying progressed, the client would become increasingly upset because he was not "completely absorbing" all the material spread out in front of him; this prompted him to study through the night and up until the time of the exam. It became readily apparent that at the core of the client's evaluative anxiety were the unrealistically high standards he set for his own performance.

The therapeutic approach utilized in this case followed many of the procedures outlined above. The primary focus was to have the client recognize that he was approaching his current situation in a most unrealistic way; this was causing him to become anxious and engage in unrealistic behavior, which only complicated matters further. As therapy progressed, the client began to adjust his standards in light of the realistic expectations associated with his current situation, and he also developed a more appropriate approach to studying for exams. He obtained a B average by the end of the academic year, and agreed to register for a lighter course load during the following year. The client was seen occasionally during his final year in college, and reported feeling under less pressure academically than ever before. Despite his more easygoing attitude toward academic work, he eventually graduated from college with honors.

In a follow-up interview with the client one year after graduation, he indicated that it was unquestionably the training he had received in rational restructuring that contributed toward his anxiety reduction. Although he had been relatively adept at self-relaxation, it was only temporarily beneficial because he was generating constant anxiety with his unrealistic self-statements. With such clients, rational restructuring, as opposed to relaxation training or systematic desensitization, would seem to be the treatment of choice.

● ATTRIBUTION

An interesting development in recent years is the attempt to apply findings from experimental social psychology to therapeutic behavior change. One such effort has been within an area that is known as "attribution theory" (Davison & Valins, 1969; Valins & Nisbett, 1971). Generally speaking, this theory—or better, group of loosely related hypotheses—addresses itself to the possible importance that certain beliefs have in behavior change and maintenance. For example, Nisbett and Schachter (1966) showed that normal human subjects would tolerate more electric shock if they believed that part of the arousal they experienced was due to a pill they had ingested rather than to the shock itself. In a related study, Valins and Ray (1967) demonstrated that snake phobic subjects could be better induced to approach snakes if they could be deceived into believing that they were not aroused emotionally when viewing slides of snakes.

As we have pointed out elsewhere (Davison & Wilson, 1973b; Davison, Tsujimoto, & Glaros, 1973; Goldfried & Merbaum, 1973), however, there is serious question about the *clinical* utility of such findings. This point was originally brought up by Nisbett and Schachter themselves when they stated that:

> Since we would not expect that an individual undergoing *extreme* pain, fear or rage could easily be persuaded to attribute the accompanying physiological arousal to an artificial source, there should be limits placed on the generality of these notions (1966, p. 228).

Furthermore, there have been several unsuccessful attempts to replicate the original Valins and Ray findings (Suchinsky & Bootzin, 1970; Kent, Wilson, & Nelson, 1972; Rosen, Rosen & Reid, 1972). For these reasons, we are reluctant to attach as much validity to attribution as we would to some of the other concepts and procedures reviewed in this chapter. It would, however, be premature to discount entirely the clinical utility of attribution in behavior therapy.

Empirical Support

The literature in clinical psychopharmacology suggests that people tend to regress to pretreatment levels of functioning after discontinuing psychoactive drugs such as tranquilizers (Kamano, 1966). In an analog study focusing on this problem, Davison and Valins (1969) led subjects to believe that their ability to withstand uncomfortable electric shocks had been markedly increased by the ingestion of a "fast-acting vitamin compound." In fact, the amperage of the shocks delivered after the "drug" had been taken was surreptitiously reduced. Half the subjects were then told that they had received a placebo, while the remainder continued to believe that a drug had effected their apparent improvement in shock-taking. As predicted, subjects who had been disabused of the cognition that the drug was responsible for their improvement tolerated more shocks afterwards than those who were led to believe that the drug had accounted for the change.

This attribution effect has been carried further with a group of insomniacs (Davison, Tsujimoto, & Glaros, 1973). In this experiment, subjects were presented with a treatment package composed of chloral hydrate (1000 milligrams) and self-produced relaxation instructions, as well as scheduling procedures (i.e., setting specific times to settle down to sleep). Following treatment, half of the subjects were told that they had received an optimal dose of the drug, while the others were informed that the dosage they had received was too weak to have been responsible for any improvement. All subjects were instructed to discontinue the drug but to continue with the relaxation and the scheduling procedures during the posttreatment week. As in the Davison and Valins study, those who could not atrribute their changes to the drug better maintained their therapeutic gains.

Taken together these two experiments suggest that belief in the efficacy of one's own efforts can contribute to the maintenance of treatment gains. However, in their discussion of the results of the insomnia study, Davison and his colleagues point out that it would be unwise to overgeneralize from these experimental findings, as the absolute improvement could not be regarded as clinically significant. Furthermore, within this paradigm, the therapist is faced with the dilemma of creating a significant treatment effect that is vague enough to permit the clinician later on to persuade his client that he had played the major role in his improvement.

Keeping in mind the tentativeness of these findings, we offer below some possible applications. Some of what we will suggest is probably part of the armamentarium of many behavior therapists, although it is perhaps not applied in a systematic or deliberate fashion. What follows, then, might best be viewed as a heuristic for clinical investigation.

Applications of Attribution

Assessment Therapy

As we suggested in Chapter 2, one of the ways behavioral assessment differs from traditional assessment procedures is in its close relationship to therapeutic intervention. We have found clinically that many clients achieve some comfort when the assessment conveys the idea that their problems are due to learning experiences rather than to presumed "mental illness," and also when they learn that there is potential for gaining some control over their behavior.

A case example might illustrate this notion. Davison (1968) treated a client complaining of a reliance on sadistic fantasies for sexual gratification. Since age eleven, he had derived sexual gratification only from masturbating to fantasies of torturing young women. Prior to any specific behavior therapy intervention, the therapist attempted to alleviate the client's concern about the problem itself by describing unusual experiences that can be induced in normal human beings by various psychological manipulations, such as sensory deprivation. He further suggested that the working assumption in the therapy would be that the client's own peculiar reliance on sadistic fantasy had come about in some kind of normal, social learning fashion, and it would be approached in a manner consistent with this construction of the problem. Thus, rather than viewing his difficulty as a sign of unconscious conflicts, the client was able to reconstrue his problem in less frightening terms and thereby achieve some significant relief in the very first session: "Boy, am I glad to hear *that!*"

The suggestion is, then, that behavior therapists may have within their very orientation and diagnostic practices a potentially useful therapeutic tool, helpful in alleviating undue concern on the part of the client about the seriousness of his difficulties. At the same time, it must be emphasized that no claims are made about the validity of the particular social learning conceptualization, for it may in fact be that a given problem is due not to social learning but rather to some kind of organic disease. Knowledge of the etiology of human psychopathology is incomplete (Davison & Neale, 1974).

Attribution of Physical Symptoms

We have treated several clients for fear of heart attack. Typically a client is referred by a physician for therapy after complaining of heart palpitations and shortness of breath that have no organic basis. Often the individual is excessively anxious about certain situations, experiences physical symptoms that are similar to those occurring during a coronary, and interprets these tension reactions as signs of an impending heart attack. Along attributional lines, a therapist may be able to reconstrue these symptoms for the client and to embark on some kind of anxiety-reduction program to further strengthen the nonorganic hypothesis. Thus, one of our clients was taught simply to relax when anxious; this intervention reduced the palpitations and thereby the fear of heart attack.

Another example is seen in a case report by Davison (1966) in which a client diagnosed as paranoid schizophrenic was enabled to reconstrue "pressure points" above his forehead in naturalistic terms, thereby removing the paranoid flavor of his ideations and verbalizations. This man had come to believe that spirits were influencing him by applying pressure on his right temple. The therapist suggested to the client that these sensations might be a part of an anxiety reaction to specific situations involving decision making. A regimen of *in vivo* desensitization aimed at reducing the particular anxiety reactions was employed. As the client saw himself able to control his tensions, that is, the "pressure points," he changed his interpretations of these sensations, attributing the feelings to an anxiety reaction rather than to external spirits. This reinterpretation not only had the advantage of being amenable to behavior therapy, but also helped the client stop behaving in a paranoid way, at least for a short time.

Self-Control Attribution

The attribution literature reviewed earlier suggests that if a client views himself as largely responsible for his improvement in therapy, he is more likely to maintain these gains. This consideration is particularly important in operant conditioning programs (see Chapter 10), where the difficulties in generalization and maintenance present a challenge to behavior therapy. Presumably, people whose behavior is shaped by external reinforcers might attribute the treatment changes only to this external influence and therefore not generalize their changed behaviors to the posttreatment or follow-up situations. Perhaps therapists should be sensitive to such attributions and communicate to their clients following treatment-produced change that their new behaviors are due less to external reinforcements than to their own efforts to change.

The client's perception of his role can be taken into account in other aspects of therapy. For example, with relaxation training, we typically tell the client that our contribution has been that of a guide or teacher, whereas the important control over muscle tensions has been due to the client's own efforts. When employing psychoactive drugs, the clinician can minimize the importance of the drug per se by emphasizing the client's attempts at coping. Finally, most therapists, at the end of a successful treatment program, have to decide how they will respond to the gratitude expressed by clients. While it no doubt helps one's ego to believe he has been the important factor in somebody's improvement, it nonetheless may be better if a therapist takes *little* credit for what has happened, and focuses instead on the client's important contributions to the therapeutic gains.

● SUMMARY

This chapter describes some of the ways cognitive factors may play an important role in the control and modification of behavior. One use of cognitive relabeling is in those instances where a client's emotional reactions are mediated by automatic, irrational self-statements. Using Ellis' rational-emotive therapy as a point of departure, we have placed rational restructuring more within a learning framework, and have systematized procedures for modifying what essentially are well-learned, but maladaptive, "sets". A case illustration is provided, in which rational restructuring proved to be more successful in anxiety reduction than was systematic desensitization. Another use of cognitive relabeling focuses on how an individual explains his own emotional reactions or overt behaviors, and even the behavior change process. Some of the clinical applications of attribution theory are discussed.

Chapter

Problem Solving

Because of the complex and ever-changing nature of our society, people continually find themselves confronted with challenging problems. Depending on the complexity of the situation and the possible negative consequences of inadequate coping, these problems may be trivial or crucial. Thus, ranging from such minor dilemmas as trying to decide what shoes to wear in the morning, to more significant issues, such as dealing with an unreasonable employer or a troubled spouse, our daily lives are replete with situational problems that we must solve in order to function effectively.

Obviously, people differ greatly in how they can handle problems, no matter what their degree of complexity or seriousness. Much of what we view clinically as "abnormal behavior" or "emotional disturbance" may be more usefully construed as *ineffective behavior* with its negative consequences, such as anxiety, depression, and the creation of secondary problems. A problem-solving approach can prove to be a useful means of dealing with many situational challenges.(As used in the present context, *problem solving* is defined as a behavioral process, whether overt or cognitive, which (1) provides a variety of potentially effective responses to the problem situation, and (2) increases the likelihood of selecting the most effective response from among these various alternatives.)

The relevance of problem solving to therapy is based on two assumptions: (1) ineffectiveness in coping with problem situations, with its personal and social consequences, often results in emotional or behavioral disorders requiring psychological treatment; and (2) a person's general effectiveness may be facilitated by training in general skills that would allow him to deal independently with the challenges of day-to-day living.

In many respects, problem-solving training may be viewed as helping the individual develop a "learning set" (Harlow, 1949), thus increasing the likelihood of coping effectively in a wide range of situations. In this context, problem-solving training may be thought of as a form of self-control or independence training. The major difference is that in problem solving the essential aspects of the technique (i.e., the problem-solving procedures) are performed without prior awareness of the most effective response, whereas in the typical self-control procedure, the response to be controlled is selected in advance (Goldfried & Merbaum, 1973). The major objective in problem solving is to *identify* the most effective alternative, which may then be followed by other self-control operations to stimulate and maintain performance of the selected course of action. Thus, problem solving becomes a crucial initial phase in a more general self-control process, often described by such terms as "independence," "competence," and "self-reliance."

● THEORY AND RESEARCH

Although research discloses wide differences among individuals in how they solve problems, there is a remarkable degree of agreement among various theorists and investigators about the operations involved in effective problem solving (D'Zurilla & Goldfried, 1971). The following five stages represent a consensus view: (1) general orientation, (2) problem definition and formulation, (3) generation of alternatives, (4) decision making, and (5) verification.

By specifying stages of problem solving, we do not imply that this is exactly the way problem solving is, or should be, carried out in real life. A person may move back and forth from one stage to another—for example, he may be working on decision making and then go back to problem definition for more information before making his decision. Moreover, with complex problems, one may be working simultaneously on several subproblems, each at a different stage of development. The following discussion should be viewed *not* as a description of how problem solving usually takes place, but instead as a heuristic for organizing therapeutic procedures.

General Orientation

It has long been recognized that an individual's orientation to a situation can greatly influence the way he will respond. An orientation that encourages independent problem-solving behavior includes the set or attitude to (1) assume that problem situations constitute a normal part of life, and recognize the possibility that one can cope with many of these situations; (2) identify problem situations when they occur; and (3) inhibit the tendency to respond to one's first impulse.

To the extent that an individual anticipates being able to cope independently with his problems, even though no appropriate course of action may be immediately apparent, there is greater likelihood that he will be successful in finding an adequate solution (Bloom & Broder, 1950). Similarly, research findings indicate that an individual's expectation of being able to control his environment can greatly increase the likelihood that he will in fact attempt to cope with difficulties when they do occur (Lefcourt, 1966; Rotter, 1966). The overriding importance of feeling in control has been demonstrated in a host of experiments (Geer, Davison, & Gatchel, 1970; Glass & Singer, 1972).

Even if one is optimistic about his ability to handle situations effectively, it may not always be easy to *identify* problems when they arise. The usual process of problem recognition has been vividly described by Miller, Galanter, and Pribram (1960):

> In ordinary affairs we usually muddle ahead, doing what is habitual and customary, being slightly puzzled when it sometimes fails to give the intended outcome, but not stopping to worry much about the failures because there are too many other things still to do. Then circumstances conspire against us and we find ourselves caught failing where we must succeed—where we cannot withdraw from the field, or lower our self-imposed standards, or ask for help, or throw a tantrum. Then we may begin to suspect that we face a problem (p. 171).

As the quote implies, one of the most important identifying features of problem situations rests within the individual's emotional reaction itself. Rather than dwelling on this upset, the emotional reaction may be viewed constructively as a *cue* to shift one's attention to the problem situation which may be producing it.

Along with being able to identify problems as they occur, it is important to maintain an inhibitory set prior to any overt response (Dewey, 1910; Dollard & Miller, 1950; Osborn, 1963; Parnes, 1967; Simon, 1957). Findings by Bloom and Broder (1950) indicate that less successful problem solvers tend to be impulsive and quick to give up if a solution is not immediately apparent. Similarly, Dollard and Miller (1950) maintain that the first step in all but the most simple types of reasoning is to "stop and think." They point out that if a person responds immediately when confronted with a problem, there may not be sufficient time for those cue-producing (i.e., cognitive) responses to occur that could help him select an effective course of action.

Although important in successful problem solving, this general orientation or set represents but a small part of the entire process. The more central stages of the problem-solving process are described below.

Problem Definition and Formulation

Unlike problem solving in the laboratory setting, most problem situations in the real world are "messy"—that is, ambiguous and lacking in necessary facts and information. Thus, in the real-life setting, the person must (1) *define* all aspects of the situation operationally, and (2) *formulate* or classify elements appropriately.

According to Skinner (1953), an important advantage of *defining* a problem in operational terms is that it points up the crucial stimuli that might increase the availability of an effective response. By stating a problem concretely, the individual forces himself to make relevant what may have seemed irrelevant at first glance. The importance of *formulating* issues has been stressed by Gagné (1959) and Mowrer (1960), who argue that the individual in a problem-solving situation is *not* responding directly to external stimuli, but rather to mediational cues. For example, a problem situation may be formulated as a conflict between a goal and some obstacle standing in the way of that goal, or between two or more goals (Osborn, 1963; Parnes, 1967). Once the problem has been defined and formulated, the individual is ready to begin generating alternatives.

Generation of Alternatives

Generating alternative solutions is typically considered to be at the core of problem solving. The major task during this stage is to come up with a range of possible responses, among which may be found effective ones.

Much of the research in this area relates to Osborn's method of "brainstorming." Originally developed in 1938 as a procedure for facilitating "idea finding" in group sessions, brainstorming has four basic rules:

(1) *Criticism is ruled out.* Adverse judgment of ideas must be withheld until later.

(2) *"Free-wheeling" is welcomed.* The wilder the idea, the better; it is easier to tame down than to think up.

(3) *Quantity is wanted.* The greater the number of ideas, the greater the likelihood of useful ideas.

(4) *Combination and improvement are sought.* In addition to contributing ideas of their own, participants should suggest how ideas of others can be turned into *better* ideas, or how two or more ideas can be joined into still another idea (Osborn, 1963, p. 156).

There have been several reports supporting the efficacy of brainstorming, based both upon uncontrolled training programs and experimental studies (D'Zurilla & Goldfried, 1971). These findings indicate that brainstorming is more likely to generate effective responses than is the attempt to produce *only* good quality alternatives.

To eventually judge the quality of a response alternative, it must be presented at an appropriate level of specificity. As a means of getting more specific, the problem solver can first generate as many general alternatives (i.e., "strategies") as possible. He may then move on to decision making and select the best strategy or strategies. Finally, he can return to the generation-of-alternatives phase to produce as many specific alternatives (i.e., "tactics") as possible for carrying out the selected strategies.

Decision Making

By generating a number of alternative courses of action, the problem solver has, in a sense, exchanged old problems for new ones. With only one available solution, there is obviously no need to go through the decision-making phase. With only one option to choose from, however, the likelihood of selecting the most effective course of action is diminished. Although research indicates that brainstorming instructions result in more good quality alternatives, some findings by Johnson, Parrott, and Stratton (1968) have suggested that people may not always be able to identify the best of the alternatives they have generated.

In the process of determining the "goodness" of any particular course of action, past work on decision making has made extensive use of the "utility" concept, in which making a choice involves (1) a prediction of the likely consequences of each course of action and (2) a consideration of the utility of these consequences in dealing with the problem as formulated (D'Zurilla & Goldfried, 1971).

In discussing the generation of alternatives, we have differentiated between "strategies," or general courses of action, and "tactics," or the specific ways these alternative courses might be implemented. In selecting the best strategy, focus is on the likelihood of *resolving the major issues*; in selecting tactics, the focus is on the likelihood of effectively *implementing the strategy*. For example, in a situation where someone needs money to support his family, the evaluation of the strategy ("try to find additional work") would depend on an estimate of how well it might resolve the person's conflict. The tactic ("place an advertisement in the paper"), on the other hand, would be judged on its likelihood of locating additional work.

Up until this point in the problem-solving sequence, the individual has been operating primarily at a cognitive level. Unless the individual actually engages in some direct action, however, he may remain obsessively "lost in thought" and fail to enter the final stage of problem solving, namely, verification.

Verification

Perhaps the most relevant description of this stage of problem solving comes from the work of Miller, Galanter, and Pribram (1960). In conceptualizing the relationship between an individual's plans and his actions, they propose a Test-Operate-Test-Exit (TOTE) unit, whereby an individual's problem solving is guided by the extent to which the outcome of his activities is congruent or incongruent with a given standard. If, after engaging in some cognitive or behavioral operations, the individual "tests" or matches the progress he has made and decides that it is congruent with a standard, he then stops or "exits" from these activities. If, on the other hand, he finds the match to be incongruent, he continues to "operate" until a successful match is obtained.

In order to deal with a problem situation at more than a hypothetical level, the individual must carry out the selected course of action, observe the consequences of his actions, and match the real outcome against his expected outcome. If the match is satisfactory, the problem-solving process can be terminated, and the individual "exits." If the individual finds the match unsatisfactory, however, he continues to "operate" (i.e., returns to problem definition and formulation, generation of alternatives, and/or decision making), repeating this procedure until a satisfactory match is obtained, at which point the problem-solving process is terminated. The entire problem-solving process is outlined schematically in Figure 1.

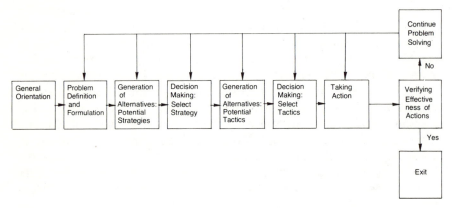

Figure 1.

● IMPLEMENTATION OF PROBLEM SOLVING

At this point, the reader may feel overwhelmed by the complexity of the problem-solving model described thus far. We have made it a point of presenting the problem-solving sequence in considerable—even obsessive—detail, not because we expect that each and every step will have to be covered during problem solving, but to provide a heuristic by which the therapist may implement the training process. In our own clinical experience with the procedure, we have found that some individuals tend to be vague and abstract in the way they define and formulate problems; other clients tend to be "tight," and have difficulty generating alternative courses of action; still others have difficulty anticipating consequences.

Depending on the particular deficiency existing in any given case, more or less emphasis would be placed on each of the various problem-solving phases.

During the training process, various behavior change procedures are used, such as modeling, prompting, and reinforcement. During the early phase of training, the therapist can demonstrate the problem-solving procedures while the client passively observes. Since problem solving occurs at the cognitive level, the therapist should verbalize all of his thoughts. As the client gradually takes a more active role in problem solving, the therapist can begin to function primarily as a supervisor-consultant, asking and answering questions to guide the client, encouraging and evaluating *in vivo* applications, and reinforcing successive approximations to effective problem-solving performance. Consistent with the emphasis on self-control, the client can also be encouraged to reinforce his own successful performance.

General Orientation

Training begins with a discussion of the rationale, course of treatment, and its anticipated benefits. The client can be helped to understand why problem situations are likely to occur (e.g., changing roles, new environments), and given the expectation that he can learn to cope independently with most of these challenges. Depending on the client, a certain amount of rational restructuring (see Chapter 8) may be helpful. The set to recognize problem situations when they occur, and the set to inhibit the tendency to react "automatically" without carefully thinking things through should also be stressed. The client may be sensitized to the problem situations in his life by discussing the general areas of daily living in which such difficulties might occur (e.g., family relationships, job situations, health). As an initial homework assignment, the client can be asked to self-monitor problem situations. Since such situations, prior to their resolution, are likely to produce emotional reactions (e.g., feelings of uncertainty, confusion, frustration), the therapist can point out that these feelings can serve as a useful signal for him to look for the events (cognitive and external) that may be responsible for these feelings.

The function of this general orientation is to provide the client with an *initial* set of expectations. Once the individual begins to practice the problem-solving strategy and is successful in coping effectively with the actual problem situations, these expectations should be strengthened.

Problem Definition and Formulation

Since many clients tend to describe their problems abstractly, they may have to be taught to provide the details necessary for an operational definition of the problem. In many instances, not only *external* situational events, but also *internal* events (i.e., thoughts, feelings) will be important for a complete description of the situation. Sometimes the client might also have to seek out additional facts and information that may not be immediately available. In many respects, this process can be compared to what behavior therapists do during the assessment phase of treatment. One important difference is that with problem solving, the therapist trains the client to apply this assessment to his own problems.

The following clinical transcript illustrates how a general description of a problem situation becomes defined in operational terms.

Client: I've been depressed and upset lately.

Therapist: How long have you been feeling this way?

Client: Oh, for about the past month or so. I think a lot of it is due to the fact that my husband has started working late. I really should feel very grateful, because we really do need the money.

Therapist: In what way do you feel your upset is related to your husband's working late?

Client: Well, I've been feeling more and more lonely, nervous, and generally upset in the evenings, waiting for him to come home. I don't like being alone at night. Also, by the time my husband does get home, he's usually so exhausted that he goes right to bed.

Therapist: So your contacts with him are limited?

Client: Very much so. I really miss having the chance to sit down with him and talk about what's gone on during the day. He feels pretty much the same as I do about this. Also, neither of us is very happy about the fact that our sex life has fallen off.

Therapist: And what do you feel this is due to?

Client: Sheer fatigue on his part. Our sex life has always been good up until now.

Therapist: So, one of the things that is of great concern to you involves the minimal contact—sexual and otherwise—that you've been having lately with your husband.

Client: Also, I just don't like being alone every night; I'd much prefer being with someone else. I actually do have a number of friends, and enjoy being with them.

Therapist: So it's not just your missing husband. It's also being generally lonely.

Client: I guess so. You know, I think another thing that has been bothering me about staying at home at night is the fact that we live on a dark and isolated street. I guess I am afraid that someone might find out that I'm alone every night, and try to break in.

Therapist: Do you know of any cases where this has happened?

Client: I have read about a number of robberies occurring not too far from where I live.

Therapist: Before your husband started working late, did you have any of these concerns?

Client: Not really. I think an awful lot of the difficulty is basically due to a very bad situation. I just don't know what to do about it.

Once the situation has been defined operationally, the client should *formulate* the problem by identifying her major goals, and then those issues or conflicts that make the situation problematic. In the example above, the client's goals included the desire for social interaction during the evening, more communication with her husband, the feeling of safety in the evening, and more sex during the week. The major issues in this case involve goals and the obstacles opposing them: desire for company versus being alone at night; desire for conversation versus husband's fatigue; desire to feel safe versus being alone and afraid that someone will break in; desire for sex versus husband's need to get to sleep.

The initial specification of goals and issues is a critical first step in the treatment program, and may itself be sufficient to make the client aware of possible solutions. When the solution is not obvious, the client can move on to the next stage and learn to identify possible response alternatives.

Generation of Alternatives

In having the client generate response alternatives, the distinction can be made between "strategies" and "tactics." Depending on the client, alternate labels may be required in assisting him to make this differentiation (e.g., *what* to do vs. *how* to do it, general approaches vs. specific actions). During this phase of the problem-solving process, the client is instructed to brainstorm possible solutions at the strategy level. The following transcript illustrates this procedure:

Therapist: OK. Now we seem to have a clearer picture of the kinds of things that are making life difficult for you. Let's see if you can come up with some possible solutions. Do you remember the brainstorming rules I told you about?

Client: I think so. Let's see, I'm supposed to think of as many possibilities as I can, no matter how silly or impractical they may seem at first.

Therapist: That's right. Just let your mind run free. Even though you come up with a possibility, it doesn't necessarily mean that you would ever really want to carry it out.

Client: OK.

Therapist: Also, at this particular point, I don't think you really have to worry about being too specific. Try to think of general approaches to handling the situation; later on, we can start looking at specific ways to carry out some of these approaches.

Client: I'm not sure if I completely understand what you mean.

Therapist: Well, for example, let's suppose that you decided that one possible solution was "I would find a babysitter." That's describing a possibility at a very general level; it indicates *what* you would do, not *how* you would go about doing it. For example, in getting a babysitter, you could contact a relative, look in the classified section of your local newspaper, call some friends to find out if they know anyone who is available, or any one of a number of other specific ways of carrying out the general approach of "getting a babysitter."

Client: I see what you mean.

Therapist: [*Before actually getting her to start generating alternatives, I ought to review the four issues that we formulated a little bit earlier. Since they are not all that independent, I won't bother to have her brainstorm on each issue separately, but instead present them all at once.*] Fine. Now thinking at this general level, I'd like you to come up with as many possibilities as you can think of; I'll note them down as you mention them. Remember, don't make any attempt to evaluate them at this point. Although you really can be as creative, or even ridiculous, as you want in thinking of possibilities, keep in mind the four major concerns you have about your current situation: Having company at night, more communication with your husband, feeling safe in the evening, and more frequent sexual relations.

Client: Let's see . . . I can get someone to visit me during the week. I can go out myself in the evening. I could get a stronger lock for my door, or maybe even put in a burglar alarm system. Maybe I can ask my husband to put in some bright lights outside of our house. Let's see . . .

Therapist: [*The pause and the look on her face make me feel that she may be running into some difficulty. Maybe she's making some premature evaluations; at least all her alternatives up to now seem to be fairly sensible. Perhaps I should remind her about deferring judgment until later.*] Try not to hold back. Just include anything that comes to mind, no matter how foolish it may seem.

Client: Well, I suppose I could always keep a gun in the house (*laughs*). Or maybe complain to the police, and see whether or not they could have the area patrolled better. Many of the other people on the street have told me that they're also concerned about the number of robberies lately, so maybe we could all get together and sign a petition or something. I think if we all complained, it might be more effective.

Therapist: [*That sounds like a really good idea. On the other hand, she seems to be getting too specific at this point; I prefer she stay at a strategy level.*] It certainly sounds reasonable. Why don't you hold off on the specifics for a while; we can get into that a little bit later. For now, let's stay at the general level.

Client: All right. I guess I was just getting carried away. About the problem of my husband not being too interested in sex when he gets home, I guess there might be things I could do to help put him in the mood. Maybe we could have intercourse at other times, such as early in the morning or weekends. Although I probably would never do it, I could always have an affair. Maybe my husband and I could also find time to talk to each other at other times as well, like by telephone during the day, or early in the morning. . . . I don't think I can think of anything else.

Therapist: [*She could use a little bit of prompting at this point. Perhaps I can provide her with an alternative that I thought of a few minutes ago.*] Let's keep at it a little bit more. How about the possibility of your husband looking for a better paying job?

Client: I doubt if he could find one. Oh, but I'm not supposed to think about those things, right?

Therapist: Right.

Client: Well, maybe he can work on Saturday instead of weekday nights.

Once it appears that most of the available response alternatives have been identified by the client, she is ready to make some decision about the best strategy to pursue. Apart from the therapist's judgment that most potential courses of action have been covered, there are no criteria for when this phase of problem solving should be ended.

Decision Making

In moving to decision making, the client must predict which of the possible strategy-level alternatives are worth pursuing. A general guideline is to have the client anticipate the likely consequences of each strategy, and then evaluate how useful such consequences are for resolving the problem situation. Before considering consequences in detail, however, the client should first eliminate any obviously poor alternatives, since the deferment of judgment directive may have produced clearly untenable solutions.

In deciding on alternatives, the client should review each possibility and ask the question: "If I were successful in carrying out this particular course of action, what would be the likely consequences?" To assist the client in identifying possible consequences, the therapist can instruct him to consider consequences of both a personal and social nature, as well as on a long-term and a short-term basis.

Obviously, the problem solver cannot predict all possible consequences. For any outcome considered, one can only guess how likely it is to occur (e.g., highly likely, likely, or unlikely). Similarly, in evaluating the utility of any consequence, it is only reasonable to ask the client to make gross judgments of the value assigned (e.g., very good, good, neutral, bad, and very bad). Depending on the particular client's ability to make fine distinctions, a more detailed evaluation may be feasible. In such instances, a written checklist may be used (see pages 200–202). After carefully weighing the various alternatives, the client should select a strategy that appears to have the best payoff, in the sense of resolving the major issues while maximizing other positive consequences. The following clinical excerpt illustrates some of these points.

Therapist: [*Before going into detailed decision making, why don't I just get her to screen out any alternatives she obviously does not want to pursue further?*] Let's look at the alternatives you've come up with, to see if you can arrive at some decision as to which will be worth considering further. To begin with, are there any which you would want to reject out of hand?

Client: Well, I doubt if I would really want to have an affair. As I mentioned before, my husband and I get along quite well. It's just that the situation we find ourselves in is very bad. I wouldn't want to do anything which would endanger our marriage.

Therapist: Are there any other alternatives that might be eliminated?

Client: I don't think so.

Therapist: [*In having her evaluate the strategies she's come up with thus far, she should operate on the assumption that she will be able to come up with a good tactic for implementing it.*] OK. Let's look at each of these possibilities, trying to anticipate what the likely consequences would be if you *were* successful in following through with it. In trying to estimate the possible consequences, think along the lines of what the implications might be for you, as well as anyone else you care about, such as your husband, children, friends, relatives—

```
                      PROBLEM-SOLVING CHECKLIST

1. Problem Definition and Formulation

   a. Definition of situation, including important details:

      Background: Although most of my courses at college are in the
      afternoon, I have one required course that meets at 8:00 in
      the morning.  After the first few weeks of school, I began
      attending this class less and less regularly.  I have gotten
      into the habit of studying late, and have a lot of trouble
      getting up to meet the class.

      Specific Problem Situation: It's halfway through the semester,
      and I've missed two weeks of my 8:00 class - about six consecutive
      class meetings.  I'm really afraid to go back, because I feel I
      will be too far behind in the work and might not understand
      what's going on.


   b. Formulation of conflicts or issues:

      __Should return to class__   vs.   _Might not understand what's going on_

      __Study late at night__      vs.   _Have to get up for early morning class_

      _____       vs.   _____

2. Brainstorming general courses   3. Deciding on a strategy (or strategies)
   of action (strategies):            ( ++ = very good; + = good; 0 = neutral;
                                        - = bad; -- = very bad.)

                                      Consequences of Strategy
                                                              Final
                                      For self    For others  Selection

   a. Return to class and try to catch a.  --          0         _____
      up on course work on my own.

   b. Return to class and get help      b.  +           0            √
      from others in catching up
      with course work.

   c. Continue as I am, but try to      c.  -           0         _____
      fake my way through the exams.

   d. Ask some friends what they        d.  -           0         _____
      think I should do.

   e. Return to class and make sure     e.  +           0            √
      I don't miss any future classes.

   f. Drop the course.                  f.  --          -         _____

   g. Try to keep up with course work   g.  --          -         _____
      and take final exam, but not
      actually attend classes.

   h. _____    h._____   _____     _____


      _____
```

both immediate consequences and long-term ones. (*Referring to written notes.*) Let's consider first the possibility of your going out in the evening.

Client: All right. I think I would enjoy getting out of the house to be with some friends. I don't think it would affect my husband one way or the other, although I would have to arrange for a

4. Brainstorming specific ways of carrying out strategy "b".	5. Deciding on specific ways of carrying out strategy (++ = very good; + = good; 0 = neutral; - = bad; -- = very bad).		
	Consequences of Specific Behaviors		
	For self	For others	Final Selection
a. Look for a tutor.	a. _+_	0	_____
b. Ask the instructor if he would give me extra help in the course.	b. _0_	_-_	_____
c. Ask the instructor how he thinks I might best make up the material.	c. _++_	_0_	✓
d. Ask some friends to explain the material I missed.	d. _+_	_-_	_____
e. Borrow some notes from a friend and try to catch up before returning to class.	e. _-_	_-_	_____
f. Borrow some notes from a friend but return to class immediately.	f. _+_	_-_	_____
g. Sneak into the instructor's office and steal his lecture notes.	g. _--_	_-_	_____
h. Find someone who has taken the course and borrow his lecture notes.	h. _+_	_0_	_____
i. _____	i. _____	_____	_____

babysitter. That could run into money if I do it on a regular basis. If I did go out at night, I'd probably be worried about the children's safety; you know, the whole business about the robberies in the neighborhood. It would depend on whether that problem could be solved or not.

Therapist: [*Hmm. I guess I should have seen that earlier. The issue of the robberies in the neighborhood has to be dealt with before we can go about evaluating the effectiveness of responses for dealing with the other issues.*] OK, that's a good point. Maybe it would be best to start off considering possible ways of handling that situation. Why don't we look at that for a while, and then come back to consider some of the other possibilities.

Client: Right. Let's see. I think I mentioned something about getting together with a number of other people on the street to see if we could get the police to do something about the situation. It's hard to know exactly what the results would be. I guess a lot depends on how we carry it out. But, assuming that we handle it right, I can't see anything but good coming of it.

6. Brainstorming specific ways of carrying out strategy "e".	7. Deciding on specific ways of carrying out strategy. (++ = very good; + = good; 0 = neutral; - = bad; -- = very bad).		
	Consequences of Specific Behaviors		Final
	For self	For others	Selection
a. Completely rearrange my study habits so as to get to bed earlier.	a. +	0	
b. Get to bed earlier only on the nights before the early morning class.	b. ++	0	√
c. Switch to a section that meets later in the day.	c. 0	0	
d. Put my alarm clock on the other end of the room so I can make sure I get up on time.	d. +	-	
e. Get a friend to wake me up on time to get to class.	e. +	-	
f. Study through the night so that I can be sure to be awake early in the morning.	f. --	-	
g. Have a friend tape-record the lecture for me.	g. +	-	
h. _____	h. _____	_____	_____
i. _____	i. _____	_____	_____

Therapist: [*I don't think she's considering the time and effort involved as a potential negative consequence. I'll point that out to her and see what she says.*] How about the time and effort involved?

Client: As far as I'm concerned, that wouldn't be much of a factor.

Therapist: Suppose you were to evaluate this alternative then. Would you say it was very good, good, neutral, bad, or very bad?

Client: Offhand, I would think of it as a very good possibility.

Therapist: OK, fine. Let's go on to another possibility.

In situations with several major issues, it is rare for any one strategy to resolve the entire problem. More likely, several different courses of action will have to be followed. The therapist should also bear in mind that some problem situations are not amenable to any really "good" solution. This is particularly the case in handling crises (e.g., the loss of a spouse), where the evaluation of alternative solutions would have to be made on a relative rather than absolute basis.

Once a strategy or set of strategies, is chosen, the client is asked to return to the generation-of-alternatives stage to produce specific behaviors, or tactics, for implementing each strategy. The same procedures involved in generating strategies should be used here. For example, in the case of the strategy, "Get someone to visit during weekday evenings," the client generated the following tactics: "Ask my mother to visit me during the evening"; "Arrange a card game one night a week"; "Give a cooking course"; and "Invite friends for dinner occasionally." Having generated a number of specific alternative behaviors, the client can again engage in decision making, this time to select the most effective tactic for implementing each of these strategies.

Sometimes, in the process of generating or evaluating alternatives, the client comes up with a solution far more effective than anything yet considered. In studying various ways to cope with the problem of being home alone during the evening, for example, the client in the above example hit upon a solution that seemed better than anything she had yet considered. This occurred as she was attempting to make a decision about the best tactic for implementing the strategy of "going out more frequently during the evening." The interaction was as follows:

Client: If I were able to take an adult education course, I could get involved in working on ceramics and other similar activities. I've done that in the past, and I know I would enjoy it very much. This would only take up one, or at best two, nights a week. Anything more than that would involve spending too much on babysitters, which is something we can't afford at this time. But maybe there's a way to deal with that, perhaps by looking for some part-time job I could have a few nights a week. That would have a number of positive consequences: not only would I be able to get out more frequently, but I could also earn some money.

Therapist: [*Why didn't I think of that? She seems to have inadvertently hit upon an alternative that also bears directly on the origin of the entire problem situation: The reason her husband has been working late is because of their financial situation. Should I point it out to her or not? Maybe it's best to wait a bit and see if she's able to see the connection herself. It won't hurt that much to smile and offer a minimal verbal acknowledgement].* Mhm.

Client: The more I think about it, the more I like the idea. In fact, I might be even better off if I could look for a job during the day. That would really be much better in a number of ways. If I were able to get a job, even if it were just part-time, that would mean that my husband wouldn't have to work evenings. He's only doing it for the money, and I know he dislikes the situation as much as I. A part-time job would probably be better, especially if I could find something during the time the kids are in school.

Therapist: *[I'm really glad I didn't say anything. I think that's a great idea. I hope she sees it the same way.]* How does this solution compare to the others you've considered thus far?

Client: I like it much better. It doesn't do anything about the robberies in the neighborhood, but I think that could be handled separately. The more I think of it, the more I realize that getting a job would be the best way to approach the situation. In fact, I'm surprised I didn't think of it before. If for some reason I can't find a job, I guess I can fall back on some of the other possibilities we've discussed.

Therapist: *[I don't think that the previous problem solving has gone to waste, in the sense that she now has some contingency plans, should she have any difficulty finding a job that would be able to pay enough to handle the financial situation. Time for her to brainstorm possible tactics for finding a job.]* That's true. Why don't we now consider some of the possible ways you might be able to locate a job.

Verification

Up to this point, the client has been operating purely at a cognitive level. Despite the strong emphasis on thinking, the primary objective is to facilitate doing. Consequently, once the client has decided on what she believes to be the most effective course, the therapist should encourage her to act on this decision, and then to *verify* how effective the action has been. Verification essentially involves observing the consequences of one's actions. If the client is satisfied with these consequences, the problem-solving process can at last be terminated. Should the solution fail to resolve the situation satisfactorily, the client would have to resume the problem-solving process to arrive at a better answer.

In some instances it might not be appropriate to expect the client to be capable of carrying out the most effective course of action. This is particularly true with clients who are either too anxious to behave in certain ways, or who lack the ability to do so. Obviously, then, the therapist must make a careful assessment of the client's inhibitions and response capabilities to decide whether he can respond in certain ways without receiving additional treatment, such as desensitization, rational restructuring, or behavior rehearsal.

As with therapeutic procedures described in previous chapters, the client is frequently given homework, that is, he is encouraged to practice problem solving between sessions. To assist him in carrying out problem solving *in vivo*, record forms such as that presented on pages 200–202 can be most helpful.

● APPLICATIONS

One of the most appropriate applications of problem solving is with a so-called dependent client who cannot cope with problem situations on his own, but can perform quite effectively when the therapist tells him exactly what to do. Such clients may have an adequate repertoire of general performance skills, but may be deficient in independent problem-solving ability. The major goal of treatment with this client should be to teach him new problem-solving skills and not merely to feed him an unending series of "solutions." Another client might have good problem-solving skills but might be unable to use them because of emotional inhibitions. With clients like this, a graded-tasks approach to problem-solving training and implementation might produce a disinhibiting effect through a process similar to *in vivo* desensitization. Many people show a combination of difficulties (i.e., deficits and inhibitions), involving not only problem solving but also response execution. With such clients, problem-solving training would typically be combined with other behavior therapy techniques, such as behavior rehearsal or systematic desensitization.

An illustration of this last type of difficulty is an eighteen-year-old female freshman who was having considerable trouble adjusting to college. She had never lived away from home prior to going to school, and had come from a home environment where she was always considered the "baby" of the family. The client was eventually referred to the university clinic by her roommate, who was finding it increasingly difficult to satisfy the continual demands for help. In describing her adjustment problems, the client related a wide array of situations with which she was unable to cope—such as not being able to decide on what courses to take, when and where to study, how to spend her free time, and a host of other day-to-day concerns. When faced with such situations, the client's immediate response was either to ask her roommate what to do, or to call home for advice. Since one of the major interfering factors was the client's fear of being alone, it was apparent that problem-solving training could not be implemented immediately. She was too afraid to be in her room alone, and even had difficulty walking across campus by herself. Consequently, a program of relaxation training and *in vivo* desensitization was instituted before problem-solving training could take place. In addition, the client had to learn to become more assertive with her parents, for they continued to undermine her attempts at independence. Complications such as these are not uncommon with highly dependent individuals.

Another area where problem-solving training may be appropriately employed is with psychiatric patients prior to their discharge. Particularly when someone has been hospitalized for a long period of time, the transition in role status is likely to present difficulties in his adjustment to a nonhospital setting. Even when the discharged patient has been able to overcome many of the problems which originally led to hospitalization, he may experience a variety of difficulties making the adjustment. If nothing else, he will be returning to an environment that is likely to have changed considerably during the time he was hospitalized. Thus, training in problem solving would be indicated to help him cope independently with situational problems involving his job, living arrangements, social contacts, and other circumstances which he must handle to make it on the outside. Training in problem-solving skills may also be used with other populations where a dramatic shift in environment or role status is involved, such as paroled prisoners and ex-drug addicts (Copemann, 1973).

Problem solving has been used to help adolescents and children to more effectively handle various conflict situations. Kifer, Lewis, Green, and Phillips (1973) have described the use of problem solving to assist predelinquent adolescents and their parents in mutually arriving at decisions. Problem solving has also been used to facilitate leadership training in adolescents (Almedina & Rubin, 1974), and to foster peer cooperation among children at the grade school and kindergarten level (Schneider & Robin, 1975; Shaftel & Shaftel, 1967; Spivak & Shure, 1974).

Problem solving is especially appropriate when the consequences of an ineffective response might be serious or even disastrous. In such instances, the intent is not so much to provide the client with problem-solving training as to serve as a framework for intervention. Questions involving divorce, marriage, change in occupation, and other similar life decisions fall into this category. This is particularly true of suicide, where a problem-solving approach can help the person think through and consider alternative solutions to an apparently insurmountable crisis.

Finally, problem solving may be applied within a broader therapy program, to help the client become more independent toward the end of therapy. As the time for termination approaches, a client may experience difficulty in relying more on his own resources and less on the advice and direction of the therapist. Indeed, with the growing emphasis in behavior therapy on the importance of self-control (Goldfried & Merbaum, 1973), the use of problem-solving principles has great potential for training the client to function, in effect, as his own therapist.

● SUMMARY

Some clients may be effectively helped by training in problem-solving skills. The five problem-solving stages discussed in this chapter are: (1) general orientation, (2) problem definition and formulation, (3) generation of alternatives, (4) decision making, and (5) verification. This therapeutic approach can be conceptualized as a form of self-control training, for it is directed toward the goal of helping the client think for himself. Thus, problem-solving training would appear to be relevant with overly dependent clients who rely excessively on the guidance and suggestions of others, and with children and adolescents struggling to function on their own. On the assumption that problem situations generally arise when individuals are in the process of undergoing radical role and/or environmental changes, the problem-solving approach would be important in assisting, for example, discharged psychiatric patients, paroled prisoners, and ex-drug addicts in making the transition to their new status. Additional applications may be made in crisis intervention, and in helping the soon-to-be terminated client to depend less on the advice and direction of the therapist and more on his own resources.

Chapter

Reinforcement Procedures

This chapter focuses on procedures that attempt to alter behavior by manipulating its consequences. The emphasis, then, will be on what is generally termed the operant approach. Before describing the therapeutic procedures themselves, we shall briefly review some of the key concepts underlying this general approach to behavior change.

● REINFORCEMENT

Technically, an event is regarded as a reinforcer if it increases the probability of the behavior it follows. A *positive* reinforcer is an event which, when presented to the individual, increases the behavior in question. An event that achieves the same end by virtue of its removal is termed a *negative* reinforcer.

In clinical practice, the therapist infers something the client likes, and considers it a potential positive reinforcer. For example, we generally assume that a client who respects his therapist will regard approval from him as something positive, as something to work for—in other words, as a positive reinforcer. With a child, the assumption can usually be made that approval from a nurturant adult will be positively reinforcing. Negative reinforcement is illustrated by a parent picking up a crying child; the parent's behavior would be negatively reinforced by the cessation of whining. There are many subtleties involved in the choice of a reinforcer at a given point in time; these will be discussed below.

● PUNISHMENT

In discussing the concept of punishment, it is important to differentiate it from negative reinforcement, as described above. In the case of negative reinforcement, we *remove* a negative event, contingent upon the presence of some *desirable behavior* we wish to increase. In the case of punishment, on the other hand, we *present* a negative state of affairs contingent on certain *maladaptive behaviors*. To state it another way, the purpose of negative reinforcement is to increase the frequency of certain desired behaviors; the purpose of punishment is to decrease the frequency of undesired behaviors.

Behavior can be reduced in frequency by any one of three basic punishment procedures: the presentation of an aversive event, the removal of the person from a situation where he would otherwise be able to earn reinforcers (i.e., time-out), and the deduction of a certain amount from a person's collection of reinforcers (i.e., response cost).

A clinical example of punishment as an aversive event is a frown from the therapist when the client does or reports something that is judged maladaptive or undesirable. With a child, this at times might take the form of a shout or even a slap from a guardian. An example of time-out is isolating a child in a room separate from the classroom where positive reinforcement has been available; during the isolation the child is unable to participate in positively reinforcing activities. An example of response cost is taking away a given amount from a child's accumulated total of goodies, contingent on a behavior one wants to weaken.

● EXTINCTION

An extinction procedure reduces the probability of behavior by withholding reinforcers that customarily have been presented. For example, if we have determined that attention from a teacher is maintaining the acting-out of an elementary school child in the classroom, we could instruct the teacher to stop attending to such behavior in hopes that it will extinguish. Extinction is often facilitated by simultaneously reinforcing the occurrence of an incompatible response. Thus, the teacher who ignores a child's inappropriate behavior can be advised to praise the child when, for example, he is sitting in his chair and doing his work. As an aside, it is interesting to note that most discipline in school settings tends to inadvertently reinforce undesirable behavior because some teachers seem to pay less attention to a child working appropriately than to one who is acting out. It should also be mentioned, however, that the teacher's attention may, for a particular child, act as a *punishing* event, reducing the frequency of the behavior; for another child, or for the same child on another occasion, attention may inadvertently reinforce the behavior. Once again, the clinical worker has to judge at the time what the client's most likely reaction will be to a particular intervention.

● OTHER OPERANT CONCEPTS

There are several additional terms commonly used in the operant literature. *Shaping* refers to the gradual training of a complex response by reinforcing closer and closer approximations. For example, a retarded child might be taught to make his bed by first reinforcing him for fluffing up his pillow, then for pulling the top sheet forward, and so forth. Each segment of the complex behavior is a *successive approximation* of the final target behavior. Indeed, the essence of the operant approach might well be seen as the analysis of complex behavior into manageable units of chained responses. Related to these concepts are *fading* and *prompting*. Consider, for example, teaching an autistic child to speak. It is often useful, at the beginning of training, to utter a word loudly while encouraging the child to imitate. This verbal prompt would then, over trials, be faded, or gradually removed as the child becomes more and more adept at speaking.

The conceptual framework of the operant approach in behavior

therapy is deceptively simple. Implementation represents a challenge to the ingenuity and persistence of the clinical worker or
teacher. The remainder of this chapter considers theoretical and
applied issues that are seldom treated explicitly in discussions of
clinical behavior therapy.

● OPERANT CONDITIONING WITH ADULTS

Outpatient Settings

Since operant conditioning depends on environmental contingencies, one might wonder whether this approach has any significant applicability to adult outpatient settings, where the therapist is
able to exert direct influence only during a therapy session. We
believe that it does.

Often the therapist will suggest that a client try out certain
behaviors between sessions. As a client is reporting a reasonably
successful effort, the therapist generally nods or otherwise
expresses approval of the client's attempts, all of which hopefully
will reinforce his extra-session behavior. It is important to have
the client recount as many details as possible of the new behavior
performed between sessions, so that the various steps in the behavioral chain can be commented upon favorably.

This raises an interesting question: Just what is it that is being
reinforced? Stated in strict operant terms, we may observe that the
therapist is reinforcing verbal statements by the client. However, is
it only the verbal report that we regard as the important behavior to
be reinforced? Not at all, for the real target is what is taking place
on the outside, as when an inhibited client successfully asks to have
his undercooked steak taken back to the kitchen for additional
broiling. The actual targets, then, are those behaviors that are *symbolically* produced during the therapy hour, so that these symbolic
representations can be observed by the therapist and reinforced
when appropriate. Thus, any reinforcement that takes place under
conditions other than those in which a behavior is actually occurring takes advantage of the unique human capacity to symbolize, to
make the past (or for that matter the future) present.

In addition, the therapist can direct the client to try out new
behaviors in the natural environment, *between* sessions, in such a
fashion as to be reinforced by others. In this way the therapist
becomes more a consultant to the client than the kind of direct
"shaper" that one sees in institutional settings or with children.

Another issue relates to the topography of the reinforcer: What form should the reinforcer take at a particular time for a particular client? What is it that guides the therapist at a given point in time to reinforce a client in a particular way? Shall it be a nod of the head, a reflection of the client's feeling (Truax, 1966), a smile, or perhaps even a period of attentive silence? Here is yet another example where the therapist must be a *Menschenkenner*, that is, someone who understands people, and especially the particular client, so that his hunch about what is likely to be interpreted by the client as a reinforcer will be correct. We at times have had a well-intentioned smile interpreted as a sarcastic sneer by a client who happened to be upset when he was reporting a successful between-session behavior.

There is nothing mysterious or unusual here, especially if we recognize that researchers have to make judgments, admittedly simpler ones, about what reinforcer to use. For example, those who experiment with rats will never use color as a cue, for the simple reason that laboratory rats are color-blind. In verbal conditioning studies with humans, even disagreeing with an individual can function as a reinforcer under certain circumstances (Davis, 1971).

What happens to the therapist-client relationship when a therapist feels he must punish a particular behavior during a session, whether it be a verbal representation of the actual target behavior, or an ongoing behavior exhibited in the session? A therapist need not convey dislike or contempt for a client when he disapproves of his behavior. Hopefully the relationship is such that the client is prepared to interpret the therapist's behavior as in the client's interest, even when it is bitter medicine to swallow.

Another area important for the implementation of operant procedures in the outpatient setting is the therapist's shaping of the client's self-reinforcement. It is important first of all that the client commit himself to undertaking a particular therapeutic regimen, whatever it is. The client is then instructed to comment favorably to himself whenever he has behaved in a particular way between sessions. Whether the client will in fact fulfill the terms of the contract by (1) accurately evaluating his behavior and (2) reinforcing himself for emitting it depends a good deal on the commitment to therapy that the client has come to feel. The therapist may have to train the client in self-reinforcement, for example, by asking him how he felt after he engaged in a particular behavior, and by pointing out that a self-statement such as "I felt pretty good about myself" is appropriate. Some clients may reinforce themselves very infrequently, in which case rational restructuring may be needed to convince them that a given effort is, in fact, praiseworthy. Of course, reinforcement can also take the form of allowing oneself to have a piece of luscious chocolate cake or to partake of some other pleasurable activity only after a page of manuscript has been completed (a strategy that the present writers have used on more than one occasion).

In a conjoint marital therapy situation, the therapist may have to spend much time teaching couples to reinforce each other for specific behavioral changes between sessions. For example, one can extract from the husband the promise to comment favorably on caring statements from the wife, while at the same time urging the wife to reciprocate by demonstration of physical affection.

Controlled Environments

Much has been written about the heterogeneity of institutionalized patients (e.g., Davison, 1969). If we were to draw a sharp substantive distinction between hospitalized and nonhospitalized people, we would run the risk of decreasing our effectiveness by overlooking procedures that might be proven useful for outpatients. For example, a severely anxious person might enter the psychiatric section of a Veterans Administration hospital rather than remain on the outside for therapy because he is entitled to veterans' benefits if hospitalized. Numerous other factors naturally would enter into a decision about entering a hospital, and these factors may very well be more important than the specific behavior exhibited by the client. We should be wary, therefore, of regarding in a qualitatively different way a person who is being seen on a psychiatric ward rather than on an outpatient basis. One might, for example, contemplate systematic desensitization for an institutionalized patient, even one carrying a schizophrenic diagnosis. Thus, much of what has been written in this book may be relevant to the therapist's approach to institutionalized adults.

While the judgment may seem harsh, we would suggest that operant approaches used to date with the great mass of inpatients reflect effective hospital management more than a thoroughgoing therapeutic approach to problem behaviors. Thus, for a regressed schizophrenic to make his bed in the morning may represent a definite improvement, but he may nonetheless have to remain institutionalized. Moreover, a patient's behavior as shaped within the hospital should correspond to real-world demands. As we have argued elsewhere (Gagnon & Davison, in press), token economies may very well be reinforcing the wrong things, for they teach people that good behavior usually pays off, and that one gets what one deserves. It may be that what society calls "sanity" entails the toleration of injustice as far as the correspondence between what our behavior merits and what in fact it obtains in reinforcement terms. That is, effective functioning in noninstitutional settings may well depend on the ability *not* to expect to receive what one believes he has earned.

To describe fully the procedures employed in token economy programs would go far beyond the scope of this book. Fortunately, detailed descriptions of token economies are available elsewhere (Ayllon & Azrin, 1965; Kazdin & Bootzin, 1972; Schaefer & Martin, 1969). Essentially, a token economy consists of at least the following elements: (1) careful specification of behavior that will be reinforced, e.g., making one's bed before 8:00 A.M.; (2) a clearly defined reinforcer with a clearly understood value, e.g., a green-colored token worth five points; (3) a set of back-up reinforcers that the token represents, e.g., a visit to the canteen costing 30 points; (4) a trained administrative staff that can observe the patient's behavior and apply reinforcement contingencies promptly and accurately. A properly run token economy is characterized also by (5) careful record-keeping on each patient so that staff personnel can know whether a given behavior from a particular patient merits a reinforcer. For example, when encouraging bed-making, a staff member would want to reinforce a more regressed patient for even straightening his blanket slightly, whereas a more advanced patient would be required to tuck in all corners and have his pillow neatly fluffed and in place.

● OPERANT CONDITIONING WITH CHILDREN

General Considerations

Our emphasis in this section should not be construed as an overall endorsement of the operant approach for all childhood problems. For example, a counterconditioning approach would be more appropriate for children who demonstrate a variety of fears. Nonetheless many childhood problems seem to be amenable to analyses along operant conditioning lines.

With children, we generally have greater potential control over the environment since they are under the surveillance of adults for great amounts of time. Further, the behavior of children tends to occur far more often than that of adults in locations that allow for operant manipulation.

This appearance of greater *potential* control, however, must not blind the therapist to the very real practical difficulties in achieving *actual* control over a child's environment. Whether the therapist must enlist the cooperation of a teacher, a principal, a hospital administrator, the staff on a psychiatric ward, or one or both of the child's parents—in all instances persuasive skills are needed to work successfully with the ultimate controllers of the child's behavior. As we have seen in many other areas of clinical behavior therapy, one of the greatest challenges to the behavior therapist is insuring that procedures are in fact implemented by the appropriate individuals.

Outpatient Settings

Operant behavior therapy with children in home settings can be viewed in the context of three specific steps: (1) presentation of rationale; (2) training of the social change agents; and (3) maintenance of behavior change after termination.

Presentation of Rationale

Many parents do not take kindly to the thought that their children's behavior can be controlled in seemingly mechanistic ways. There may be a negative reaction to having human behavior construed in the same terms used for animals. Clearly, it is important to explain the nature of scientific metaphors in understandable terms and to make clear that one is hardly engaging in a "humans are nothing but rats" argument (Davison & Stuart, 1975).

Another possible source of resistance from parents is the implication that, since they are to play such an important role in changing their child's behavior, they are therefore responsible for having produced the undesirable state of affairs in the first place. Here it is necessary simply to point out that the procedures effective in changing a behavior bear no necessary relationship to the reasons the behavior arose initially (Davison, 1969; Rimland, 1964). In working with the parents of autistic children, for example, one does not have to believe that these problems originated in faulty learning experiences. As we have pointed out elsewhere (Davison, 1965), even an organic view of the nature of autism can be consistent with an operant approach to altering certain behaviors in such children.

Another way that cooperation can be facilitated is to remind the parents that reinforcement and punishment are already in use in the household, pointing out that the therapy is designed primarily to make such control more consistent and effective. If the parents counter that reward procedures have already been tried without success, it is important for the therapist to evaluate what in fact was done and, in all likelihood, suggest that the well-intentioned effort lacked the necessary knowledge and skill for maximally effective application.

Parents complaining about their children's behavior may come to therapy with the expectation that their involvement will be minimal, perhaps extending no further than sitting in the waiting room while therapy is ministered to the child. Clearly, this misconception must be watched for and corrected. Should the parents seem to lack motivation, the therapist can always point out that a 24-hour-a-day professional therapist is impractical and quite expensive. Instead, the parents can work as aides under the therapist's guidance and supervision.

Some parents' predilection for aversive control—common among some teachers as well—can be coupled with an objection to the use of rewards as "bribes." This argument often goes as follows: "Why should I dangle goodies in front of Leonard? He ought to be doing these things anyway, without special favors being used to get his cooperation." This kind of objection can be discussed both philosophically and pragmatically. We try to make clear to the parents that the word "bribe" is appropriate for situations in which one person is attempting to take advantage of another, without that person's interests in mind. This is to be contrasted with reward or reinforcement, which is a technical aid for helping the child acquire skills necessary for survival and social living.

Once the parents accept the general reinforcement approach, it may be helpful to introduce any one of several good manuals currently available. A book we have found to be particularly helpful is Patterson and Gullion's *Living with Children* (1971); it describes a number of child behavior problems in operant terms and explains basic operant concepts. The use of such ancillary materials leads us into a second aspect of outpatient operant work with children.

Training of Change Agents

The concepts and operations that must be conveyed to parents are readily explained with folksy examples from the therapist's clinical practice or, better still, from the specifics of the clinical problem at hand. As in all other areas of behavior therapy, considerable ingenuity is called for by both therapist and parent in translating a given theoretical concept into a practical intervention.

It is of paramount importance to teach the parents careful observation of the behavior to be changed. Thus, a child's "aggressiveness" must be operationalized in terms of specific aggressive behaviors under specific circumstances. One may very well find that a "highly aggressive" child behaves aggressively when only the father is home and not when both parents are home. It can be useful to present an "A-B-C" paradigm for the observation of the child's behavior. "A" refers to the antecedent conditions, such as "When he sat down for dinner, . . ." "B" indicates the actual behavior in question, such as ". . . he began at once to spin in his chair . . ." while "C" refers to the consequences of the behavior, such as ". . . until I yelled at him to stop."

The concept of shaping is similarly important, especially if the parents despair of achieving a particular long-term goal. Thus, a child's insistent refusal to clean up his room can be broken down into manageable units of behavior that can be worked on one at a time.

Perhaps of greatest importance to convey to parents is the necessity to reinforce desirable behavior as promptly as possible following its emission, as well as to extinguish or ignore undesirable operant behavior. It is worth noting at this juncture that the therapist should not assume that a particular thing will be reinforcing to every child under all circumstances. Thus, sugarcoated M & M candies may be ineffective for a child who is satiated on such candies by a noncontingent regime provided by a generous relative or neighbor.

The methods for teaching parents or teachers operant concepts and operations are highly diverse. *At any rate, one should never assume that simply describing a procedure is going to result in the change agent's following those instructions.* What one actually has to do is alter the behavior of the change agent, so that these new behaviors will exert the desirable influence on the child. Thus, parents, teachers, and other appropriate change agents have to be taught to modify their way of responding to the child, so that the child presumably will behave differently as a function of changed adult behaviors.

It is possible that a parent may be too anxious in a particular situation to apply a given procedure. Thus, a parent highly fearful of the child's injuring himself might be reluctant to ignore cries from the playground that are clearly operant in nature. The clinician might then find himself in a therapy relationship with the parent, perhaps even including desensitization to particular child behaviors.

A frequent challenge is to persuade a parent to ignore obvious "temper tantrums" by a child who has learned that such behavior is highly aversive to the parent and typically achieves a desired goal or reinforcer. Parents must be forewarned that the beginning of an extinction program is likely to lead to temporary increases in such operant outbursts.

The use of numerous examples as well as direct observation and modeling (perhaps during home visits) are important. There are many ways to facilitate this process of instruction. In addition to suggesting the aforementioned book by Patterson and Gullion, the therapist should solicit specific relevant examples from the parent or teacher. The change agent should be encouraged to "find" his own child in the various chapters, which describe children who are negativistic, combative, overactive, dependent, frightened, and withdrawn.

If one-way screen facilities and a wireless earphone ("bug-in-the-ear") are available, it is possible not only to role-play with the change agent, but also to observe and monitor interactions with the child. Homework assignments between sessions, with concomitant careful recording by a parent of specific interactions and outcomes, are of obvious utility. Naturally, the therapist must be careful to prescribe parental changes so that good outcomes are likely. In addition, as is common throughout all behavior therapy, the outcomes of specific interventions provide important assessment material for subsequent changes in strategy. It is also worth emphasizing that the therapist is asking a great deal from the parent when, for example, the parent is urged to ignore Elizabeth's whining rather than attend to it. Many parents are quite unaware of how they reinforce much of their children's undesirable behavior; long-standing habits of parents cannot be expected to change overnight.

The following question can perhaps help the behavior therapist make realistic and ethically proper judgments about what kinds of interventions to suggest to parents who are struggling with problems of their children: How does he raise his own children, or deal with youngsters for whom he has responsibility? For example, how does a given behavior therapist handle crying from his two-year-old if he is certain that the child is dry, well-fed, and in no physical pain? How difficult is it for the professional to place his own offspring on extinction? And what strategies does he adopt to inhibit himself from the all-too-human tendency to go to the wailing toddler and comfort him?

The following transcript is from a session in which a mother was instructed to ignore the operant whining of her child while the therapist observed through a one-way screen:

(*Mother sitting, reading a newspaper, while Andrew, her-five-year-old "hyperactive" son, is playing about 20 feet away with some blocks.*)

Mother: I really like that building you've made, Andrew.

Andrew: I don't like it at all.

Mother: Well, that's OK.

Andrew: (*Whining*) Well, why did you say you liked it?

Mother: (*About to respond when therapist speaks to her via the earphone.*)

Therapist: Go back to your newspaper and do not respond.

Andrew: (*Whining still more loudly*) Hey! Why don't you answer me?

Mother: (*Once again looks up from her paper as if about to respond.*)

Therapist: Even though it may be difficult, go back to your newspaper, please, and let's see if this passes.

Andrew: (*Turns back to his blocks and plays quietly. After a few minutes*) Mommy, would you help me with this building?

Therapist: Now go and play with him since he is not whining.

Mother: (*Walking towards Andrew*) I'd like that very much Andrew, because you asked me so nicely.

Therapist: That was fine.

This relatively simple exchange made immediately clear to the mother how she had become involved with her son in an interactional pattern where she responded with attention to his whining.

The many technological aids currently available, including video tape equipment, can be used effectively by the resourceful behavior therapist, once the basic framework for conceptualization and intervention is acquired.

An innovation that we have found useful under some circumstances is to have several sets of parents meet in a group so that each can profit from the instructions and experiences of the others. As in all group therapy, individual participants are often encouraged by shared experiences; in this type of group, parents can derive some needed social support for their efforts to change their own behavior and subsequently that of their children. As an aide in leading such groups, the guide by Becker (1971) is quite useful. Like the Patterson and Gullion book, it contains numerous down-to-earth examples of child management problems and how they can be analyzed and altered in an operant fashion. Frequent quizzes help the reader ensure that he has mastered material before proceeding.

Most praiseworthy about this clearly written book by Becker is its attention to interpersonal factors in reinforcement. For example, an entire chapter is devoted to how to reinforce, pointing out the seemingly obvious but indispensable necessity to convey caring and warmth to a child while rewarding good behavior. The reader is given specific operational hints in establishing good relationships, such as touching, hugging, having the child sit in the lap, and so forth. Another noteworthy feature of Becker's training manual is its emphasis on teaching the child rules, for example, "If you make a mess, you'll have to clean it up." This emphasis on rules encourages the child to reason things out for himself, facilitating the self-direction which is the ultimate goal of any behavior therapy intervention.

Maintenance of Behavior Change

One of the most neglected aspects of all approaches to therapy is the problem of maintaining behavior change following termination. As we have pointed out elsewhere in this book, the continuing existence of a therapy relationship can foster and maintain a desire on the part of the client to work toward a desired goal. However, it is a challenge to our ingenuity and to the client's resources to continue using the behavioral techniques found effective during therapy (Goldfried & Merbaum, 1973). This is clearly the case in outpatient work with children. Will the parents continue the appropriate operant reinforcement regime worked out in therapy once the therapeutic contract has been terminated? Much to our dismay, we have found on follow-ups after several months that a home situation had deteriorated, apparently due to parental failure to maintain the desired contingencies. We find it ethically sound and pragmatically effective to forewarn parents and teachers of this potential tendency to neglect new habits. There is no point in allowing a parent or teacher to believe that his responsibility as a change agent ceases once the presenting problems are handled. Hopefully, the newly taught behaviors of parents will become "second nature" through continued practice in therapy. It may also be advisable to phase out therapy sessions gradually rather than to terminate abruptly, so that the parents know that they will have to keep the therapist informed of their interactions with their child. The therapist should also encourage the parents to devise their own techniques or to use old techniques in new settings with their child.

Controlled Environments

As we have seen in our review of reinforcement procedures with adults, a behavior therapist may also work with children in relatively controlled settings, such as psychiatric wards, day-care centers, or classrooms. Clearly, the comments already made on reinforcement procedures in general are exceedingly relevant in working with children under more controlled conditions.

As an in-depth example, consider some of the problems and potentialities in working with "normal" children in classrooms. As we have so often found to be the case, we must be concerned initially with obtaining the cooperation of the school system and, in particular, the classroom teacher. This can involve meetings with a school committee, with the principal, or with an entire teaching staff. Ultimately, a quasi-therapeutic relationship must be established with the teacher, whereby the therapist has to enlist the teacher's cooperation in changing his behavior so that ultimately the behavior of one or more of the children can be modified. Without such cooperation even the most sophisticated of operant technologies is doomed to failure.

It is not unusual to find that a teacher, upon learning the basic outlines of reinforcement procedures, will say that he already uses reward and punishment. Of course he does. What the behavioral consultant does is to introduce a degree of systematic application and objective measurement that probably has not characterized the reward and punishment procedures already used by the teacher. The manner in which the therapist introduces the enterprise as a whole can be very important. No matter how skilled the clinician may be in operant theory and technology, chances are the teacher knows a good deal more about the actual goings-on in a classroom. In other words, translations from theoretical principles to clinical reality will probably come more from the teacher than from the consulting "expert." It thus makes sense for a number of reasons to introduce oneself—and view oneself!—as a willing consultant to meet the teacher's needs and to work with him to improve his effectiveness in the classroom and, in general, to make his job easier and more gratifying.

Many teachers feel that they should accede to every request for help from every student. If, however, a student has the intellectual ability to meet a particular school demand, the teacher might very well be unwittingly preventing the child from functioning independently. It may be necessary to convince the teacher that he can more appropriately help a particular child by ignoring requests for assistance if he judges beforehand that the child can in fact perform a particular activity without help.

While a given child might behave quite differently at home than he does at school, it is nonetheless advisable to try to recruit the cooperation of the parents. Indeed, recent ethical and legal controversies suggest that such consent from the parents will be an essential part of any behavior change regimen. It may be necessary, for example, to use, as backup reinforcers for tokens earned by the child in a classroom, activities or treats that only a parent can rightfully provide, such as taking the child to the movies or buying the child a much-desired bicycle.

An occasional source of resistance on the part of some teachers relates to the artificiality they feel in doling out their praise and attention in a planned fashion. As O'Leary and O'Leary (1972) have pointed out, some teachers may feel that spontaneity and natural warmth are lost when a child is deliberately appraised for what he is doing and then systematically reinforced or ignored. A possible strategy in defusing this resistance is to remind the teacher of the controls that already exist in a classroom and of the benefits that the child (and hence the teacher as well) can achieve by the strengthening or elimination of certain behaviors. Moreover, the therapist might point out to the teacher that expressions of liking and approbation, although presented in a deliberate fashion, can nonetheless become quite spontaneous and sincerely felt, particularly as a child begins to improve.

As is the case in changing any sort of behavior, teachers, being only human, will occasionally fail to reinforce appropriately. Should this happen at the beginning of a behavior change procedure, the resulting intermittent reinforcement might well retard the acquisition of desirable behavior. However, if such application

Timing is critical

of contingencies takes place after a particular behavior has been fairly well established, this unplanned intermittent reinforcement will probably serve to strengthen the behavior even more than would a continuous reinforcement schedule. This is merely another way of saying that the teacher's less-than-perfect performance might actually be beneficial in a reinforcement regimen.

Yet another way that the teacher's knowledge of the school situation becomes important is in planning the details of a reinforcement regimen. What does this particular child like to do that might be made contingent upon desired behavior? Chances are that the teacher will be in an excellent position to provide this crucial information.

In assessing the problems to be dealt with, it is useful to keep in mind that the average lay person tends to describe behavior more as a function of inherent traits rather than being situation-specific and heavily influenced by particular setting conditions and reinforcement contingencies. Thus, the therapist should not be satisfied with a description of a child as "aggressive" or "withdrawn". The teacher must learn to specify more precisely the kinds of behaviors that are taking place and under what circumstances they occur. An advantage to working in a controlled setting is the possibility of observing the child directly. The therapist might wish to time-sample a particular child's activities during a classroom activity so as to obtain for himself a better understanding of the variables of which the behaviors are a function. It may come as a surprise to a teacher that a child regarded by him as withdrawn might act quite aggressively on the playground during recess. While this may be obvious to the experienced clinician, it is by no means obvious or even accepted by most people.

In deciding what kind of reinforcer to introduce into a classroom, we agree with a caution voiced by O'Leary and Drabman (1971) that naturally occurring reinforcers should be utilized before introducing the artificiality and complexity of token economy procedures. The therapist might, for example, explore the utility of encouraging the contingent application of praise or other privileges in a classroom setting. Not only is this less disruptive to the ongoing program in the school, but it avoids having to move away from the artificiality of a token program as a consultant prepares to leave the school setting. Playing paddle ball in the playground, dusting erasers, being leader of the day—all take place in most classrooms and are likely to be there long after the clinician leaves. Green and yellow tokens, on the other hand, are seldom a part of normal classroom programs.

Some Ethical Considerations

There are several ethical questions when working with children: How old does a child have to be to merit the final say on which of his behaviors are to be changed and how? Consider a bright ten-year-old who is acting up in school. Suppose further that both the teacher and the boy's parents want him to sit more quietly so that he can derive more from the academic program as well as contribute to the overall decorum of the classroom. Should this child's approval for a behavior change regimen be elicited? What if the child so much enjoys his horsing around in class that he refuses to participate? Indeed, under such circumstances, could we even expect meaningful change to take place, or might we not encourage the child to behave appropriately only while the teacher is watching? Would we feel different if the child had a borderline IQ? Or if the child were 15, or 6? What if the child is committed to a mental institution? In Chapter 13, we will deal more intensively with this and related ethical conundrums.

● APPLICATIONS

The range of behavior problems amenable to operant analysis and intervention is very broad indeed. In the operant behavior therapy literature the difficulties that have been handled with some degree of effectiveness include bed wetting, poor reading habits, aggressive behavior, withdrawn behavior, thumb sucking, nail biting, extreme shyness, faulty toilet habits, low activity level, and interpersonal deficits (O'Leary & Wilson, 1975).

Whatever the topography of the behavior, it is of paramount importance to make an adequate assessment of the controlling variables. Just because a child cries seemingly inappropriately does not mean that such behavior should be ignored. Consider a ten-month-old baby who begins crying because a diaper pin has opened and is sticking into his side. Clearly one would not want to ignore such pain-related behavior. The operant approach as a whole, often presented as a simple, straightforward matter of reward and punishment, is in actuality as challenging and difficult in its conceptualization and implementation as any other mode of therapeutic intervention described in this book.

● SUMMARY

This chapter examined the operant approach within behavior therapy. With its focus on the consequences of behavior, the operant orientation seems particularly appropriate under conditions of high environmental control, as is the case with children and with institutionalized populations. The framework itself is deceptively simple; as we have encountered throughout the book, considerable ingenuity and *Menschlichkeit* are demanded in translating the abstract principles into meaningful clinical interventions. Special emphasis was placed on the interpersonal context in which any operant manipulation takes place; for example, a smile from the therapist, though intended as a reinforcer, might, for some clients at certain times, be interpreted as a sign of superciliousness. Moreover, some clients object to the idea that their behavior, or that of their children, is under environmental control; suggestions were proposed for handling these frequent clinical challenges.

PART 123

DECISIONS FOR CLINICAL APPLICATIONS

Chapter 11

Selected Clinical Problems

With the exception of those infrequent occasions when a client's presenting problem is relatively simple (e.g., fear of dogs), the therapist's decision-making process will not be nearly so straightforward as much of the behavior therapy literature suggests. More typically, a client's difficulties will have to be approached with a variety of procedures, depending on those variables that are assumed to be controlling the problem in question. Thus, as will be illustrated below, individuals incapacitated by anxiety will be approached differently, depending on what the therapist believes underlies their anxiety. What follows may sound very much like the search for "underlying causes" that behavior therapists are mistakenly alleged to overlook. The fact of the matter is that, like other applied scientists, the behavior therapist searches for the strongest controlling variables, many of which are not obvious from a cursory examination of the presenting problem

(Bandura, 1969; Davison & Neale, 1974; Goldfried & Pomeranz, 1968; Lazarus, 1965).

We would like to emphasize that much of the material presented here is necessarily based on our combined clinical experiences, and those of our colleagues. While continuing advances in assessment and comparative outcome research will contribute to a more empirically based set of decision-making procedures, the current state of affairs requires the clinician to work in a heuristic fashion on the basis of his own clinical experience. While we openly admit the utility of clinical experience in directing the decision-making process, we are also sensitive to the potential dangers in such an approach to assessment and therapy. To declare that a given conceptualization or procedure is useful because it "works clinically" is, at best, an interim state of affairs —one that we hope will be replaced by findings stemming from controlled clinical research.

Since we intend this chapter to be illustrative of a general approach to conceptualizing and treating clinical problems, we shall make no attempt to be encyclopedic in our coverage. We wish to illustrate *a way of thinking*, not to present a handbook for the clinical management of problem behaviors.

● A DECISION-MAKING HEURISTIC

Although many of the preceding chapters outlined behavior therapy techniques in a relatively straightforward fashion, we would again like to emphasize the obvious, that human beings are complex, and that the treatment does not always advance so smoothly as one might wish. In addition to limitations in our current pool of techniques, problems of clinical intervention may be due to an incomplete behavioral analysis.

Assessment is one of the most crucial as well as one of the most difficult steps in the behavior change process. Without determining the current maintaining variables for any problem behavior, the therapist can easily waste time and effort in pursuing functionally irrelevant targets. In Chapter 2, we described the general approach to carrying out a behavioral analysis: attention should be paid to potential situational antecedents, organismic variables, response variables, and situational consequences. Such information is crucial in deciding what should be changed. In planning how to effect such change, the decision-making process includes other considerations, such as relevant client variables (e.g., can the client imagine a scene and become anxious?), or pertinent situational conditions (e.g., is it possible to enlist the cooperation of the teacher in handling a child behavior problem?). This general decision-making heuristic will be illustrated below with problems of anxiety, depression, unassertiveness, negative self-concept, and identity crisis.

● ANXIETY

It is often assumed that the presence of anxiety dictates systematic desensitization as the treatment of choice. Although we in no way deny the dramatic behavior change that may result from the skillful and creative use of desensitization, it should not be assumed that such methods are called for in every case of anxiety. Clinical anxiety may be roughly classified as follows: (1) that which seems to have been classically or vicariously conditioned; (2) that which is due to instrumental deficits; (3) that which results from self-generated anxiety-eliciting statements; (4) that which stems from self-induced behaviors, and (5) that which is due to an untenable aspect of one's life situation.

Conditioned Anxiety

Relatively simple phobias are assumed to be directly related to past conditioning experiences—either classical or vicarious in nature—so that the anxiety or avoidance responses are directly linked to specific sets of stimulus situations. In such instances, some form of desensitization would be appropriate, whether it be via imaginal presentation of items, *in vivo* exposure, modeling, or some combination of these. In the absence of clear-cut research data attesting to the relative effectiveness of one therapeutic procedure over another for particular types of phobias, the behavior therapist must rely on these considerations: whether or not the client can clearly imagine a scene and become anxious during the process of imagination; whether the client can be taught to relax; and whether he can be coaxed into graduated *in vivo* exposures to the feared object.

Instrumental Deficits

Sometimes a person's anxiety in, or avoidance of, certain situations may result from the lack of certain skills; this deficiency places him at a disadvantage under certain circumstances. A person may be anxious in interpersonal situations, for example, because he lacks the basic social skills necessary to interact with others. Included here are those people who are shy and retiring in their social interactions, as well as those who are aversive and obnoxious to others. Also included are people who do not interact well with others because their behavior is inappropriate. For the therapist to desensitize such clients, or to attempt in some other way to directly reduce their anxiety in interpersonal situations, might create what Bandura (1969) has described as "relaxed incompetents." A more appropriate therapeutic approach would be to have the client self-monitor situations in which such anxiety occurs, or perhaps to have him ask peers about his impact on others, and then to help him learn more appropriate behaviors, using modeling and behavior rehearsal procedures. Depending on the client's level of anxiety and the distortion of his view of the reactions of others toward him, desensitization and/or rational restructuring may also be required as supplemental procedures. Further, problems involving the lack of appropriate social skills seem to lend themselves particularly well to group treatment. Here, the therapeutic procedure would involve not just individually oriented therapy within a group setting, but using the group in ways that would effectively simulate real-life situations.

Anxiety-Arousing Self-Statements

Anxiety reactions and avoidance behavior may frequently result from internal, often ruminative thought processes that someone engages in while evaluating or labeling a particular situation. As we have suggested in Chapter 8, however, such mislabeling may be so overlearned that the person may not deliberately and overtly distort the situation. The therapist must make some *inference* about the likelihood that inappropriate self-statements are mediating the anxiety. In so doing, the clinician must use his judgment to determine whether, given the client's social skills and what the therapist believes to be the realistic demands of the situation, the client might be distorting. We have observed this distortion most often in social-evaluative situations, where the individual misconstrues others' evaluation of him and unrealistically undermines his own performance. With such a client, we have been impressed with the effectiveness of a rational restructuring approach (Kanter, 1975): the client is taught to evaluate more appropriately the demands of given situations and his ability to function in them.

Self-Induced Behaviors

Closely related to the above situations are instances where anxiety is a direct result of someone's overextending himself. A person who has taken on too much responsibility is likely to be placed under considerable pressure. The college professor with a tight and rigid work schedule is likely to find himself in a perpetual state of tension. More often than not, however, his overextended schedule stems from unrealistic self-demands. If a person's behavior is dictated by many "shoulds" and "musts," anxiety is likely to result. A rational restructuring of these self-induced demands is called for.

Untenable Environment

There are times when people may be anxious primarily because of their environment or general life situation. Such an assessment is clearly relative, for individuals are likely to differ in their capabilities to cope with situational demands. However, there nonetheless exist certain types of conditions that are likely to cause difficulty for most individuals. Take, for example, the child who is continually anxious because of overly harsh parents; or the woman who is upset by the unreasonable behavior of her psychotic spouse; or the anxious executive who is overworked, not because of his own unrealistic demands, but because of the expectations of his superiors.

Modifying the environment, or suggesting that the client remove himself from it, should be considered only after attempts have been made to have him learn to cope directly with it. A key issue here is the definition of the "untenability" of the environment, for such a label is related to the coping ability of the individual as well as to value judgments by both client and therapist. In the final analysis, it is up to the therapist—*in close collaboration with the client*—to make this evaluation. While the therapist's value system plays an important role in judging an environment to be untenable, his own ethical system plays an even stronger role in deciding what should be done. If the woman with a psychotic husband believes in the sanctity of marriage and her obligation to stay in the relationship, the therapist is faced with a difficult ethical dilemma: Should he try to persuade the client to change her views? Obviously, there is no easy answer.

● DEPRESSION

Considering the very high incidence of depression, it is somewhat surprising that it is one of the least explored areas in behavior therapy. For the most part, behavior therapists have attempted to understand depression by focusing on the external behavior of the client; they have suggested that depression is due to the relative absence of reinforcing consequences in a person's life (Ferster, 1965). Although this conceptualization has some value, it is probably incomplete. To begin with, a functional approach to understanding maladaptive behavior runs the risk of overlooking possible physiological determinants. In the case of so-called endogenous depression, the possibility of physiological, chemical, and hormonal imbalances cannot be overlooked (Davison & Neale, 1974); especially for this kind of depression—which is typically severe—appropriate antidepressant medication must be considered.

Even within a functional viewpoint, a conceptualization of depression based solely on external reinforcements remains incomplete; showering a depressed client with gifts and other forms of reinforcement may not alleviate the problem. We favor a more comprehensive view, whereby depression may result from *a perceived absence of any contingency between the person's own efforts and the reinforcing nature of the consequences that follow* (Seligman, 1975). We believe it is crucial to add the cognitive component, particularly since depression is not solely characterized by a low rate of behavior. It is not uncommon to find well-functioning individuals who are depressed. Of paramount importance is the person's *perception* of his ability to control his world. This perception has been described as an attitude of "helplessness and hopelessness." Within this conceptual viewpoint, the general therapeutic strategy would be directed toward helping the client recognize that he can, indeed, control events around him. The precise therapeutic procedure would depend on which variables are controlling the depression.

When the search for potential physiological determinants has proved to be negative, depressive reactions may result from any one or a combination of the following factors: (1) the individual's *efforts* to bring about positive reinforcement are inadequate; (2) the individual's *perceptions* of his ability to control his world are distorted; or (3) his *environment* is unresponsive, in the sense of containing few reinforcements.

Inadequate Efforts

An individual's belief that he cannot control his world may be accurate: objectively, he may be unable to cope with the demands of his particular environment. Even here, however, it is important to determine exactly *why* this ability is lacking. It may be that appropriate skills are simply not in the client's behavioral repertoire; in this case behavior rehearsal, modeling, prompting, and other procedures for overcoming *behavioral deficits* would be in order. If the client's inability to cope with his environment is a function of *inhibitions*, a therapeutic procedure focusing on the direct reduction of anxiety would be called for, whether in the form of desensitization or, if the inhibitions are cognitively mediated, rational restructuring.

In suggesting the use of rational restructuring for depression due to an inability to function, we would like to emphasize that the procedure is employed as a means of reducing the client's inhibitions, thereby allowing him to cope more adequately with his environment. We would *not* use such a therapeutic procedure to have the client reevaluate his self-worth without first making attempts to increase behavioral competence. With one of our clients whose primary complaint was depression, it became evident that her unhappiness was a function of her social isolation, which in turn was due to poor social skills. Although some therapists might have concentrated on helping this client recognize that she was a worthwhile person regardless of what she did, our initial approach was to facilitate competent behavior.

Even where the primary focus has been to get the client to cope more effectively with his environment—either by overcoming certain behavioral deficits or by removing inhibitions—his depression may not be alleviated. We have seen clients change objectively without concomitant change in self-concept. Consequently, techniques that will allow the person to obtain a more realistic picture of his newfound level of functioning (e.g., self-monitoring, therapist and peer feedback) would be in order.

Perceptions of Incompetence

This brings us to the person who comes to therapy with what appears objectively to be an adequate level of functioning. Although the consequences of his behavior would typically be judged to be reinforcing, the individual is nonetheless depressed.

Unlike the type of client described above, such a person can cope, but he does not value the consequences he earns. In such instances, we have operated on the assumption that the problem lies mainly with unrealistically high standards for self-reinforcement. Thus, it is the distorted perceptions of the individual that should be the primary target, for hardly anything that the client does would be "good enough" to "deserve" a reinforcer. With clients such as these, we would suggest the use of rational restructuring.

Unresponsive Environment

An objectively competent individual may accurately perceive his ability to cope with his environment, and yet depression may occur simply because the environment does not yield reinforcements, regardless of his efforts. For example, it is not unreasonable to expect depression to result from the loss of a loved one who had been a principal source of reinforcement.

Sometimes the absence of reinforcers is complicated with other factors. Take, for example, an encyclopedia salesman whose feeling of comptence depends on his ability to get people to pay large sums of money for something they do not need or want. Consider also the woman who receives little gratification from a life at home that is limited to changing diapers, cooking meals, and accommodating herself to the wishes of her husband. If such people are depressed because they find themselves doing something that is not personally rewarding, the therapist can suggest that they attempt to find other satisfactions, or learn to like what they are doing. Which approach to take will clearly depend on both the client's desires and the therapist's social conscience and ethical system.

Other borderline cases present difficulties in determining whether or not the environment or the individual's perceptions should be the primary target. We have seen depressed persons who, although quite competent themselves, are functioning in an environment where other individuals might be at least as competent. A bright student who attends an extremely good school with many other outstanding students may be dissatisfied with his own efforts. Because of the excellent performance of those around him, he may find that his environment does not provide him with sufficient reinforcement. Here too, we can suggest that he change his environment, for example, by transferring to another school, or that he somehow rationally reevaluate the nature of his self-worth within a broader context than that of students at his particular school.

Some General Considerations

There are other complications in working with depressed clients. For example, agitated depression has traditionally been viewed as a category separate from the lethargic, vegetative type. In cases of agitated depression, it is frequently unclear whether anxiety is inhibiting the person from effective coping, or instead is the individual's reaction to his impaired functioning. The former state of affairs would justify an anxiety reduction approach, whereas the latter would warrant attempts to deal with behavior deficits, inappropriate perceptions of abilities, and/or the unresponsive environment.

An even more prevalent complicating factor is the vicious cycle that the depressed person often has gotten himself into: He perceives himself as unable to obtain reinforcement—for whatever reason—which he then construes in a negative way, further undermining his own view of his ability to get things done. An initial step would be to help the person behave so as to obtain *some* kind of reinforcement, perhaps by means of graded tasks, overt or cognitive behavior rehearsal, and continual instigation and reinforcement by the therapist. Determining if the individual can be helped to function at a reasonable level provides invaluable assessment information on the relative roles of behavioral deficits and inhibitions, unrealistic self-evaluations, and the unresponsive nature of the environment.

● UNASSERTIVENESS

As frequently construed within the behavior therapy literature, unassertiveness involves a behavioral deficit. Because the unassertive individual has been assumed to lack certain behavioral skills, the therapeutic procedure of choice has typically been behavior rehearsal. Indeed, as we pointed out in Chapter 7, "assertion training" has frequently implied some form of behavior rehearsal.

In our view, this conception of unassertive behavior is incomplete. We have seen numerous clients who have been able to increase their assertiveness without the aid of any skill training. We have also seen unassertive clients who we thought had generalized behavioral deficiencies but who could in fact, engage in assertive behavior under certain circumstances. Take, for example, a client who has an inordinate amount of difficulty asserting himself with peers and authority figures, but has no difficulty speaking out to his spouse or children. Or a person who is unassertive with everyone except one close friend. Can we legitimately label something a "behavioral deficiency" if we observe the behavior occurring on at least one occasion, or would it be more useful to conceptualize the problem as an inhibition in all instances except this one interaction? This seems to be, as yet, an unresolved dilemma.

In our own work with unassertive clients, we have identified at least five variables of functional importance: (1) the person may not know *what* to say or do; (2) the person may not know *how* to say or do something; (3) anticipatory anxiety may inhibit the person from saying or doing something of an assertive nature; (4) the client may have vague and perhaps unrealistic concerns of something "bad" happening if he asserts himself; and (5) moral or ethical beliefs may lead the person to believe that it is not "proper" to assert oneself.

Absence of Information

When someone's unassertiveness is due to lack of information about what should be said or done under certain circumstances, a deficiency may be said to exist. Lack of knowledge about appropriate behavior would not require any direct behavior rehearsal procedures. Instead, some form of information giving is needed. This may entail the therapist discussing what is to be done in certain social circumstances, provided that he is aware of the social mores of the client's cultural milieu. If the therapist is not aware, as was true when one of us was seeing an unassertive nun in therapy, assistance from some representative person familiar with the client's environment (e.g., friend, co-worker, spouse) may be called for.

Behavioral Deficit

Unassertive behavior resulting from a lack of knowledge of what to say or do may be accompanied by an actual behavioral deficiency: the client may not know *how* to assert himself appropriately. The individual's tone of voice, body posture, eye contact, and a host of other variables related to style of responding lend themselves to retraining via modeling, behavior rehearsal, and periodic feedback.

Anticipatory Anxiety

When the client's anxiety prevents him from emitting what might be appropriately assertive behavior, the anxiety could be reduced by desensitization or coping relaxation. Even when the client lacks both the information and actual skills for asserting himself, anticipatory anxiety may also play a role. Under such circumstances, direct attention to anxiety reduction would facilitate any behavioral shaping process.

Unrealistic Expectations

Quite often unassertive behavior seems to be maintained by the expectation that standing up for one's rights will have negative consequences. With such clients, the lack of assertiveness might be more appropriately conceptualized as a problem of social-evaluative anxiety. Specifically, these individuals are frequently afraid that if they assert themselves, others will think less of them. We have typically approached such clients with some form of rational restructuring, either according to the guidelines described in Chapter 8, or by simply convincing them that they are wrong. Unassertive people are frequently impressed when they realize that by *not* asserting themselves, the consequences they are trying to avoid may *actually occur*. For example, the reason many people are reluctant to engage in assertive behavior is that they are afraid others will no longer like or approve of them. In fact, by not asserting themselves, they may *lose* the respect of their friends and colleagues.[1] The realization that assertiveness is likely to help them reach their goals, along with instigation and reassurance by the therapist, can in itself get such clients to modify their behavior.

Moral and Ethical Concerns

Some individuals may be reluctant to assert themselves because they feel that it is somehow "improper." Such concerns differ somewhat from those mentioned in the previous section. For example, the client may believe that it is wrong to express certain

[1] Women are probably in a different situation, for, as discussed in Chapter 13, their increased assertiveness may not invariably meet with approval.

feelings. Such misconceptions may be stated in only vague terms. For example, one client was reluctant to assert himself to a close friend, for he felt it was not proper. As it turned out, the client had never thought through what the consequences of assertion might actually be; as he began to discuss them with the therapist, it soon became apparent that the feared negative consequences were mythical.

There are times when the consequences anticipated by an unassertive individual are more clearly moral or ethical in nature. If the therapist is knowledgeable about the client's moral guidelines, he can discuss the issues himself. Otherwise, outside experts likely to be more credible to the client (e.g., ministers, priests, rabbis) might be called upon for assistance.

Some General Considerations

As is the case with other problem behaviors, it is not always easy to determine which variables may be operating in any given instance. By the time the adult client arrives for professional help, a number of variables might be functionally operative. For example, if the individual has been inhibited from asserting himself for some period of time, actual gaps in his behavioral repertoire may have developed, so that he now lacks the ability to assert himself adequately in given situations. Conversely, an individual possessing a behavioral deficiency for any length of time may also become inhibited about asserting himself, particularly in light of past negative feedback he may have received from others.

Considering the complexities involved in any given case, we sometimes favor a "shotgun" approach in dealing with unassertive behavior. Tactically, one of the easiest things to do is to have the client begin by self-monitoring assertive behavior. Information resulting from this monitoring will prove useful regardless of the specific therapeutic approach eventually decided upon. Hopefully, it may also be reactive in the sense of facilitating assertiveness, particularly if the client keeps daily observations of both assertive and unassertive behavior.

At our present stage of knowledge, the only way we can suggest to actually determine which variables are most important in maintaining assertive behavior is to directly ask the client involved. Sample questions might include: What might you say or do if you were in this kind of situation? Can you demonstrate to me exactly how you would go about saying or doing it? If you were completely calm, how do you think you would respond in that situation? What do you think would happen if you actually asserted yourself in this situation? What might other people think of you if you asserted yourself? According to whose moral or ethical standards do you think such behavior is inappropriate?

● NEGATIVE SELF-CONCEPT

Although the tendency to devalue one's self-worth is found along with various other clinical problems, it nonetheless is worthy of separate consideration. Clients frequently complain about lack of self-confidence, inferiority feelings, a sense of inadequacy, all of which may be construed as a negative attitude about their own behavior. In many respects, the variables associated with negative self-concept are similar to many of those underlying depression. We have observed three parameters—certainly not mutually exclusive—associated with complaints of inadequacy feelings: (1) the person's behavior may be objectively less than adequate; (2) his standards for evaluation may be overly severe; or (3) he may simply be unaware of the impact he is having on his environment.

Behavioral Ineffectiveness

It could well be that a person's feelings of inadequacy are realistic, if he is not very effective in many of his interactions with his environment. In the absence of any standardized measures of competence, the clinician must draw on his own estimate of what in fact is effective in the person's social milieu, and perhaps also make use of ancillary reports from outsiders who may be familiar with the person's social situation. As is true in so many other clinical instances where a client is not emitting the appropriate behavior, the clinician should consider the possibility that a skill deficit exists, or that the behavior is in the repertoire but is in some way being inhibited. Skill training and/or anxiety reduction procedures would be used, depending on the assessment.

Unrealistically High Standards

Since the notion of self-worth has a strong evaluative component, there is always a possibility that the person is being overly harsh on himself. If his standards for effectiveness are unrealistically high, chances are the person will seldom be satisfied by his performance. Rational restructuring procedures would be useful in such instances.

Misperception of Effectiveness

Even when an individual's behavior is objectively adequate and his standards for self-evaluation appropriate, a negative self-concept may result from unawareness of his positive impact on the environment. We have encountered this when a client has recently acquired a new behavioral repertoire, but continues to believe he is ineffectual. Treatment under such circumstances can consist of feedback that may bring his perceptions more in line with reality. This is more than simple reassurance and support, for it entails concrete and detailed feedback, giving specific examples of how competently he is in fact behaving. The client can be instructed to observe himself in various situations, and to note the difference between his newfound abilities and his behavior in the past. Further, audio and video tape feedback may be used to demonstrate to the individual how he appears to others. Finally, the therapist can provide frequent summaries and descriptions of the client's more effective functioning in various situations.

● IDENTITY CRISIS

The term "identity crisis" is admittedly fraught with surplus meaning. In the most general sense, it refers to difficulties in establishing meaningful life goals. Although the concept of identity crisis is a construct derived from another theoretical system, it nonetheless merits attention from all clinicians.

From the vantage point of the behavior therapist, it is less profitable to focus on a detailed analysis of such feelings—which are typically stated in vague terms alluding to the meaning of life—than to attend to the antecedents of such subjective reactions. In carrying out a behavioral analysis of identity crisis, it becomes readily apparent that the conceptualization is similar to that described for depression and negative self-concept. The major difference, however, is that identity crisis frequently is related to certain changing role conceptions in the client. Although identity crises are most poignantly encountered in adolescents, our complex and dynamic society makes never-ending demands for changes in behavior throughout our lifetime. As a result, questions such as "Who am I?" and "Where am I going?" constantly assail us.

Dollard and Miller's (1950) concept of the "learning dilemma" seems to relate to identity crisis, in that the individual's previous behavior no longer seems to work or pay off. Thus, what we see as identity crisis may be the affective reaction of an individual who does not feel he is in control of his world. In more severe forms, we find the feelings of hopelessness and helplessness associated with depression. Often the individual's role definition or conception has changed so that he has difficulty functioning as he did in the past. In adolescence, the previously dependent youth is suddenly required to behave in ways that are different from what he is accustomed to. Similarly, the successful businessperson or professional who has worked long and conscientiously to "make it" may find himself at a loss once his objectives have been reached. And the person who, after working all his life, moves into retirement finds himself in a role requiring behaviors not familiar to him, and not requiring skills that he has spent a lifetime acquiring.

In treating an identity crisis, the therapist would work to undo whatever behavioral deficits are interfering with the individual's performance, to change attitudes regarding his ability to cope, and/or to reduce inhibitions that prevent effective coping that might otherwise exist. The focus here is on the particular task requirements associated with the new role the individual finds himself in. Information giving, problem solving, role playing, and desensitization may all be required.

Inextricably tied to the notion of identity crisis are concerns regarding values. Assuming that a person is capable of engaging in certain behaviors, one must invariably ask whether or not he *wants* to behave in given ways. Although the therapist's own values and biases will likely play a role in dealing with certain issues, it nonetheless is possible to focus on the client's concerns. For example, they may be understood as the positive or negative consequences the client attributes to a given course of action, whether they be short- or long-term consequences, or consequences for himself or for significant others. As in all problem solving, the therapist's task is to help the client evaluate potential courses of action and estimate the likely consequences of each. What we frequently construe initially as a problem of "values" may turn out to be related to a person's having overemphasized certain sets of consequences while ignoring others. What is important or meaningful in one person's life may be trivial in another's. For example, some individuals devote their energies to achievement and external signs of "success," while others work more toward personal intimacy. Although the therapist can be of considerable assistance in pointing out consequences overlooked by the client, the ultimate decision regarding the direction he wants his life to take obviously should be left to the client himself.

● SUMMARY

This chapter represents a kind of distillation of the entire book. A therapist must ultimately try to apply his knowledge in concrete ways to a wide range of clinical problems. In this chapter we have tried to portray the behavioral clinician's decision-making processes. The overall emphasis is on identifying the strongest controlling variables, for the therapist's judgment here leads inexorably to clinical interventions that will have varying degrees of utility. The decision-making processes engaged in by behavior therapists are, to our minds, at least as complex as those of other therapeutic approaches. These processes have been illustrated with the clinical problems of anxiety, depression, unassertiveness, negative self-concept, and identity crisis.

Chapter 12

Extended
Case Illustration

Most published case reports can lead one to believe that behavior therapy is a simple and straightforward approach to be used only in clear-cut cases. Many of the so-called simple cases that appear in print were probably taken out of context, partly because of space limitations, but also because complicating issues might have detracted from the major points the report was meant to convey. The purpose of the case illustration in this chapter, in contrast, is to give a more faithful picture of behavior therapy.

We have deliberately selected a fairly complicated case because it serves to demonstrate the subtleties frequently associated with the assessment of relevant problems, the setting of priorities for treatment goals, and the need for a variety of techniques. To provide the reader with a vivid, detailed, and realistic view of the ongoing considerations of this case, we present a session-by-session review based on our therapy notes. Identifying features have been changed to protect the confidentiality of the client, and substantive changes have been made for illustrative purposes.

● PRESENTING PROBLEMS AND HISTORICAL BACKGROUND

The client, whom we shall call Ann, is a thirty-five-year-old woman married to a successful dentist, a mother of two children (five-year-old daughter and seven-year-old son), and a part-time secretary. The major problems, as presented by the client, consisted of feelings of depression, severe and seemingly pervasive anxiety, lack of incentive, inability to function independently, and marked feelings of helplessness and inadequacy.

The client, who is the only female and youngest in a family of three children, was born and raised in a large midwestern metropolitan area by middle-class Protestant parents. Her father died of a heart attack when she was fifteen years of age, but her maternal uncle, who had been living with them, continued to stay on with the family. The client describes both her mother and uncle as being highly critical and overprotective, allowing her little opportunity for independent behavior.

After high school, Ann lived with her family and worked as a secretary. She continued to live at home until she was in her early twenties, at which time she married a man who was about to enter the navy. His assignment soon required a move to the west coast. This was the first time she had been away from home, and the sudden separation from familiar surroundings brought on a severe anxiety reaction. Periodic anxiety attacks and bouts of depression occurred over the years. Ann was seen by psychiatrists on four different occasions and was treated primarily with drugs. She became most acutely upset when she, her husband, and two children moved into a new home. The client was referred to the present therapist by an internist.

● COURSE OF TREATMENT

The following is a description of the course of treatment over 51 sessions within a period of two years:

Session 1

The client was extremely anxious during this initial contact, sitting on the edge of her chair for most of the session. She made me nervous just to look at her. She looked very pale and was generally unkempt.

We spent most of the session reviewing demographic and historical information. It became apparent early in the hour that Ann's appraisal of her problems is only serving to make matters worse: She's afraid that she may be "going crazy" and that something is wrong with her "nerves." In light of numerous medical examinations that showed her to be in good physical health, I tried to disabuse her of her concerns regarding any physical disability, and additionally offered some encouragement that she could, indeed, be helped. She's unquestionably highly motivated for therapy, and gives me the impression of being willing to go along with my suggestions.

One more observation: At the end of the session, the friend who had accompanied her to the session expressed great concern to me about Ann's welfare, and hoped that something might be done to help. Despite the fact that the client is a thirty-five-year-old woman, my general feeling is that my client is a child, not an adult.

Session 2

Assessment continued, with most of the time spent in expanding on the Personal Data Form, which Ann had mailed to me earlier in the week. Her written description of the major complaints is as follows: "I suffer from anxiety and depression. I have heart palpitations and a terrible feeling in my head—not a headache. Each day is such an effort to get through. I don't put make-up on or take care of myself as I used to. Every little problem becomes so magnified to me now. I've lost interest in everything. I'm trying desperately to take care of my children and not neglect them. I am so preoccupied with my symptoms I can hardly think of anything else."

Her lack of independence and unassertiveness appear to be long-standing, dating back as far as she can remember. In addition, she has always been sensitive to criticism, and becomes particularly upset when her husband is impatient with her. Although feelings of anxiety are always present, they are much more severe when she is alone at home, or out socially. I gave her a homework assignment to list specific anxiety-provoking situations; in addition to serving an assessment function, this information would be useful for hierarchy construction, should desensitization seem appropriate.

Ann seemed a bit less apprehensive during this session, and went along with my suggestion that she sit back in the chair and

try to make herself more comfortable. It's apparent that before anything else can be attempted therapeutically, something has to be
done about her high level of anxiety. I described relaxation procedures, but didn't have enough time to actually begin today.

During these initial sessions, it was apparent that she felt she
had absolutely no control over her world; she also made frequent
requests for support and encouragement (e.g., "Can you help
me?"). In searching around for some readily modifiable aspect of
her behavior that could produce some positive consequences and
give her some hope, I suggested that she make an attempt to smile
at people she had contact with during the following week, and
simply notice their reactions. I tried not to present this as any
major therapeutic strategy, but simply as a way of illustrating that
she potentially had much more effect on her environment than she
thought. She agreed to try.

Session 3

Ann brought in a list of anxiety-provoking situations, and about
10 minutes were spent transferring these onto hierarchy cards.
She *did* follow through on the "smiling" homework in one instance,
and was successful in eliciting a positive reaction from a clerk; I
encouraged her to continue this little assignment. Most of the
session was spent in tension-relaxation training; she reported
going from 90 to 25, with some difficulty in relaxing her face and
legs. She was to practice with the tape daily till our next session.

Sessions 4 and 5

Either the relaxation procedures are having a positive effect, or
she's responding favorably to the demand characteristics of the
therapy; perhaps both. Whatever the reason, Ann appeared more
relaxed during these two sessions, as well as more lively and alert.
In addition to practicing relaxation with the tape, she has been
attempting to relax herself *in vivo* even though I had cautioned her
not to just yet. She has also continued smiling at others and actually found it helpful in striking up a conversation on one occasion.
I offered my encouragement, but hastened to put these changes in
the perspective of a gradual, step-by-step progression. These sessions were also spent working on hierarchy items, which consisted
of social-evaluative situations as well as instances where she had to
be at home alone.

Session 6

Ann arrived 15 minutes late for the session and explained that the person who was to drive her had been delayed. It turns out that she has never come to any of our sessions by herself, but always had somebody drive her. I could kick myself for not having picked up on this earlier. In any event, she reported that she did very little by herself, managing to arrange her life so that friends and relatives were quick to reinforce her dependent behavior.

Ann complains of recently becoming more depressed. She's concerned about feelings of pressure in her head, has difficulty conversing with others, and is starting to neglect her physical appearance again. All this is making her acutely anxious, and she's afraid that she might be having a "nervous breakdown." Although I tried to convince her otherwise, I am concerned that she may need to be hospitalized if matters get much worse. We both decided to increase the frequency of sessions to twice a week, and to postpone any work on systematic desensitization. Instead, we'll focus on her depression. The therapeutic strategy will be to get her to gradually increase her ability to function more independently. She can always avoid those situations that make her anxious, but can do very little to deal with her depression. For openers, I suggested she try to do some things by herself, like driving to the next session alone.

Session 7

She began by proudly reporting that she drove to the session by herself with minimal anxiety. Also, she reported one instance when she went shopping alone. I was delighted to hear all this and made it a point to let her know how I felt.

As part of an ongoing attempt to disabuse Ann of her concerns about being "mentally ill," I emphasized that her feelings of depression were the result of her inability to cope. I also stressed that she should gauge her progress more in terms of the changes that occurred since she began therapy, rather than all that she has yet to accomplish. I also encouraged her to tell her husband of her successes along the way; hopefully, he will serve as an additional source of reinforcement.

Ann had not been practicing her relaxation between sessions, complaining that it was inconvenient for her to do so; there always seemed to be somebody in the house. Although I stressed the importance of practicing relaxation on a daily basis, it is becoming evident that deliberate steps (assertion training?) are going to have to be made to minimize the "help" that others around her seem to be giving.

One of her major concerns appears to be her inability to cope with managing her house. She typically puts off all cleaning until Monday, when a relative comes over to help. Her general approach to chores needs some structure and organization. For example, upon waking each morning, she typically lies in bed and becomes depressed over the fact that the house is a mess. This causes her to feel even more depressed and immobilized, to the point where she now experiences difficulty even getting out of bed. To break this vicious cycle, we used some covert behavior rehearsal. Ann imagined herself getting up in the morning, making the bed, tidying up the bedroom, and getting washed and dressed. She rehearsed this sequence twice, concurrently verbalizing aloud exactly what she was doing. Ann agreed that she would, in fact, try out this behavior sequence tomorrow morning; I asked her to call me when she was through.

Phone Contact

Ann called me this morning as planned and reported following through on what she had rehearsed covertly. She awoke at 7:00 A.M. feeling somewhat jittery. She stayed in bed a while, ruminating about her difficulties, but soon got up and followed through on the routine she had rehearsed. I, of course, was quite pleased and encouraged her to make some attempt to plan the rest of the day. She added that knowing she had to phone in was helpful.

Session 8

Ann missed one scheduled session, reporting that her sister had paid her an unexpected visit. She looked much more relaxed this session, smiled more, and related a number of success experiences. She's more willing to place herself in social situations, and is becoming more and more successful at carrying out relaxation *in vivo*. In addition, the morning routine is becoming more natural, with the dread of facing a new day having diminished considerably. We spent some time discussing the importance of her refusing the help offered by friends and relatives.

Ann cognitively rehearsed her plan for an entire day, while I offered periodic suggestions that she relax any time she experienced tension. The last 5 to 10 minutes of the session were spent in testing her ability to relax (which was good), and I then gave her a tape recording of an abbreviated version of relaxation instruc- *13* tions (letting go without initial tensing).

Sessions 9, 10, and 11

She followed through on what she had rehearsed cognitively, and was enthusiastic about her success. In fact, she accomplished even more than she had planned. Ann told her husband of her progress, and he, too, was most pleased. It was also quite obvious that she gets considerable pleasure in telling me of her progress. I feel the same way and told her so. She's been practicing her relaxation, and reports good success (down regularly to 25). She generally feels in much better control of herself socially; in fact, a review of the hierarchy resulted in the elimination of several ✓ items of a social-evaluative nature. We spent some time on hierarchy construction, although her progress to date may very well *14* make systematic desensitization unnecessary.

I used cognitive rehearsal to prepare her for the forthcoming *15* weekend. She reports feeling somewhat unhappy although she's clearly not as unhappy as she used to be. She's beginning to function more adequately, yet still does little during the course of the day that she truly enjoys. We discussed some possible reinforcing ✓ activities. The whole question of her satisfaction with her role as housewife should certainly be discussed.

Sessions 12 and 13

Ann called to cancel a session, stating that her sister had again paid her an unexpected visit. She had a few good days since I saw her last week. She went out to dinner with friends. In addition, she prepared dinner for her mother and sister, which was the first time she had ever done so for anyone in her new home.

She seems to be less fearful about being alone at home. I explained the need for her to gradually spend more periods of time *16* alone, and also for associating such solitude with more pleasurable activities (e.g., knitting, reading). Although she's been making *17* concerted efforts to do so, well-meaning friends and relatives always seem to interfere. I pointed out the need for greater asser- ✓ tiveness on her part, and as a beginning, suggested that she keep *18* a daily record of those situations where she was, and was not, assertive.

Session 14

Ann canceled her regularly scheduled appointment because of a snowstorm. When she arrived for today's session, she had all sorts of good things to report from the previous week. As a result of her self-monitoring, she has begun to assert herself more than usual (e.g., offering her opinion to co-workers, disagreeing with her husband). We used those situations in which she was not successful in asserting herself to discuss how she might behave differently.

She reports utilizing relaxation *in vivo* on a regular basis, adding that it's becoming more and more automatic. In particular, she's been attempting to remain relaxed while at home alone, with relative success. She is also making inroads on her housework chores and is becoming better organized at work.

Sessions 15 and 16

Ann canceled a regularly scheduled session, indicating that she had to wait at home for a furniture delivery. These cancellations are really getting to me. I'm letting her get away with it, but I'm not quite sure why. I reiterated the importance of attending each session, and urged her to rearrange her other commitments so that she would be able to do so.

Her efforts to assert herself are becoming increasingly successful. For example, she insisted that a salesclerk find the exact item she wanted rather than accept the one he had initially offered to her, necessitating his looking for the article in the stockroom.

A review of the hierarchy items revealed that social-evaluative anxiety no longer seems to be a problem! It's difficult to say exactly what this was due to—perhaps the use of relaxation *in vivo*; her increased assertiveness probably has something to do with it as well. The primary source of anxiety at this time, then, involves being at home alone. I encouraged her to gradually spend longer periods of time by herself.

Ann continues to report that she is not very happy. Despite her mild dysphoric feelings, however, she nonetheless continues to function. I again stressed the importance of her becoming involved in more pleasurable activities. As a start, she said that she would be interested in taking up knitting again—a pastime she had enjoyed some years ago. She cognitively rehearsed going to the knitting store on Saturday to obtain the necessary materials, and also knitting for some time at home on Sunday.

Session 17

Ann canceled the session because her in-laws had come to visit; she felt uncomfortable about leaving them alone. I think my reluctance to be more firm about missed appointments has been a concern that she would be unable to assert herself to her unexpected visitors. I no longer think she's that unassertive. Thus, I told her that, except for legitimate reasons, I would have to bill her for future cancellations. She seemed to accept this as reasonable.

She wasn't able to get to the knitting store as planned because she was busy preparing for Christmas vacation. She had been feeling a little better this past week, mentioning that at a recent party she had socialized more than she had ever done before. Ann continues to be more assertive, and is receiving generous reinforcement from others, including her husband. Because of holiday preparations, there was little opportunity for her to remain at home alone.

Sessions 18 and 19

Ann spent two hours at home alone one afternoon, which represents the longest duration to date. She spent most of this time straightening up the house, and felt little anxiety. When shopping for food, however, she still needs to be accompanied by her uncle.

Ann was finding all sorts of excuses to avoid looking into potentially pleasurable activities. She admitted to feeling guilty about doing things for herself, thinking that her primary obligation was to her family. We'll have to explore this at the next session.

Session 20

Most of the session focused on her feelings of guilt over enjoying herself. She admitted a generally negative opinion of herself, adding that she really didn't deserve much pleasure. In an attempt to have Ann focus more realistically on her own worth, I insisted that she defend herself as a person by describing her positive traits. She enumerated a number of favorable characteristics (e.g., being a capable parent, loving her children, being sympathetic to friends, being more effective at work, and generally becoming more assertive). I urged her to keep these qualities in mind in any future subjective evaluations of her self-worth. Toward the end of the session, Ann made a firm commitment that she would finally get to the knitting store before our next session.

Interim Summary

At this point, we seem to have broken the vicious cycle between depression and her inability to function. Nonetheless, she still needs to incorporate more reinforcing activities into her life. She seems to be adept at using coping relaxation to handle her interpersonal anxiety and fear of being alone at home. Because of this, I have pretty much given up the thought of systematic desensitization. Ann is obviously very dependent on me, a fact that undoubtedly enhances my ability to instigate and reinforce her behavior between sessions. Once a stable behavior pattern seems to develop, we'll have to start working on getting her to rely on me less. There have been times when I've been tempted to call her husband in and involve him more in his wife's therapy. What has kept me from doing so, however, is that Ann might attribute any change resulting from this as being due to forces beyond her control. Everybody seems to be doing things to "help" her, and I would prefer to get her to cope on her own if I can.

Session 21

Despite a series of obstacles, she finally made it to the knitting store! She had gone there only to find that they had moved. Her inquiries at neighboring stores failed to reveal the new location. She persisted, nonetheless, until she was finally able to find another store. Her active attempts at coping represent a marked departure from previous behavior and have resulted in a good deal of self (and therapist) satisfaction.

Although Ann continues to make progress along the lines of increased assertiveness, she finds herself having difficulty expressing her ideas to one of her particularly assertive friends. We rehearsed several times a situation in which she successfully defended her role as homemaker and mother against the arguments offered by her friend. This led into a discussion of Ann's role perception and her guilt over engaging in pleasurable activities. Prior to having her children, she had always worked full-time and in recent years had experienced difficulty learning how to be a homemaker. I raised the possibility that some of her depression might be the result of her devoting too much of herself to home and family. We went into this issue at great length, after which she came to the conclusion that she *wanted* to be a homemaker but that she could not yet do so comfortably and successfully. At the most, she would only want to continue working part-time.

She agreed to spend a half hour during the week either reading or knitting, and doing so immediately before going to work. The entire behavior sequence was cognitively rehearsed.

Session 22

She spent the half hour knitting, but didn't enjoy it as much as she would have liked. Her mind kept wandering, thinking of all the things that had to be done around the house. She presents her current situation as still "moving into" her new home, feeling that she never had really organized things. After these various chores are completed, she feels that her mind will be free to pursue more enjoyable interests. There's probably a certain amount of reality associated with her distraction, and it might be best for me to back off a bit temporarily in getting her to pursue leisure-time activities.

Ann spent some time reporting on her successful use of relaxation *in vivo*, and on examples of increased assertiveness.

Session 23

An unforeseen event resulted in Ann having to spend the entire day alone at home. Her cousin, who typically helped her clean the house on Mondays, called her at the last minute to say that she was ill. Ann's immediate thought was, "How am I ever going to get through the day?" She became very anxious and wanted to run immediately out of the house. Instead, she remembered to relax herself and keep busy. Despite the basic unpleasantness of remaining at home, the very fact that she lived through the day offered her considerable hope that she could eventually eliminate this problem.

Sessions 24, 25, and 26

Ann reports spending more and more time alone at home, experiencing only minimal anxiety. It seems as if that full day at home alone may have done the trick. So much for total therapist control over *in vivo* exposures. From time to time, she has had to assert herself to keep others away. She's just about finished working on her projects around the house. She's also been doing more reading and knitting lately, and feels much less guilty about doing things for herself. Her personal appearance has become more important to her, and she is in the process of buying some new clothes. She also finds herself dwelling less on areas of difficulty which still remain, and complains less to others. For the most part, these last few sessions have been devoted to reporting and planning.

Sessions 27 and 28

She has finally completed the "moving in" process at home, and reports having "no more excuses" about not pursuing other things in life. In addition to her own activities, she feels that it would be important for both her husband and herself to spend more time together; some possibilities were discussed.

Because she continually self-monitors, her occasional lapses into a dependent role cause her to become annoyed at herself. Fortunately, she reacts to this annoyance by forcing herself to be more independent and assertive, especially to her husband.

Although her current level of functioning represents a substantial improvement over past behavior, she continues to speak negatively about herself. Much to my dismay, Ann persists in asking: "When will I ever get better?" The change in self-image appears to have lagged behind overt behavior change; hopefully her attitude will improve if she is able to appreciate how well she is getting on.

Sessions 29 and 30

Ann related a number of instances in which she asserted herself. On one occasion she insisted that a man move his truck from in front of her driveway so that she could leave, in spite of his wanting to complete his delivery first. Being alone no longer seems to be a problem, as this occurs fairly regularly for varying lengths of time. She's been knitting and reading without feeling any guilt. Things continue to go well at work.

I had urged her to keep a diary of her effective behavior, and to use this in order to get a more realistic perspective on her adequacy as a person. She did so, and found it most helpful in updating her view of herself.

For the first time since Ann moved into the house, she held a dinner party. She handled most of the work herself, did not feel undue pressure, and reported enjoying herself very much. To top things off, she was massively reinforced by friends who commented on what a "relaxed hostess" she was. It was at this point that I suggested that she think along the lines of reducing the frequency of our sessions from twice to once per week.

Session 31

For reasons that are not immediately clear, Ann reports feeling depressed during the past few days (a reaction to my suggestion about cutting back frequency of sessions?). Although she's able to function fairly well, she reverted back to having somebody drive her to this session. The primary focus today was on having her reevaluate her negative self-image (e.g., "I have an inadequate personality") in light of her new strengths and abilities. I'll have to devise a more systematic approach to getting her to adopt a more realistic self-image. The next session was scheduled after Ann's two-week vacation.

Sessions 32, 33, and 34

Her vacation went fairly well, although she experienced marked anxiety as she returned home. I told her that I sometimes feel this way after vacations, and that it is not an atypical reaction. It appears as if her current difficulties are self-imposed, in the sense that she has been overlooking her positive attributes and instead has been spending a good deal of time thinking about her remaining deficiencies. My suggestion that she stop ruminating and attempt to divert her attention to current matters appeared to help somewhat. Consequently, I decided to follow this up with more formalized thought-stopping procedures, which she reported being able to use to good advantage between sessions.

Three procedures were used in an attempt to have Ann focus on her more positive characteristics: (1) Whenever she assumed a helpless and dependent role during our sessions (e.g., "How shall I handle this situation?") I switched roles with her, requiring her to provide the solution to her own query; (2) I had her keep a daily record of those events which she felt she handled effectively, and we reviewed these during each session; and (3) I provided her with periodic feedback during the sessions, via tape recorder, of those instances where she spoke about herself in a positive way.

Despite what appears to be a setback, I feel that she possesses enough strength to warrant cutting back to one session a week.

We agreed to do so, at least on a tentative basis. Her dependency on me, although put to good therapeutic advantage in the past, now has to be phased out.

Sessions 35 and 36

She reports feeling less depressed lately, which suggests that the thought stopping, as well as my encouraging her to look at herself in a less jaundiced way, may have been helpful. She's currently taking steps toward expanding her social life, which she feels will go a long way in combating what currently appears to be a low-level state of depression.

During one of the sessions, she presented a very realistic picture of her current status, indicating that for the first time in her life she is beginning to behave like an adult. She added that although it may take a good deal of time, she is nonetheless optimistic that she will achieve the kind of independence she wants. She also construes setbacks as being only temporary, and probably insignificant in the more global picture. Fortunately, the session was being taped, which gave me an excellent opportunity to offer her immediate and vivid feedback on what she had said.

Sessions 37 and 38

Ann and her husband were away for a week, visiting his parents. She felt very relaxed during the trip, and enjoyed herself much more than she had anticipated. Rather than being upset by the letdown she felt upon returning home, she was able to attribute this to the feeling most anyone might expect upon returning from vacation.

She continues to function well in her many day-to-day activities. Her fear of being alone and her other anxieties are no longer a problem.

Unfortunately, the low-level depression continues to exist. As she puts it, "The joy of life is not there." We discussed at great length what could provide her with greater happiness. Among the things that she feels would make her happy are more frequent contact with friends, greater attention paid to her physical appearance, and having her husband spend more time around the house. This last item led into a lengthy discussion of her relationship with her husband, who seems to have mixed feelings about her increased assertiveness. Although my immediate inclination is to call him in for a session, I'm afraid this might feed into her dependency, so I encouraged her to discuss this with him directly.

Sessions 39 and 40

These have been the best two sessions to date. Ann looked well, smiled, was very animated and enthusiastic in her speech, and generally reported feeling very good about things.

She is becoming more involved with friends, and has taken steps to spend more time with her husband. She hired a cleaning woman, and is able to sit around the house relaxing frequently without feeling guilty. Things are also going well on the job.

She and her husband have had a couple of lengthy discussions about her increased assertiveness. Some of these ended in arguments, but she did hold her own. There is obviously a lot to resolve here, so I'll be keeping tabs on things. I'm not sure at this point whether I'll have to have him come in for a session.

Interim Summary

Her fear of being alone no longer seems to be a problem, a fact that she attributes to the full day she had to spend by herself. She also seems to be more comfortable socially. Her increased assertiveness seems to be helping her move toward greater independence in two ways. She is able to keep well-meaning friends and relatives from rushing to her assistance, thereby giving her more of an opportunity to attempt things on her own. Further, her assertiveness allows her to cope with everyday matters more effectively. A factor contributing to her assertive behavior is that she continually self-monitors, attempting to behave more assertively when she notices herself lapsing into a more passive role. Although the subjective picture of herself has seemed to lag behind overt behavior change, she is beginning to get a more realistic view of her new-found abilities. It's probably not too early to start working on terminating by gradually cutting back on the frequency of our sessions and also by using problem solving to get her to rely more on her own resources. A lot will depend on whether her husband will become receptive to her growing independence.

Sessions 41, 42, 43, 44, and 45

The therapeutic strategy during each of these sessions was to have Ann "report in" on the events of the previous two weeks. With the exception of one minor setback, her behavior pattern appears to be fairly stable. Even the one setback was useful therapeutically: although she initially became concerned ("I'm getting sick again"), she quickly identified herself as simply being a bit nervous, and was then successful in relaxing away these feelings. I tried to point out that this "setback" was in a way fortunate, in that it provided her with the opportunity to cope independently. This, I suggested, should make her less apprehensive about any problems in the future, and should also contribute to her overall feelings of competence.

For the most part, the problems brought up during these sessions were realistic, such as how to cope with an unreasonable neighbor and how to resolve differences with her husband. In contrast to my directiveness during our earlier sessions, I made a concerted effort to avoid offering her my own suggestions on these matters, instead assisting her in coping by herself through problem solving. With termination approaching, she has to be taught to deal with these things on her own. It appears less and less likely that I'm going to have to see the husband. The next session was scheduled in five weeks.

Session 46

Things continued to go well. The next session is scheduled in five weeks.

Session 47

The client phoned a week after our last session, feeling very anxious and depressed. Her children had just returned to school after summer vacation, and she was experiencing difficulty reestablishing the behavior pattern she had gotten into prior to the summer. As a result, she was afraid that she was "back to where I was before." A special session was scheduled.

Ann related the sequence of events leading to her upset. Toward the end of the summer, she had left the children with her mother for a few days so that she and her husband could visit some friends. Upon returning home, she began to think of the vacation ending and of the many impending responsibilities. Her upset was then compounded by the following factors: Her daughter had just entered first grade, and was refusing to go to school because of her very strict teacher. Ann became upset, and was then concerned about being upset, because I had told her that she was better. This led her to think: "Even *he* doesn't know how sick I am."

To make matters worse, her husband offered little sympathy,

and even became somewhat angry over her difficulties in coping. Although I acknowledged that her husband could have been more supportive, I also pointed out that, in contrast to the past, he was annoyed at her *lack* of independence. She seemed slightly encouraged to hear this.

I urged Ann to place the current situation in a more realistic perspective, stressing that even the most competent of individuals experience problems when they have to cope with a new routine. I gave her examples to back this up, each of which illustrated how initial difficulty was followed by successful coping. A session was scheduled for the following week.

Session 48

We began with ten minutes of relaxation training, followed by my reminder that she attempt to apply this skill in stressful situations. In describing the problems her daughter was having at school, it became apparent that the primary source of difficulty was the teacher. Although a petition of complaints was being filed by several other parents, Ann demonstrated a remarkable degree of assertiveness by indicating that she would prefer to speak with the principal directly, as she feels this would be more effective.

Session 49

Her meeting with the principal did, indeed, turn out to be effective. Her daughter was assigned to a different class, which completely eliminated the difficulties. Ann looked more cheerful, and reported feeling much better. She has been using relaxation *in vivo*, and has been asserting herself in a number of situations. However, she observed that her style of asserting herself tends to be somewhat timid. After she noted this, she made attempts to try out a more self-assured manner of speaking. I reinforced her for her self-correcting ability. In light of this, I doubt that behavior rehearsal is necessary.

We got into a discussion of the effect the therapy has been having on her marriage. There have been many changes, not the least of which is the husband learning to live with a more independent Ann. She realizes that she can deal with him more directly and she is beginning to talk to him on a more equal basis. Not surprisingly, this is making waves. However, she expresses confidence that the two of them can work it out on their own.

By mutual agreement, the next session was set up in six

months. I emphasized that should any problems arise during the interval, she make every effort to cope with them on her own before getting in touch with me.

Session 50

Ann changed the color of her hair, and wore it in a much more attractive style. All in all, she looked quite good. The contrast with how she looked at the outset of therapy is striking.

Ann's relationship with her husband has continued to improve. They went skiing together, and she was anticipating taking tennis lessons. They were generally involved in many more things together, and were starting to entertain more at home. Ann made it a point of noting how very much she enjoyed being able to use the dishes and silverware they had gotten as wedding gifts, which had been put to use in the past only on very few occasions. The marriage has become stormier and at the same time more intimate and meaningful.

Ann reports using problem solving regularly, with no difficulty following through on her preferred course of action, including those events that involve self-assertion. We agree that she will contact me in six months time, which will be shortly after the summer. Hopefully, the change in routine will not throw her as it did last year.

Session 51

Everything has gone fairly well over the past several months. The only negative thing she could point to was the fact that having the children around all summer gave her a feeling of being tied down. This is an interesting contrast to her previous fear of being alone! I inhibited my natural inclination to tell her how she could handle this situation and instead suggested that she make use of her problem-solving skills to prevent this from recurring in the future. With the children having just entered school again, she experienced some initial difficulty reestablishing the behavior pattern associated with the school year. But the important thing is that she worked it out on her own. I reiterated the usefulness of the problem-solving approach in handling life's difficulties, and urged her to make use of this approach in helping her to function independently.

Both Ann and I felt that there we could now formally terminate. I will be contacting her in six months for a routine follow-up.

Follow-up Contacts

Ann told me in today's session that all had been going quite well over the past six months. We went into the specifics of her successful coping. Inasmuch as I was about to leave the country for a year, I gave her my address should she want to contact me.

I telephoned Ann approximately one year later. Although I suggested that we set up a session to discuss her continued progress, Ann felt that she had reached the point where this was really not necessary. I was somewhat surprised by her self-confident stand on this issue. My initial feelings of being rejected and put down were rapidly replaced by a more realistic recognition of how very far Ann had come.

● FORMULATION OF PROBLEMS AND OVERVIEW OF THERAPEUTIC PROCEDURES

It might be helpful to step back a bit and summarize what went on in this case—particularly the way the client's problems were formulated, and the procedures deemed most appropriate in bringing about behavior change.

Ann was an intelligent, but unassertive and dependent woman who, in many respects, had behaved much like a young and helpless child during most of her life. The client's problems, as presented, consisted primarily of severe and pervasive feelings of anxiety, as well as feelings of depression and lethargy. She reported that she had lost interest in, and experienced difficulty in coping with, the world around her, and often found herself reluctant even to get out of bed in the morning. She was not able to understand why these feelings "come over me," and was afraid she might be becoming "mentally ill." Because of the difficulty she had asserting herself, she also reported feelings of discomfort in having to deal with people socially. On the other hand, she had a marked fear of being alone, especially at home. In addition, her passive and helpless attitude often elicited concern and aid from friends and relatives, which only seemed to perpetuate her difficulties.

Although Ann had always tended to manifest little self-confidence and was never completely able to function independently, the greater demands placed on her over the ten years prior to therapy (i.e., periodic moves, caring for her two children, running a large house—all the while working part-time) appeared to have made her problems more acute and severe. In addition, her inability to control or understand the possible reasons for her feelings of anxiety and depression made her even more upset, in that she was afraid she "would never get well."

Although the therapeutic plan began with relaxation and desensitization, it was soon felt that the treatment of the client's depressive reaction should receive higher priority. The reasoning behind this was that she was readily able to avoid having to be by herself, but was unable to do very much about changing her feelings of depression, or the behavioral lethargy that accompanied them. In addition, she had become very much afraid that the persistence of her depressed feelings might be an indication that she was becoming very severely disturbed.

The client's feelings of depression and helplessness were conceptualized as an outgrowth of her inability to have an impact on the world around her. Consequently, rather than focusing primarily on the dysphoric feelings themselves, the treatment approach involved the establishment of greater behavioral competency. The use of encouragement, behavior rehearsal, self-observation, cognitive rehearsal, and especially problem solving, along with the therapist's reinforcement of the various activities, all contributed to the lifting of her depression.

Toward the goal of reducing Ann's anxieties and fears, it was decided initially to utilize systematic desensitization. However, relaxation training itself, as well as relaxation *in vivo*, produced striking results: She became less anxious about being home alone and found herself able to function comfortably in many social situations that previously had made her quite tense. Her increased assertiveness and overall competency may very well have contributed to this anxiety reduction.

Even though Ann began to show improvement in a number of different areas, she nonetheless persisted in referring to herself as inadequate, helpless, worthless, and so on. On the assumption that self-perceptions are based on the individual's evaluation of her behavior—either directly or through the reflected reactions and attitudes of others—it was apparent that the client was not appropriately reevaluating her own improved status. Instead of recognizing positive changes, most of her focus was on the negative features of her behavior. Toward the goal of changing her self-perceptions, the therapist employed such procedures as having her listen to tape-recorded portions of the session where she was affirming something positive about herself, having her keep a diary of her successful coping, and discussing any favorable reactions of ✓ others toward her.

A married individual's difficulties are often enmeshed in relationship issues with the spouse. In Ann's case, her husband had grown accustomed to dealing with a passive, dependent person. The increase in her assertiveness and overall independence necessitated a readjustment in their interactions with each other, and for a time it appeared that conjoint sessions might be needed. But Ann wanted to work things out without the therapist's direct involvement, and fortunately she and her husband were able to do just that.

In reviewing the therapy notes, it occurred to us that little in the way of rational restructuring was used. Although it may very well have been useful in dealing with the client's self-concept, guilt, depression, unassertiveness, and interpersonal anxiety, it was not employed. The reason for its absence is simple. At the time the client was being seen, the therapist had not yet recognized the potential effectiveness of such an approach within a behavioral framework.

It would be interesting to speculate how other behavior therapists might have gone about working with Ann. Although there unquestionably would be many points of similarity, differences would most assuredly exist as well. The fact that behaviorally oriented clinicians reading this case illustration might be able to think of alternate ways of conceptualizing the client's problems, and might decide on using somewhat different therapeutic procedures, underlines the main purpose of this chapter: To demonstrate that clinical behavior therapy involves considerably more than the routine application of techniques.

Chapter 13

The Ethics
of Behavior Change

Throughout this book we have alluded to ethical considerations in implementing behavior therapy. In this chapter we will attempt to pull together what we view as some of the more important issues.

Although it may appear otherwise from the sometimes vituperative press reports in the mid-1970s, ethical issues are inherent in *any* therapeutic endeavor, not just in behavior therapy. Whether the therapist is working within a framework that is basically psychodynamic, humanistic, or behavioral, he is constantly confronted with the necessity of making moral decisions regarding both the goals of therapy and the means used to approach those goals.

A colleague of ours was once asked, after he had changed his orientation from a psychodynamic to a behavioral one, whether he had become more concerned with ethical issues of behavior control. His immediate response was that indeed he had. On further reflection, however, he concluded that this should not have been the case. To state the obvious, we are all in the business of control. It often seems that those committed to psychodynamic or humanistic orientations prefer to regard their work as enabling their clients to change *on their own* and make their own decisions. Our position simply stated is: We cannot on the one hand argue that our availability as professionals is worthwhile and justified, and on the other hand maintain that we are *not* in the business of changing people's behavior (London, 1964). We are reminded of the paradox inherent in the controversy about the influence of television on behavior. On the one hand, networks deny any possible adverse influence that programing might have on the aggressive behavior of the viewer, and yet they turn around to sponsors and suggest that skillful advertising will affect the buying behavior of the public (Liebert, Neale, & Davidson, 1973).

The discussion of ethical issues and behavior change is hardly new in behavior therapy. One of the earliest discussants was Perry London (1964). In his early work London attempted to sensitize his colleagues to some of the moral concerns inherent in any behavior change process. Later, in a frequently cited discussion of ethics in behavior therapy, Bandura (1969) said:

> In any type of social influence enterprise there exist two basic decision systems. One set of decisions pertains to the selection of goals; these decisions require value judgments. The second set of decisions, which involve empirical issues, relates to the selection of specific procedures for achieving selected goals. In the latter domain the agent of change must be the decision-maker, since the client is in no position to prescribe the learning contingencies necessary for the modification of his behavior. But though the change agent determines the means by which specified outcomes can be achieved, the client should play a major role in determining the directions in which his behavior is to be modified. To the extent that the client serves as the primary decision-maker in the value domain, the ethical questions that are frequently raised concerning behavioral control become pseudo issues (p. 101).

It might be concluded from the above that Bandura sees little problem regarding value judgments in behavior therapy. The behavior therapist is the expert on how to change, and the client is the expert in which directions change should be made. However, the situation is not that simple, as becomes clear if one reads Bandura just a little further:

> More often, however, because clients are uncertain about the benefits they hope to derive from treatment, or because their goals are

stated too broadly, the identification of relevant outcomes must constitute the initial objective of the program. In such instances it is necessary to conduct a thorough behavioral analysis in order to *identify the social conditions governing the client's response patterns* [italics added] and the range of behavioral and situational modifications likely to promote the desired psychological changes (p. 101).

What Bandura is alerting us to here are the conditions that surround the very decision making of clients as to the kinds of changes they want to work toward in therapy.

This has been taken much further in an important book by Seymour Halleck, entitled *The Politics of Therapy* (1971).

> Any type of psychiatric intervention, even when treating a voluntary patient, will have an impact upon the distribution of power within the various social systems in which the patient moves. The radical therapists are absolutely right when they insist that psychiatric neutrality is a myth (p. 13).

> At first glance, a model of psychiatric practice based on the contention that people should just be helped to learn to do the things they want to do, seems uncomplicated and desirable. But it is an unobtainable model. Unlike a technician, a psychiatrist cannot avoid communicating and at times imposing his own values upon his patients. The patient usually has considerable difficulty in finding the way in which he would wish to change his behavior, but as he talks to the psychiatrist his wants and needs become clearer. In the very process of defining his needs in the presence of a figure who is viewed as wise and authoritarian, the patient is profoundly influenced. He ends up wanting some of the things the psychiatrist thinks he should want (p. 19).

There is an important implication to Halleck's thesis, namely that the distinction typically made between "voluntary" outpatient treatment and more coercive institutional treatment is spurious, even insidious. It is all the more undesirable in that it can mask the important fact that the clinician is invariably in a position of greater power in relation to the options available to the client. In fact, one could argue that an even greater tyranny on the part of therapists is possible when the influence processes are *not* openly acknowledged and investigated (Davison & Stuart, 1975).

For illustrative purposes, we will discuss some ethical issues in the following areas: assertion training for women, behavioral contracting in therapy with children, the treatment of homosexuality, behavior therapy conducted in institutional settings, and therapeutic frankness.

● ASSERTION TRAINING FOR WOMEN

We were consulted a few years ago by a woman in her middle thirties, the wife of a successful attorney and the mother of three children. In a pattern that is common in our society, the woman had forsaken advanced schooling in order to establish a household with a man who was clearly to become a good provider. Now she found herself depressed and frustrated because of a constricted pattern of home life that was becoming increasingly onerous to her. When she consulted us, her presenting complaint was inappropriate levels of anxiety in social situations, particularly those involving business associates of her husband. Whereas we might have approached this problem in terms of desensitization, we found ourselves questioning this as a goal; we therefore engaged the woman in discussions about her feelings of being pressed into service, as it were, on behalf of her husband's professional aspirations. With very little probing, the woman began to express considerable anger and resentment, especially at what she viewed to be the insensitivities of her husband in not appreciating her dislike for such socializing. Further questioning revealed that the woman had never allowed herself to express these resentments to her spouse. With some encouragement and behavior rehearsal, she was able to discuss her feelings of frustration with her husband. Surprisingly and happily, the husband responded in a very sympathetic fashion. By encouraging the woman to assert herself, better channels of communication were opened up within the marital unit; the woman returned to school on a part-time basis, with her husband's full support; and her "social anxiety" disappeared.

The women's movement has been saying some valid things about the goals selected by therapists for their female clients. Despite the absence of hard data, our clinical impressions are that assertion training—at least up until the mid-1970s—was not used as often for female clients as it was for males, even though it might have been warranted. Indeed, the very judgment of what is an appropriately expressive or assertive behavior by a woman is probably made on prejudicial bases; that is, a particular response by a woman is apt to be viewed as aggressive or "bitchy" and hence not adaptive, whereas the same response pattern in a man would be viewed as appropriately assertive. This is consistent with Broverman, Broverman, Clarkson, Rosenkrantz, and Vogel (1970), who found that both male and female clinicians considered the healthy woman to be more submissive, less independent, less adventurous, less aggressive, and less competitive than men. In light of societal prejudices, extra care is warranted in preparing the client for likely negative reactions to her more assertive behavior patterns.

● BEHAVIOR THERAPY WITH CHILDREN

At a social gathering some years ago, the authors heard a discussion of who the most oppressed segments of the population were. After mention of blacks, Chicanos, and women, somebody indicated that children surely were the most oppressed, having even less power and influence than other disadvantaged minorities. We find this worth thinking about, particularly in light of the problems we have become aware of when dealing with adolescents on the border between childhood and adulthood, and with younger children in terms of classroom behavior therapy procedures (Winett & Winkler, 1972).

We were once consulted by the parents of an especially precocious six-year-old who, perhaps because of the influence of an older sibling, had decided that most of the work in the first grade was nonsense and could be readily dispensed with. After talking with the child, it became terribly clear that he was an unusually talented boy. If we were to construe ourselves simply as the agent of the boy, we should have found ourselves attempting to intervene with the school to relieve the teacher's pressures that this child acquire reading skills. However, because of the age of the child and because of what in our view were the serious negative consequences of his not learning to read, we used our influence to persuade him that indeed it was worth learning how to read. On the other hand, if the child had objected to joining a play group because he was not particularly happy there, even though his parents wanted him to go, we would have been reluctant to side with the parents, the reason being that the negative consequences of his *not* joining the group were not terribly serious.

What would have happened if this client were a twenty-year-old junior in college and if his parents had come to us in a similarly distraught state, complaining that their son wanted to drop out of school? In this instance, we probably would not have used our power position to persuade the young man that he must remain in school at all costs. We would rather have directed our attention more to the parents.

The working principle that guides our decision making in intervention with children and young adults involves at least two important factors: the age of the child and the consequences of his continuing to do what is presumably problematic. We are aware that other therapists might analyze such situations differently, but that would only prove our point: It is not a straightforward matter to decide how to intervene in childhood clinical problems.

● BEHAVIOR THERAPY FOR HOMOSEXUALITY

Moving from Halleck's basic thesis that the idea of therapeutic neutrality is a myth, the argument has been developed by Davison (in press) that therapists should discontinue their efforts at altering the sexual preferences of adult homosexuals even when an individual comes to a therapist "voluntarily" and announces a desire to change.

As suggested in a survey by Davison and Wilson (1973a), behavior therapists do not regard homosexuality as inherently abnormal or even undesirable. And yet, nearly all the behavior therapy literature on homosexuality concerns programs for altering that pattern of sexual response. Even though data fail to show that adult homosexuals are more disturbed than matched heterosexual controls (e.g., Evans, 1970; Hooker, 1957), therapists nonetheless tend to approach homosexuality at best as undesirable, and certainly worthy of change. Thus far it would seem that therapists are acting in a humane way, solely on behalf of their client's interests. But, as Halleck has pointed out, the very existence of such therapeutic programs tends, in the larger political context, to confirm the bias that such patterns of behavior are maladaptive and even sick. "How can we honestly speak of nonprejudice when we participate in therapy regimens that by their very existence—and regardless of their efficacy—condone the current societal prejudice and perhaps also impede social change?" (Davison, in press).

The argument has been carried even further by Begelman:

> . . . the point of the activist protest is that behavior therapists contribute significantly to preventing the exercise of any *real* option in decision making about sexual identity, by further strengthening the prejudice that homosexuality is a problem behavior, since treatment may be offered for it. As a consequence of this therapeutic stance, as well as a wider system of social and attitudinal pressures, homosexuals tend to seek treatment *for being homosexuals*. Heterosexuals, on the other hand, can scarcely be expected to seek voluntary treatment for being heterosexual, especially since all the social forces arrayed—including the unavailability of behavior therapy for heterosexuality— attest to the acknowledgment of the idea that whatever "problems" heterosexuals experience are not due

to their sexual orientation. The upshot of this is that contrary to the disclaimer that behavior therapy is "not a system of ethics" (Bandura, 1969, p. 87), the very act of providing therapeutic services for homosexual 'problems' indicates otherwise (Begelman, 1975, p. 180).

In other words, the above arguments suggest that the existence of sexual change regimens for homosexuals, particularly in the absence of similar efforts to help homosexuals live more happily as homosexuals, restricts the range of "free choice" for homosexuals, even those who come "voluntarily" for change (see Silverstein, 1972). The issue is similar to that mentioned above in assertion training for women. If there are few therapists available who are willing to entertain a particular set of goals for a particular kind of problem, then how can one speak meaningfully of free choice in the decision by a client to work toward a particular kind of behavior change?

As with all ethical issues, the above solution is not without its problems. As Davison (in press) has questioned, who is the therapist to make such important decisions for outpatient clients? One answer would be simply to agree with Halleck's thesis that we already make such decisions, and that we should simply be aware of them and hopefully deal more honestly with the political implications of what we do, even with voluntary clients. But what about the homosexual client who might conceivably want to change not out of societal pressures and prejudices but out of a sincere desire for those things that are usually part of the heterosexual package —spouse and children? Who are we to deny such an individual the possibility of fulfilling his desires? If we are not willing to take a stand against such an eventuality, we might consider helping such an individual to expand his sexual repertoire so that he can function with women (or with men, in the rare case of a lesbian who wants to change). However, as Davison has proposed, this should be done only if researchers and clinicians commit themselves to help heterosexual individuals expand their repertoires into the homosexual if we can determine somehow that they *really* want to change.

Even if one finds it impossible to accept the extreme forms of these arguments, they should at least alert clinicians to other problems that homosexuals might have and that could conceivably have nothing at all to do with their sexual preferences. For example, it is entirely possible for a homosexual to be alcoholic, and for his drinking problem to be as unrelated to his sexual orientation as a drinking problem found in a heterosexual. We would suggest that our *biases* lead us to construe the drinking problem of a homosexual in terms of the sexual preference, something we would never do in thinking of heterosexuals. Or, as Gagnon and Simon (1973) have put it:

> . . . the homosexual's sexual object choice [has been allowed] to dominate and control our imagery of him. We have let this single aspect of his total life experience appear to determine all his products, concerns and activities. This prepossessing concern on the part of nonhomosexuals with a purely sexual aspect of the homosexual's life is something we would not allow to occur if we were interested in the heterosexual . . . the mere presence of unconventional sexuality seems to give the sexual content of life an overwhelming significance. [But] homosexuals . . . vary profoundly in the degree to which their sexual commitment and its facilitation become the organizing principle of their lives (p. 137).

● SOME ETHICAL AND LEGAL PROBLEMS WITH INSTITUTIONALIZED POPULATIONS

The year 1974 witnessed a concerted attack in the press and in Congress on behavior therapy in institutionalized settings. In our opinion, many of the criticisms were well taken, aimed as they were at poorly conceived and insensitively administered "behavior modification" programs. We want to state at the very outset, in the strongest possible terms, that simply administering a punishment to a patient does not mean that one is doing behavior therapy. Thus the reprehensible practice in an Iowa prison of punishing misbehavior by an injection of apomorphine is hardly to be considered a sensible application of learning principles.

Unfortunately these attacks have often been directed at the behavior therapy enterprise as a whole. Clearly, when we are dealing with populations that have little choice about participating in therapy programs, very special ethical issues arise, though we suggest that they are not different in quality from the ethical conundrums already reviewed above with outpatients. We discuss here four of the many issues that have been recently delineated (Davison & Stuart, 1975).

Absolute Versus Contingent Rights

Recent court decisions, as Wexler (1973) has pointed out, should alert therapists to limitations in the kind of behavior therapy that entails the contingent administration of rewards, such as in token economies. Some clinicians, in their attempts to make institutionalization rehabilitative rather than merely punitive or custodial, have sought to offer inmates and patients access to some of "the good things in life" as a *consequence* of adaptive behavioral changes. This has necessarily meant the denial of such amenities as a private room, with a gradual restoration of these privileges when good behavior occurs. If, however, patients and prisoners are viewed as having an absolute right to such privileges, treatment programs will have to be devised with a greater degree of ingenuity so as not to violate constitutionally guaranteed rights. Wexler suggests, for example, that rather than denying a patient food even temporarily, we might offer an inmate the choice among hard-boiled, soft-boiled, or scrambled eggs.

Choice of Goals

Questions have also been raised about what goals behavior therapists have a right to work toward with institutionalized people. As even a cursory reading of the token economy literature will show, much attention has been paid to increasing the productivity of residents in hospital and prison maintenance programs. This presumably has been done for purposes of rehabilitation and also to distract the inmate from the monotonies of institutional life. However, as the *Wyatt vs. Stickney* decision becomes more generally applied, such goals may be viewed as involuntary servitude. In other words, patients and inmates may have to be paid a minimum wage if their work-activities contribute to the smooth functioning of the institution.

Again, this is not without its problems, as Wexler has pointed out. If directors of institutions have to be concerned with maximum efficiency, they might then choose to hire outside people, who are generally functioning better, if they have to pay a minimum wage for such institutional jobs. The argument will have to be made by professionals that such activities are in fact rehabilitative with only secondary benefit accruing to the institution. We agree with many that the case has not yet been adequately made.

The Right to the Best Possible Validated Treatment

There has been much discussion of the rights that mental patients have to treatment, particularly if they are involuntarily committed to an institution. After all, if society deprives a citizen of his freedom, is it not the responsibility of society to help prepare this person for meaningful functioning outside the institution?

Davison and Stuart have argued that, since so little is known about the best way to devise institutional treatment programs, the most ethical imperative should be to *require* both descriptive and evaluative research in institutions. That is, responsible program administrators should be required to seek and compare the effectiveness of alternative programs. Thus, rather than regarding institutional evaluative research as a potential violation of the rights of residents, such research efforts might be seen as *mandatory* aspects of responsible institutional management. This suggestion goes against most current thinking.

Consent to Treatment and Research

In the 1970s, the Department of Health, Education and Welfare issued several sets of guidelines for the conduct of research with human subjects. These require, in various forms, informed consent on the part of any human being participating in research. In such cases where the individual is judged incapable of making an informed decision (such as in the case of a retarded child or committed mental patient), a legal guardian or the courts are to make such decisions.

Clearly, the scientist's need to know must be balanced against the possible harm or humiliation to a participant in a particular experiment. The answers are far from clear, but one scheme, suggested by Davison and Stuart (1975), is that we construe a continuum of a consent-giving process ranging from a situation where a subject need not even be informed that he is in an experiment all the way to a subject having to sign a consent form in the presence of witnesses with a full disclosure of the objectives and methods of the research. Factors that would bear on the necessary level of protection might be four in number: the level of potential benefit to the subject, the level of risk, the validity of the procedure, and the extent to which a subject can give informed consent at all.

For example, if participation in an experiment is likely to be of no benefit to the subject and likely to put him at high risk, then we would have to be extremely careful in insuring that the would-be subject have as full an understanding as possible regarding the nature of the experiment. This would make it very difficult for a researcher to expose a prisoner to a potentially lethal dose of radiation when that particular individual is not suffering from a physical disorder that could conceivably be helped by the experimental treatment.

As another example, it is reasonable to assert that a prisoner is less able to give "free informed consent" to participating in a research project than a person who is not institutionalized against his will. Other things being equal, we would have to be far more cautious in allowing the prisoner to participate in a risky experiment than we would for someone who could be expected to exercise less coerced decision making.

● THE QUESTION OF THERAPEUTIC FRANKNESS

There is a thorny and fascinating question regarding the degree of honesty in ethical clinical practice. Can one make the bald statement that the therapist must always be honest with a client? This seems impossible, as much as we might like it to be the case. For example, if a therapist is asked by a desperate, suicidally depressed person whether there is any hope for him, and if the therapist feels pessimistic, is he ethically bound to tell that client exactly what is on his mind? Does one serve the client's best interests by sharing with him the despair that the therapist himself might have at that particular time?

If we succeed in helping a client, and if we continue to see our own role as important in this therapeutic gain, are we being unethical by suggesting afterwards that his own efforts were far more responsible than any assistance the therapist lent—assuming of course that the attribution of change to one's self contributes to greater maintenance of behavior change than construing one's improvement as due to an external agent (see Chapter 8)?

Finally, consider the question of timing. Nearly every experienced therapist has decided during a therapy session to hold back on a comment, interpretation, or some other kind of intervention in the belief that the time was simply not right. Does the exercise of such professional judgment necessarily expose the therapist to charges of deceit and dishonesty?

Once we have been entrusted with the task of helping the client, we believe that this overriding responsibility should often take precedence over complete therapeutic frankness.

● A NOTE ON SOCIETAL INVOLVEMENT

Recent years have witnessed an increased interest in and a growing tendency toward community involvement. Impatient with the fee-for-service model of outpatient practice, many health professionals argue that we should go forth into the community and take mental health to larger groups. We believe that professionals should be concerned with preventative intervention, but we see difficult questions inherent in this tack. What right do professionals have even to suggest to others how they can live better lives unless they are first consulted by them? What duty do we have to change what we believe to be sources of societal oppression? What goals should we help others work toward? Should we encourage greater levels of achievement in society, or deeper levels of intimacy?

Another concern relates to the current state of our technology. Most readers would probably agree that we are just beginning to learn how to change individual human behavior in an enduring fashion. The issue then becomes whether we know any more about how to effect beneficial changes in large units of behavior that have as their "client" groups of people such as a neighborhood or an elementary school. While there is much to say about focusing on these large units, we feel it imperative to raise the question of whether we might be premature in trying to introduce behavior change procedures that can possibly affect such large numbers of people.

Although the community trend is important, we must be particularly sensitive to the ethical issues involved.

● SUMMARY AND IMPLICATIONS

As we stated at the beginning of this chapter, behavior therapists do not have a monopoly on ethical difficulties. Any attempt by one human being to change the behavior of another, particularly in the name of mental health, is fraught with moral implications. We have attempted in this chapter to outline a few of the difficulties faced by the practicing behavior therapist. We would argue that each of these problems is important also for therapists of other persuasions, and hence should be of interest to readers of this book who are not heavily involved in behavior therapy.

Above all, those of us in the helping professions have a good deal more to learn than we already know. To snuff out clinical and experimental research efforts at this point in time would be a tragedy. And yet, we have to admit in all candor that some of our colleagues have not always been as acutely aware of their ethical imperatives as they should be.

We would suggest that behavior therapy has little to apologize for, particularly in the context of the history of other therapeutic enterprises. While there have indeed been follies committed in the name of behavior therapy, we would argue that it is behavior therapy that has most conscientiously and objectively pursued new knowledge, that we harbor precious few cherished myths about what we do, and that we are critical of our own endeavors.

There are many human problems that would seem amenable to the mode of scientific analysis that is the essence of behavior therapy. We need not demean the human being by our concepts and methodologies. Indeed, the benefits already realized justify considerable optimism that increased knowledge of how we behave will enable people to increase their alternatives and truly fulfill their potential. We hope and recommend that professionals continue to devote the necessary energy to the important challenges.

References

Agras, W. S. Transfer during systematic desensitization therapy. *Behaviour Research and Therapy*, 1967, 5, 193–199.

Alberti, R. E., and Emmons, M. L. *Your perfect right.* (2nd ed.). San Luis Obispo, Calif.: Impact, 1974.

Alexander, F., and French, T. M. *Psychoanalytic therapy.* New York: Ronald, 1946.

Almedina, J., and Rubin, A. *Environmental design: Community psychology.* Unpublished manuscript, State University of New York at Stony Brook, 1974.

Aronson, E., and Carlsmith, J. M. Experimentation in social psychology. In G. Lindzey and E. Aronson (Eds.), *The handbook of social psychology. Volume 2. Research Methods.* Reading, Mass.: Addison-Wesley, 1968.

Ausubel, D. P. *The psychology of meaningful verbal learning.* New York: Grune & Stratton, 1963.

Ayllon, T., and Azrin, N. H. The measurement and reinforcement of behavior of psychotics. *Journal of the Experimental Analysis of Behavior*, 1965, 8, 357–383.

Ayllon, T., and Azrin, N. H. *The token economy: A motivational system for therapy and rehabilitation.* New York: Appleton-Century-Crofts, 1968.

Bandura, A. A social learning interpretation of psychological dysfunctions. In P. London and D. Rosenhan (Eds.), *Foundations of abnormal psychology.* New York: Holt, Rinehart and Winston, 1968.

Bandura, A. *Principles of behavior modification.* New York: Holt, Rinehart and Winston, 1969.

Bandura, A., and Kupers, C. J. Transmission of patterns of self-reinforcement through modeling. *Journal of Abnormal and Social Psychology,* 1964, *69*, 1–9.

Barber, T. X. *Hypnosis: A scientific approach.* New York: Van Nostrand Reinhold, 1969.

Bard, M., and Berkowitz, B. Training police as specialists in family crisis intervention: A community psychology action program. *Community Mental Health Journal,* 1967, *3*, 315–317.

Beck, A. T. *Depression: Clinical, experimental and theoretical aspects.* New York: Harper & Row, 1967.

Becker, W. C. *Parents are teachers.* Champaign, Ill.: Research Press, 1971.

Begelman, D. A. Ethical and legal issues of behavior modification. In M. Hersen, R. M. Eisler, and Miller, P. M. (Eds.), *Progress in behavior modification.* New York: Academic Press, 1975.

Bem, D. J., and Allen, A. On predicting some of the people some of the time: The search for cross-situational consistencies in behavior. *Psychological Review,* 1974, *81*, 506–520.

Bernstein, D. A., and Borkovec, T. D. *Progressive relaxation training.* Champaign, Ill.: Research Press, 1973.

Bijou, S. W., and Baer, D. M. *Child development. Vol. 1. A systematic and empirical theory.* New York: Appleton-Century-Crofts, 1961.

Bloom, B. S., and Broder, L. J. *Problem-solving processes of college students.* Chicago: University of Chicago Press, 1950.

Bowers, K. S. Situationism in psychology: An analysis and a critique. *Psychological Review,* 1973, *80*, 307–336.

Brehm, J. W. *A theory of psychological reactance.* New York: Academic Press, 1966.

Brehm, J. W., and Cohen, A. R. *Explorations in cognitive dissonance.* New York: Wiley, 1962.

Brooks, C. V. W. *Sensory awareness: The rediscovery of experiencing.* New York: The Viking Press, 1974.

Broverman, I. K., Broverman, D. M., Clarkson, F. E., Rosenkrantz, P. S., and Vogel, S. R. Sex-role stereotypes and clinical judgments of mental health. *Journal of Consulting and Clinical Psychology,* 1970, *34*, 1–7.

Cautela, J. R., and Kastenbaum, R. A reinforcement survey schedule for use in therapy, training, and research. *Psychological Reports,* 1967, *20*, 1115–1130.

Copemann, C. D. *Aversive counterconditioning and social retraining: A learning theory approach to drug rehabilitation.* Unpublished doctoral dissertation, State University of New York at Stony Brook, 1973.

Corsini, R. J. (Ed.) *Current psychotherapies.* Ithaca, Ill.: F. E. Peacock, 1973.

Corsini, R. J., Shaw, M. E., and Blake, R. R. *Roleplaying in business and industry.* New York: Free Press, 1961.

Davis, J. D. *The interview as arena.* Stanford: Stanford University Press, 1971.

Davison, G. C. An intensive, long-term social-learning treatment program with an accurately diagnosed autistic child. *Proceedings of the 73rd Annual Convention of the American Psychological Association.* Washington, D.C.: American Psychological Association, 1965.

Davison, G. C. Differential relaxation and cognitive restructuring in therapy with a "paranoid schizophrenic" or "paranoid state." *Proceedings of the 74th Annual Convention of the American Psychological Association.* Washington, D.C.: American Psychological Association, 1966.

Davison, G. C. Elimination of a sadistic fantasy by a client-controlled counterconditioning technique. *Journal of Abnormal Psychology,* 1968, *73,* 84–90.

Davison, G. C. Appraisal of behavior modification techniques with adults in institutional settings. In C. M. Franks (Ed.), *Behavior therapy: Appraisal and status.* New York: McGraw-Hill, 1969.

Davison, G. C. Counter control in behavior modification. In L. A. Hamerlynck, L. C. Handy, and E. J. Mash (Eds.), *Behavior change: Methodology, concepts and practice.* Champaign, Ill.: Research Press, 1973.

Davison, G. C. Homosexuality: The ethical challenge. *Journal of Consulting and Clinical Psychology,* in press.

Davison, G. C., and Goldfried, M. R. Postdoctoral training in clinical behavior therapy. In I. B. Weiner (Ed.), *Postdoctoral education in clinical psychology.* Topeka, Kansas: Menninger Foundation, 1973.

Davison, G. C., and Neale, J. M. *Abnormal psychology: An experimental clinical approach.* New York: Wiley, 1974.

Davison, G. C., and Stuart, R. B. Behavior therapy and civil liberties. *American Psychologist,* 1975, *30,* 755–763.

Davison, G. C., Tsujimoto, R. N., and Glaros, A. G. Attribution and the maintenance of behavior change in falling asleep. *Journal of Abnormal Psychology,* 1973, *82,* 124–133.

Davison, G. C., and Valins, S. Maintenance of self-attributed and drug-attributed behavior change. *Journal of Personality and Social Psychology,* 1969, *11,* 25–33.

Davison, G. C., and Wilson, G. T. Attitudes of behavior therapists toward homosexuality. *Behavior Therapy,* 1973, *4,* 686–696 (a).

Davison, G. C., and Wilson, G. T. Processes of fear-reduction in systematic desensitization: Cognitive and social reinforcement factors in humans. *Behavior Therapy*, 1973, *4*, 1–21 (b).

Dewey, J. *How we think*. Boston: Heath & Co., 1910.

DiLoreto, A. O. *Comparative psychotherapy: An experimental analysis*. Chicago: Aldine-Atherton, 1971.

Dollard, J., and Miller, N. E. *Personality and psychotherapy*. New York: McGraw-Hill, 1950.

D'Zurilla, T. J. Reducing heterosexual anxiety. In J. D. Krumboltz and C. E. Thoresen (Eds.), *Behavioral counseling: cases and techniques*. New York: Holt, Rinehart and Winston, 1969.

D'Zurilla, T. J., and Goldfried, M. R. Problem solving and behavior modification. *Journal of Abnormal Psychology*, 1971, *78*, 107–126.

Eisler, R. M., Hersen, M., and Agras, W. S. Effects of videotape and instructional feedback on non-verbal marital interactions: An analogue study. *Behavior Therapy*, 1973, *5*, 551–558.

Ekehammar, B. Interactionism in personality from a historical perspective. *Psychological Bulletin*, 1974, *81*, 1026–1048.

Ellis, A. *Reason and emotion in psychotherapy*. New York: Lyle Stuart, 1962.

Ellis, A., and Harper, R. A. *A guide to rational living*. Hollywood: Wilshire, 1962.

Erickson, M. H. Further clinical techniques of hypnosis: Utilization techniques. *The American Journal of Clinical Hypnosis*, 1959, *2*, 3–21.

Estes, W. K. Reward in human learning: Theoretical issues and strategic choice points. In R. Glaser (Ed.), *The nature of reinforcement*. New York: Academic Press, 1971.

Evans, R. B. Sixteen personality factor questionnaire scores of homosexual men. *Journal of Consulting and Clinical Psychology*, 1970, *34*, 212–215.

Eysenck, H. J. (Ed.). *Behaviour therapy and the neuroses*. New York: Pergamon, 1960.

Farina, A., Arenberg, D., and Guskin, S. A scale for measuring minimal social behavior. *Journal of Consulting Psychology*, 1957, *21*, 265–268.

Ferster, C. B. Classification of behavioral pathology. In L. Krasner and L. P. Ullmann (Eds.), *Research in behavior modification*. New York: Holt, Rinehart and Winston, 1965.

Frank, J. D. *Persuasion and healing*. Baltimore: Johns Hopkins Press, 1961.

Freedman, J. L., and Fraser, S. Compliance without pressure: The foot-in-the-door technique. *Journal of Personality and Social Psychology*, 1966, *4*, 195–202.

Fromm-Reichman, F. *Principles of intensive psychotherapy*. Chicago: University of Chicago Press, 1950.

Gagné, R. M. Problem solving and thinking. *Annual Review of Psychology*, 1959, *10*, 147–172.

Gagnon, J. H., and Davison, G. C. Asylums, the token economy, and the metrics of mental life. *Behavior Therapy*, in press.

Gagnon, J. H., and Simon, W. *Sexual conduct: The social origins of human sexuality.* Chicago: Aldine-Atherton, 1973.

Gaudry, E., and Spielberger, C. D. *Anxiety and educational achievement.* New York: Wiley, 1971.

Geer, J. H. The development of a scale to measure fear. *Behaviour Research and Therapy*, 1965, *3*, 45–53.

Geer, J. H., Davison, G. C., and Gatchel, R. I. Reduction of stress in humans through nonveridical perceived control of aversive stimulation. *Journal of Personality and Social Psychology*, 1970, *16*, 731–738.

Gittelman, M. Behavior rehearsal as a technique in child treatment. *Journal of Child Psychology and Psychiatry*, 1965, *6*, 251–255.

Glass, D. C., and Singer, J. E. *Urban stress: Experiments on noise and social stressors.* New York: Academic Press, 1972.

Goffman, E. *Asylums.* Garden City, N.Y.: Doubleday, 1961.

Goldfried, M. R. Systematic desensitization as training in self-control. *Journal of Consulting and Clinical Psychology*, 1971, *37*, 228–234.

Goldfried, M. R. Reduction of generalized anxiety through a variant of systematic desensitization. In M. R. Goldfried and M. Merbaum (Eds.), *Behavior change through self-control.* New York: Holt, Rinehart and Winston, 1973.

Goldfried, M. R. Behavioral assessment. In I. B. Weiner (Ed.), *Clinical methods in psychology.* New York: Wiley-Interscience, 1976.

Goldfried, M. R., Decenteceo, E. T., and Weinberg, L. Systematic rational restructuring as a self-control technique. *Behavior Therapy*, 1974, *5*, 247–254.

Goldfried, M. R., and D'Zurilla, T. J. A behavioral-analytic model for assessing competence. In C. D. Spielberger (Ed.), *Current topics in clinical and community psychology.* Vol. I. New York: Academic Press, 1969.

Goldfried, M. R., and Goldfried, A. P. Cognitive change methods. In F. H. Kanfer and A. P. Goldstein (Eds.), *Helping people change.* New York: Pergamon, 1975.

Goldfried, M. R., and Kent, R. N. Traditional versus behavioral personality assessment: A comparison of methodological and theoretical assumptions. *Psychological Bulletin*, 1972, *77*, 409–420.

Goldfried, M. R., and Merbaum, M. (Eds.). *Behavior change through self-control.* New York: Holt, Rinehart and Winston, 1973.

Goldfried, M. R., and Pomeranz, D. M. Role of assessment in behavior modification. *Psychological Reports*, 1968, *23*, 75–87.

Goldfried, M. R., and Sobocinski, D. Effect of irrational beliefs on emotional arousal. *Journal of Consulting and Clinical Psychology*, 1975, *43*, 504–510.

Goldfried, M. R., and Sprafkin, J. N. *Behavioral personality assessment.* Morristown, N. J.: General Learning Press, 1974.

Goldfried, M. R., and Trier, C. S. Effectiveness of relaxation as an active coping skill. *Journal of Abnormal Psychology,* 1974, *83,* 348–355.

Goldstein, A. P. *Therapist-patient expectancies in psychotherapy.* New York: Pergamon, 1962.

Goldstein, A. P. *Psychotherapeutic attraction.* New York: Pergamon, 1971.

Goldstein, A. P., Heller, K., and Sechrest, L. B. *Psychotherapy and the psychology of behavior change.* New York: Wiley, 1966.

Goodenough, F. L. *Mental testing.* New York: Rinehart, 1949.

Grossberg, J. M., and Wilson, H. Physiological changes accompanying the visualization of fearful and neutral situations. *Journal of Personality and Social Psychology,* 1968, *10,* 123–133.

Haley, J. *Strategies of psychotherapy.* New York: Grune & Stratton, 1963.

Halleck, S. L. *The politics of therapy.* New York: Science House, 1971.

Harlow, H. F. The formation of learning sets. *Psychological Review,* 1949, *56,* 51–65.

Hartmann, H. *Ego psychology and the problem of adaptation.* New York: International University Press, 1958.

Haskell, M. R. Psychodramatic role training in preparation for release on parole. *Group Psychotherapy,* 1957, *10,* 51–59.

Haugen, G. B., Dixon, H. H., and Dickel, H. A. *A therapy for anxiety tension reactions.* New York: Macmillan, 1963.

Hersen, M., Eisler, R. M., Miller, P. M., Johnson, M. B., and Pinkston, S. G. Effects of practice, instructions and modelling on components of assertive behaviour. *Behaviour Research and Therapy,* 1973, *11,* 443–451.

Hilgard, E. R. *Hypnotic susceptibility.* New York: Harcourt Brace Jovanovich, 1965.

Hilgard, E. R., and Bower, G. H. *Theories of learning* (4th ed.). Englewood Cliffs, N.J.: Prentice-Hall, 1975.

Hoehn-Saric, R., Frank, J. D., Imber, S. D., Nash, E. H., Stone, A. R., and Battle, C. C. Systematic preparation of patients for psychotherapy. I. Effects on therapy behavior and outcome. *Journal of Psychiatric Research,* 1964, *2,* 267–281.

Honigfeld, G., Gillis, R. D., and Klett, C. J. Nosie-30: A treatment-sensitive ward behavior scale. *Psychological Reports,* 1966, *19,* 180–182.

Hooker, E. The adjustments of the overt male homosexual. *Journal of Projective Techniques,* 1957, *21,* 18–31.

Jacks, R. N. *Systematic desensitization versus a self-control technique for the reduction of acrophobia.* Unpublished doctoral dissertation, Stanford University, 1972.

Jacobson, E. *Progressive relaxation.* Chicago: University of Chicago Press, 1929.

Johnson, D. M., Parrott, G. R., and Stratton, R. P. Production and judgment of solutions to five problems. *Journal of Educational Psychology,* 1968, *59,* (No. 6, pt. 2).

Johnson, W. *People in quandaries.* New York: Harper & Row, 1946.

Jones, M. C. A laboratory study of fear: The case of Peter. *Pedagogical Seminary,* 1924, *31,* 308–315.

Jones, R. G. *A factored measure of Ellis' irrational belief system, with personality and maladjustment correlates.* Unpublished doctoral dissertation, Texas Technological College, 1968.

Kamano, D. K. Selective review of effects of discontinuation of drug-treatment: Some implications and problems. *Psychological Reports,* 1966, *19,* 743–749.

Kanfer, F. H., and Phillips, J. S. *Learning foundations of behavior therapy.* New York: Wiley, 1970.

Kanfer, F. H., and Saslow, G. Behavioral analysis: An alternative to diagnostic classification. *Archives of General Psychiatry,* 1965, *12,* 529–538.

Kanfer, F. H., and Saslow, G. Behavioral diagnosis. In C. M. Franks (Ed.), *Behavior therapy: Appraisal and status.* New York: McGraw-Hill, 1969.

Kanter, N. J. *Comparison of self-control desensitization and systematic rational restructuring in the reduction of interpersonal anxiety.* Unpublished doctoral dissertation, State University of New York at Stony Brook, 1975.

Karst, T. O., and Trexler, L. D. Initial study using fixed-role and rational-emotive therapy in treating public-speaking anxiety. *Journal of Consulting and Clinical Psychology,* 1970, 34, 360–366.

Kazdin, A. E., and Bootzin, R. R. The token economy: An evaluative review. *Journal of Applied Behavior Analysis,* 1972, 5, 343–372.

Kelly, G. A. *The psychology of personal constructs.* New York: Norton, 1955.

Kelly, J. G., Blake, R. R. and Stromberg, C. E. The effect of role training on role reversal. *Group Psychotherapy,* 1957, *10,* 95–104.

Kent, R. N., Wilson, G. T., and Nelson, R. Effects of false heart rate feedback on avoidance behavior: An investigation of "cognitive desensitization." *Behavior Therapy,* 1972, *3,* 1–6.

Kifer, R. E., Lewis, M. A., Green, D. R., and Phillips, E. L. *The S.O.C.S. model, training pre-delinquent youths and their parents in negotiation responses to conflict situations.* Paper presented at the American Psychological Association, Montreal, August, 1973.

Lamaze, F. *Painless childbirth: Psychoprophylactic method.* London: Burke Publishing Co., 1958.

Lang, P. J., Melamed, B. G., and Hart, J. A psychophysiological analysis of fear modification using an automated desensitization procedure. *Journal of Abnormal Psychology,* 1970, 76, 220–234.

Lazarus, A. A. Group therapy of phobic disorders by systematic desensitization. *Journal of Abnormal and Social Psychology,* 1961, *63,* 504–510.

Lazarus, A. A. Behavior therapy, incomplete treatment, and symptom substitution. *Journal of Nervous and Mental Disease,* 1965, *140,* 80–86.

Lazarus, A. A. Behavior rehearsal vs. non-directive therapy vs. advice in effecting behavior change. *Behaviour Research and Therapy*, 1966, 4, 209–212.

Lazarus, A. A. *Behavior therapy and beyond.* New York: McGraw-Hill, 1971.

Lazarus, A. A., and Davison, G. C. Clinical innovation in research and practice. In A. E. Bergin and S. L. Garfield (Eds.), *Handbook of psychotherapy and behavior change.* New York: Wiley, 1971.

Lazarus, A. A., Davison, G. C., and Polefka, D. Classical and operant factors in the treatment of a school phobia. *Journal of Abnormal Psychology*, 1965, 70, 225–229.

Lefcourt, H. M. Internal versus external control of reinforcement: A review. *Psychological Bulletin*, 1966, 65, 206–220.

Leitenberg, H., Agras, W. S., Barlow, D. H., and Oliveau, D. C. Contribution of selective positive reinforcement and therapeutic instructions in systematic desensitization therapy. *Journal of Abnormal Psychology*, 1969, 74, 113–118.

Lewin, K. *A dynamic theory of personality: Selected papers.* New York: McGraw-Hill, 1935.

Lewinsohn, P. M., and Shaffer, M. Use of home observations as an integral part of the treatment of depression: Preliminary report and case studies. *Journal of Consulting and Clinical Psychology*, 1971, 37, 87–94.

Liebert, R. M., and Allen, M. K. The effects of role structure and reward magnitude on the acquisition and adoption of self-reward criteria. *Psychological Reports*, 1967, 21, 445–452.

Liebert, R. M., Neale, J. M., and Davidson, E. S. *The early window.* New York: Pergamon, 1973.

Lindsley, O. R., and Skinner, B. F. A method for the experimental analysis of the behavior of psychotic patients. *American Psychologist*, 1954, 9, 419–420.

London, P. *The modes and morals or psychotherapy.* New York: Holt, Rinehart and Winston, 1964.

Mahoney, M. J. *Cognition and behavior modification.* Cambridge: Ballinger, 1974.

Marston, A. R., and Feldman, S. E. Toward the use of self-control in behavior modification. *Journal of Consulting and Clinical Psychology*, 1972, 39, 429–433.

Maslow, A. H. *The psychology of science: A reconnaissance.* New York: Harper & Row, 1966.

Mathews, A. M. Psychophysiological approaches to the investigation of desensitization and related procedures. *Psychological Bulletin*, 1971, 76, 73–91.

May, J. R., and Johnson, H. J. Physiological activity to internally elicited arousal and inhibitory thoughts. *Journal of Abnormal Psychology*, 1973, 82, 239–245.

McFall, R. M., and Lillesand, D. V. Behavior rehearsal with modeling and coaching in assertive training. *Journal of Abnormal Psychology*, 1971, *77*, 313–323.

McFall, R. M., and Marston, A. An experimental investigation of behavior rehearsal in assertive training. *Journal of Abnormal Psychology*, 1970, *76*, 295–303.

McFall, R. M., and Twentyman, C. T. Four experiments on the relative contributions of rehearsal, modeling, and coaching to assertion training. *Journal of Abnormal Psychology*, 1973, *81*, 199–218.

Mead, G. H. *Mind, self, and society*. Chicago: University of Chicago Press, 1934.

Meehl, P. E. The cognitive activity of the clinician. *American Psychologist*, 1960, *15*, 19–27.

Meichenbaum, D. H. Examination of model characteristics in reducing avoidance behavior. *Journal of Personality and Social Psychology*, 1971, *17*, 298–307.

Meichenbaum, D. H. Cognitive modification of test anxious college students. *Journal of Consulting and Clinical Psychology*, 1972, *39*, 370–380.

Meichenbaum, D. H. Cognitive factors in behavior modification: Modifying what clients say to themselves. In C. M. Franks and G. T. Wilson (Eds.), *Annual review of behavior therapy: Theory and practice*. New York: Brunner-Mazel, 1973.

Meichenbaum, D. H. *Cognitive behavior modification*. Morristown, N. J.: General Learning Press, 1974.

Meichenbaum, D. H., Gilmore, J. B., and Fedoravicious, A. Group insight versus group desensitization in treating speech anxiety. *Journal of Consulting and Clinical Psychology*, 1971, *36*, 410–421.

Merbaum, M., and Southwell, E. A. Conditioning of affective self-references as a function of the discriminative characteristics of experimenter intervention. *Journal of Abnormal Psychology*, 1965, *70*, 180–187.

Meyer, V., and Chesser, E. S. *Behavior therapy in clinical psychiatry*. New York: Penguin Books, 1970.

Miller, G. A., Galanter, E., and Pribram, K. H. *Plans and the structure of behavior*. New York: Holt, Rinehart and Winston, 1960.

Mischel, W. *Personality and assessment*. New York: Wiley, 1968.

Mischel, W. Towards a cognitive social learning reconceptualization of personality. *Psychological Review*, 1973, *80*, 252–283.

Mischel, W., and Liebert, R. M. Effects of discrepancies between observed and imposed reward criteria on their acquisition and transmission. *Journal of Personality and Social Psychology*, 1966, *3*, 45–53.

Moreno, J. L. *The theatre of spontaneity*. New York: Beacon House, 1947.

Morris, R. J., and Suckerman, K. R. Therapist warmth as a factor in automated systematic desensitization. *Journal of Consulting and Clinical Psychology*, 1974, *42*, 244–250.

Mowrer, O. H. *Learning theory and personality dynamics.* New York: Ronald, 1950.

Mowrer, O. H. *Learning theory and the symbolic processes.* New York: Wiley, 1960.

Murray, H. A. *Explorations in personality.* New York: Oxford University Press, 1938.

Nawas, M. M., Fishman, S. T., and Pucel, J. C. A standardized desensitization program applicable to group and individual treatments. *Behaviour Research and Therapy,* 1970, 8, 49–56.

Nisbett, R. E., and Schachter, S. The cognitive manipulation of pain. *Journal of Experimental Social Psychology,* 1966, 2, 227–236.

O'Leary, K. D., and Becker, W. C. Behavior modification of an adjustment class: A token reinforcement program. *Exceptional Children,* 1967, 33, 637–642.

O'Leary, K. D., and Drabman, R. Token reinforcement programs in the classroom: A review. *Psychological Bulletin,* 1971, 75, 379–398.

O'Leary, K. D., and O'Leary, S. G. (Eds.). *Classroom management.* New York: Pergamon, 1972.

O'Leary, K. D., and Wilson, G. T. *Behavior therapy: Application and outcome.* Englewood Cliffs, N.J.: Prentice-Hall, 1975.

Orne, M. T. The nature of hypnosis: Artifact and essence. *Journal of Abnormal and Social Psychology,* 1959, 58, 277–299.

Orne, M. T., and Wender, P. H. Anticipatory socialization for psychotherapy: Method and rationale. *American Journal of Psychiatry,* 1968, 124, 1202–1212.

Osborn, A. F. *Applied imagination* (3rd ed.). New York: Scribner's, 1963.

Parnes, S. J. *Creative behavior guidebook.* New York: Scribner's, 1967.

Patterson, G. R. Intervention in the homes of predelinquent boys: Steps toward stage two. Paper prepared for the workshop, *Delinquent behavior: Some psychological research and applications.* American Psychological Association Convention, Washington, D.C., 1971.

Patterson, G. R., and Gullion, M. E. *Living with children.* Champaign, Ill.: Research Press, 1971.

Paul, G. L. Insight versus desensitization in psychotherapy two years after termination. *Journal of Consulting Psychology,* 1967, 31, 333–348.

Paul, G. L. Outcome of systematic desensitization. I.: Background procedures, and uncontrolled reports of individual treatment. In C. M. Franks (Ed.), *Behavior therapy: Appraisal and status.* New York: McGraw-Hill, 1969a.

Paul, G. L. Outcome of systematic desensitization. II. Controlled investigations of individual treatment, technique variations, and current status. In C. M. Franks (Ed.), *Behavior therapy: Appraisal and status.* New York: McGraw-Hill, 1969b.

Paul, G. L., and Shannon, D. T. Treatment of anxiety through systematic desensitization in therapy groups. *Journal of Abnormal Psychology,* 1966, *71,* 124–135.

Peterson, D. R. *The clinical study of social behavior.* New York: Appleton-Century-Crofts, 1968.

Peterson, D. R., and London, P. Neobehavioristic psychotherapy: Quasi-hypnotic suggestions and multiple reinforcement in the treatment of a case of post-infantile dyscopresis. *Psychological Record,* 1964, *14,* 469–474.

Pfeiffer, W. M. Konzentrative Selbstentspannung durch Uebungen, die sich aus der buddhistischen Atemmeditation und aus der Atemtherapie herleiten. *Zeitschrift fuer Psychotherapie und medizinische Psychologie,* 1967, *46,* 172–181.

Pomeranz, D. M., and Goldfried, M. R. An intake report outline for behavior modification. *Psychological Reports,* 1970, *26,* 447–450.

Rapaport, D. The theory of ego autonomy: A generalization. *Bulletin of the Menninger Clinic,* 1958, *22,* 13–35.

Reich, W. *Character analysis.* New York: Orgone Institute, 1949.

Rimland, B. *Infantile autism.* New York: Appleton-Century-Crofts, 1964.

Rimm, D. C., and Litvak, S. B. Self-verbalization and emotional arousal. *Journal of Abnormal Psychology,* 1969, *74,* 181–187.

Rosen, G. M. Therapy set: Its effects on subjects' involvement in systematic desensitization and treatment outcome. *Journal of Abnormal Psychology,* 1974, *83,* 291–300.

Rosen, G. M., Rosen, E., and Reid, J. B. Cognitive desensitization and avoidance behavior: A reevaluation. *Journal of Abnormal Psychology,* 1972, *80,* 176–182.

Rosenberg, P. *An experimental analysis of psychodrama.* Unpublished doctoral dissertation, Harvard University, 1952.

Rosenhan, D. L. On being sane in insane places. *Science,* 1973, *179,* 250–258.

Rotter, J. B. *Social learning and clinical psychology.* Englewood Cliffs, N.J.: Prentice-Hall, 1954.

Rotter, J. B. Generalized expectancies for internal versus external control of reinforcement. *Psychological Monographs,* 1966, *80,* (1, whole No. 609).

Rotter, J. B., and Wickens, D. The consistency and generality of ratings of "social aggressiveness" made from observations of role playing situations. *Journal of Consulting Psychology,* 1948, *12,* 234–239.

Russell, P. C., and Brandsma, J. M. A theoretical and empirical integration of the rational-emotive and classical conditioning theories. *Journal of Consulting and Clinical Psychology,* 1974, *42,* 389–397.

Ryan, V. L., and Gizynski, M. N. Behavior therapy in retrospect: Patients' feelings about their behavior therapists. *Journal of Consulting and Clinical Psychology,* 1971, *37,* 1–9.

Ryle, G. *The concept of mind.* London: Hutchinson, 1949.

Salter, A. *Conditioned reflex therapy.* New York: Creative Age, 1949.

Sarbin, T. R. Contributions to role-taking theory: I. Hypnotic behavior. *Psychological Review*, 1950, 57, 255–270.

Sarbin, T. R., and Allen, V. L. Role theory. In G. Lindzey and E. Aronson (Eds.), *The handbook of social psychology*, Vol. one, (2nd ed.). Reading, Mass.: Addison-Wesley, 1968.

Schaefer, H. H., and Martin, P. L. *Behavioral therapy*. New York: McGraw-Hill, 1969.

Schneider, M., and Robin, A. *Turtle manual*. Unpublished manuscript, State University of New York at Stony Brook, 1975.

Schultz, J. H., and Luthe, W. *Autogenic training*. New York: Grune & Stratton, 1959.

Seligman, M. E. P. *Helplessness*. San Francisco: W. H. Freeman, 1975.

Shaftel, F. R., and Shaftel, G. *Role-playing for social values: Decision-making in the social studies*. Englewood Cliffs, N.J.: Prentice-Hall, 1967.

Sherman, A. R. Real-life exposure as a primary therapeutic factor in the desensitization treatment of fear. *Journal of Abnormal Psychology*, 1972, 79, 19–28.

Silverstein, C. *Behavior modification and the gay community*. Paper presented at Annual Convention of the Association for Advancement of Behavior Therapy, New York City, 1972.

Simon, H. A. *Administrative behavior*. New York: Free Press, 1957.

Skinner, B. F. *Science and human behavior*. New York: Macmillan, 1953.

Spielberger, C. D. Theory and research on anxiety. In C. D. Spielberger (Ed.), *Anxiety and behavior*. New York: Academic Press, 1966.

Spivack, G., and Shure, M. B. *Social adjustment of young children*. San Francisco: Josey-Bass, 1974.

Staats, A. W., and Staats, C. K. *Complex human behavior*. New York: Holt, Rinehart and Winston, 1963.

Stanton, H. R., and Litwak, E. Toward the development of a short form test of interpersonal competence. *American Sociological Review*, 1955, 20, 668–674.

Storrow, H. A. *Introduction to scientific psychiatry*. New York: Appleton-Century-Crofts, 1967.

Stoyva, J. *Skinnerian Zen or control of physiological responses through information feedback*. Paper read at Denver University Symposium on Behavior Modification, 1968.

Suinn, R. M. The STABS, a measure of test anxiety for behavior therapy: Normative data. *Behaviour Research and Therapy*, 1969, 7, 335–339.

Sullivan, H. S. *The interpersonal theory of psychiatry*. New York: Norton, 1953.

Sullivan, H. S. *The psychiatric interview*. New York: Norton, 1954.

Sushinsky, L. W., and Bootzin, R. R. Cognitive desensitization as a model of systematic desensitization. *Behaviour Research and Therapy*, 1970, 8, 29–33.

Tasto, D. L., and Hinkle, J. E. Muscle relaxation treatment for tension headaches. *Behavior Research and Therapy*, 1973, *11*, 347–350.

Thoresen, C. E., and Mahoney, M. J. *Behavioral self-control*. New York: Holt, Rinehart and Winston, 1974.

Trexler, L. D., and Karst, T. O. Rational-emotive therapy, placebo, and no-treatment effects on public-speaking anxiety. *Journal of Abnormal Psychology*, 1972, *79*, 60–67.

Truax, C. B. Reinforcement and non-reinforcement in Rogerian psychotherapy. *Journal of Abnormal Psychology*, 1966, *71*, 1–9.

Ullmann, L. P., and Krasner, L. (Eds.). *Case studies in behavior modification*. New York: Holt, Rinehart and Winston, 1965.

Ullmann, L. P., and Krasner, L. *A psychological approach to abnormal behavior*. Englewood Cliffs, N.J.: Prentice-Hall, 1969.

Valins, S., and Nisbett, R. E. *Attribution processes in the development and treatment of emotional disorders*. New York: General Learning Press, 1971.

Valins, S., and Ray, A. A. Effects of cognitive desensitization on avoidance behavior. *Journal of Personality and Social Psychology*, 1967, *7*, 345–350.

Velten, E. A laboratory task for induction of mood states. *Behaviour Research and Therapy*, 1968, *6*, 473–482.

Wachtel, P. Psychodynamics, behavior therapy, and the implacable experimenter: An inquiry into the consistency of personality. *Journal of Abnormal Psychology*, 1973, *82*, 324–334.

Wachtel, P. *Action and insight*. New York: Basic Books, in press.

Wahler, R. G., Winkel, G. H., Peterson, R. F., and Morrison, D. C. Mothers as behavior therapists for their own children. *Behaviour Research and Therapy*, 1965, *3*, 113–124.

Wallace, J. An abilities conception of personality: Some implications for personality measurement. *American Psychologist*, 1966, *21*, 132–138.

Wallace, J. What units shall we employ? Allport's question revisited. *Journal of Consulting Psychology*, 1967, *31*, 56–64.

Weil, G., and Goldfried, M. R. Treatment of insomnia in an eleven-year-old child through self-relaxation. *Behavior Therapy*, 1973, *4*, 282–284.

Weitzenhoffer, A. M. *General techniques of hypnotism*. New York: Grune & Stratton, 1957.

Weitzman, B. Personal communication, 1969.

Werry, J. S., and Quay, H. C. Observing the classroom behavior of elementary school children. *Exceptional Children*, 1969, Feb., 461–470.

Wexler, D. B. Token and taboo: Behavior modification, token economies and the law. *California Law Review*, 1973, *61*, 81–109.

Wilkins, W. Desensitization: Social and cognitive factors underlying the effectiveness of Wolpe's procedure. *Psychological Bulletin*, 1971, *76*, 311–317.

Wilson, G. T., and Davison, G. C. Processes of fear reduction in systematic desensitization: Animal studies. *Psychological Bulletin*, 1971, 76, 1–14.

Wilson, G. T., and Evans, I. M. The therapist-client relationship in behavior therapy. In A. S. Gurman and A. M. Razin (Eds.), *The therapist's contribution to effective psychotherapy: An empirical approach*. New York: Pergamon, in press.

Winett, R. A., and Winkler, R. C. Current behavior modification in the classroom: Be still, be quiet, be docile. *Journal of Applied Behavior Analysis*, 1972, 5, 499–504.

Wolpe, J. *An approach to the problem of neurosis based on the conditioned response*. Unpublished M.D. thesis, University of the Witwatersrand, 1948.

Wolpe, J. *Psychotherapy by reciprocal inhibition*. Stanford: Stanford University Press, 1958.

Wolpe, J., and Lazarus, A. A. *Behavior therapy techniques*. New York: Pergamon, 1966.

Wolpe, J., Salter, A., and Reyna, L. J. (Eds.). *Conditioning therapies: The challenge in psychotherapy*. New York: Holt, Rinehart and Winston, 1964.

Woodworth, R. S., and Schlosberg, H. *Experimental Psychology* (Rev. ed.). New York: Holt, Rinehart and Winston, 1954.

Zemore, R. Systematic desensitization as a method of teaching a general anxiety-reducing skill. *Journal of Consulting and Clinical Psychology*, 1975, 43, 157–161.

Zilboorg, G., and Henry, G. W. *A history of medical psychology*. New York: Norton, 1941.

Name Index

Subject Index